Chutzpah
& High Heels

The Search for Love and Identity
in the Holy Land

Chutzpah
& High Heels

The Search for Love and Identity
in the Holy Land

Jessica Fishman

Yotzeret Publishing
St. Paul

This is a work of creative nonfiction. The events are portrayed to the best of the author's memory, though she has made some slight alterations to the chronological timeline of minor events in order to improve clarity. To protect the privacy of the people involved, the author has changed the names of individuals and places, as well as identifying characteristics. Conversations in this work all come from the author's recollections, though they are not written to represent word-for-word transcripts. Rather, the author has retold them in a way that evokes the feeling and meaning of what was said and in all instances, the essence of the dialogue is accurate.

The views and opinions expressed herein are solely those of the author and do not necessarily reflect the views of Yotzeret Publishing, its affiliates, or its employees.

First edition

Cover design by TotallyJamie.com
Clouds by Paz Fraizler
Author photo by Jamie Hurt

Afterword text copyright © 2017 by Rabbi Uri Regev, Esq.

Grateful acknowledgment is made to the following for permission to reprint previously published material:

Nehama, Zeev (lyrics): *Jessica*. Performed by Ethnix. © 1993 Nehama, Z., Kalinsky, T., and ACUM. Reprinted with permission of ACUM.

Publisher's Cataloging-in-Publication data

Names: Fishman, Jessica, 1980- , author.
Title: Chutzpah & high heels / Jessica Fishman.
Description: St. Paul [Minnesota] : Yotzeret Publishing, 2017.
Identifiers: LCCN 2016943621 (print) | ISBN 978-1-59287-141-4 (print) | ISBN 978-1-59287-306-7 (Kindle) | ISBN 978-1-59287-307-4 (epub).
Subjects: LCSH Israel--Social life and customs | Jews--Social life and customs | Biographies ; History--Biography ; Life histories ; Memoirs | Israel--Emigration and immigration. BISAC BIOGRAPHY & AUTOBIOGRAPHY / Personal Memoirs.

To all the women everywhere who use their chutzpah to unapologetically fight for equality, make history, and get shit done. ~~Sorry guys.~~

The Good, the Bad, and the Ugly . . . Israeli

It's 3:00 A.M. It's August. It's boiling outside.

I'm driving home from another bad date with another Israeli guy who has a big ego and a small—THUD! CLANK! BANG! The car starts making noises. Seeing that the normally busy city streets are empty, I panic. I know nothing about cars. I don't even like driving in this country. Wearing high heels and a revealing summer dress, I get out of the car. The heat from the street seeps through the soles of my shoes. I'm not worried about being raped, attacked, murdered, or robbed. In Tel Aviv, we worry about a different type of violence. But I don't have to worry about terrorism now. With just me in the street, the body count would be too low.

Hoping to fix the problem, I open the hood. I burn my fingers in the attempt and stare hopelessly at the engine. It might as well be an open heart.

I look around to find someone who can help me. Even though the streets are normally crowded, the only person I see is a man wearing a black wool jacket, black pants, a whitish-yellowish, button-up long-sleeve shirt, and a furry black hat walking past me on the sidewalk. I don't bother calling out to him. It's Friday night and I'm breaking the laws of the Sabbath in the Holy Land: I'm driving. I'm wearing a sexy, but appropriate-for-the-weather summer dress. I stare at him as he continues to pass me. He, dressed devoutly for a nineteenth-century Polish winter, looks through me, as if he knows the secret I've been trying to hide.

I know that as an ultra-Orthodox Jew, he avoids the gazes of all women, but it still feels personal and degrading. I cover my shoulders with my hands, trying to hide the truth. I shouldn't care what he thinks of me. I remind myself that there is no way he can tell just by looking at me. Maybe he is the reason that I'm in this country, but who is he to judge me? He isn't perfect. Besides, what is he doing walking around at this hour? Friday-night prayers were over hours ago and he isn't returning from a family dinner or Torah discussion in secular Tel Aviv. Did he spend the evening with a hooker? I wonder if he wore his *kippah*[1] for that.

I can't ask him for help. He won't touch a machine on the Sabbath. And even if it wasn't, he wouldn't help a stranded woman lest it cause him to have evil, sexual thoughts.

I stop looking at him and grumble to myself, "Only in Israel."

Before I have a chance to become distraught, a taxi driver pulls up like a knight in shining armor.

"Are you okay?" he asks as he gets out of the car.

Thankful, I say in Hebrew, "The car is making noises. I don't know what to do."

"Turn the car on," he orders and I obey.

After hearing the noise, he exclaims, "It's exactly what I thought. I'll fix it."

Typical Israeli man—thinking he can solve a problem before he even knows what it is. After he asks me to turn off the engine, I walk to the front of the car.

He pulls out a knife.

I don't flinch.

---

1. A skullcap worn by Orthodox male Jews at all times and by men and women in other Jewish streams during prayer. The purpose of the skullcap is to remind the wearer of God's presence.

With the knife, he yanks at something in the car and cuts it loose. Like the Prophet Elijah, he proclaims, "Your car is fine. You can drive all the way to Haifa, but get it checked first thing in the morning. That will be fifty shekels."[2]

"Are you serious?" I balk and think to myself that this man has *chutzpah*.[3]

"Of course I'm serious. I'm a mechanic by day and taxi driver by night."

I should point out that it is the middle of the night. With my hands on my hips, I ask, "If you charge for being a Good Samaritan, are you still one?"

He holds out his hand. Palm up.

Rolling my eyes, I growl, "Only in Israel."

I get back in the car and start driving.

Thirty seconds later, BOOM! THUMP! KURPLUNK! The noises are louder and scarier than before. I pull over and look around. The roads are empty. The taxi driver and my fifty shekels are nowhere in sight. I start to cry.

Who should I call? I can't call my dad; he is across the ocean. I'd needlessly worry him. Besides, what American Jew understands cars? If I need medical, legal, or financial advice I'll call an American Jew, but for car advice . . . I need an Israeli. I don't want to call the guy I was just on a date with because I'm afraid he won't pick up or would refuse to come.

Through my tears, I scan my cell's phonebook. I stop at "Bar." He has been there through thick and thin. Like me, he is a new immigrant to Israel. Well, after nearly ten years here, we aren't really new anymore.

With a French accent, Bar answers with a groggy, "Hello . . . Are you okay?" Through my sobs, I explain that I'm stuck.

---

2. $1 (USD) is approximately 4 shekels

3. Actually pronounced in Hebrew, with a guttural "ch" for an extra crude affect. Very much an onomatopoeia, chutzpah means both bravery and rudeness.

"I'm already coming," he says, using the Hebrew expression.

New immigrants always stick together.

While trying to calm down, I look up and see a young man in his car pulling up next to my car. He sees my chest heaving and tears rolling down my face. He asks me if I need help. Alone and panicking, I quickly explain that a friend is on the way.

"*Yihyeh b'seder!* Everything will be okay!" he says. During my years in Israel, I learned that a broken bone, heart, or bank account warrant this same predictable response from an Israeli doctor, therapist, or investment banker.

After asking me again if I need anything, he drives away.

Twenty minutes pass and Bar still isn't here. I look around. The roads are oddly deserted. The street light above the car suddenly burns out. My ears begin buzzing from the silence. I squeeze the wheel. My breathing speeds and gets shallower as I feel more and more stranded. My hands become tingly. I look out my window, hoping that I'll see Bar, and right next to me is another car. I didn't even hear it pull up. It isn't Bar. I begin to panic. I try to start the car again, but it won't turn over. The tinted window of the car next to me slowly opens. On the other side is the smiling face of the guy who, twenty minutes ago, told me, "*Yihyeh b'seder.*"

"I couldn't stop thinking of you crying on the side of the road," he says as he reaches out the window and hands me a box of tissues, a bottle of water, and a chocolate bar. He then drives away, disappearing as quickly as he appeared.

I may not know his name, but he makes me feel like I have a home in this country. I can't help but wonder if he would still treat me as if I belong if he knew my secret. With a smile, I sigh and think to myself, "Only in Israel." And before I have a chance to further question my place in Israel, Bar pulls up to save me from the loneliness of the night and my thoughts.

Member of the Tribe

Ten years ago, while I was in college, the thought of moving to Israel hadn't occurred to me. I pictured myself living the typical Jewish American life. I was well on my way to fulfilling this dream one cold January day in the middle of Christian Indiana.

Sitting on a pink floral couch and wearing my cutest outfit, I was trying to impress the girl sitting in front of me. My face hurt from smiling all day, but I hid it because I really wanted these girls to like me. The college rush process felt like speed dating.

"Where are you from?" the sorority sister asked me over the commotion of fifty other girls being interviewed in the same room. This wasn't an innocent question. She didn't actually care where I was born. She wanted to know if I was a member of the Tribe. I needed to be careful answering.

"Minnesota, but I have friends in Chicago and New York." I said, mentioning Jewish hot spots. As a freshman at Indiana University, I was finishing Greek Rush Week. After narrowing down the houses from eighteen to three, I had to pick which house to join. I wanted to be in one of the Jewish sororities: Sigma Delta Tau (SΔT) or Alpha Epsilon Phi (AEΦ). The former has a reputation of being nice Jewish girls, but everyone cruelly calls them Stumpy Dumpy Trolls behind their backs. The latter is known as the snobby, rich house and everyone calls them JAPs (Jewish American Princesses) to their faces.

I looked at the AEΦ pin on the girl's dress. She didn't seem like a JAP. She seemed really nice.

"Really? My cousin lives in Minneapolis: Lisa Goldenbergerwitzman. Do you know her?" the sorority sister asked. Since rush rules forbids blatantly inquiring about religion, she was playing a game of Jewish Geography.[4]

I didn't know her cousin, but I wanted the sorority sister to know I'd fit in. "Her name sounds really familiar. Maybe we went to Herzl Camp together or participated in the same USY (United Synagogue Youth) programs." I knew Jewish organization name dropping would do the trick.

Another sorority sister swapped positions with the one I was talking to. She looked familiar, but I couldn't figure out from where.

She looked at me as if she recognized me and asked, "Have I seen you at ZBT before?" ZBT was one of the Jewish fraternities.

The three forbidden topics during rush were: boys, booze, and partying.

"Probably . . . I'm a bit of a groupie." *Damn! I shouldn't have said that!* I clammed up, afraid that she'd think I was a loser.

"I'm there all of the time too. My boyfriend is in the house." She smiled. "Are you interested in any of the guys in the house?"

I shyly smiled, but before I could answer it was time to go.

With mathematical equations to statistically match up sororities' preferences with rushees' choices, rush process at Indiana University is more complex than winning the US Presidency. Thanks to some algorithms, I ended up in the JAP sorority.

When I got my bid, I couldn't wait to be friends with all the Jewish girls in the house. It would be nothing like high school in Minnesota, where I stuck out in a sea of blond-haired Lutheran and Presbyterian Norwegian descendants and guys who wore wife-beater tank

---

4. Jewish Geography is a game to figure out if Jews have common friends. This was much more challenging and rewarding before Facebook.

tops and Confederate-flag belt buckles as big as trash can lids.

*   *   *

Pledgeship didn't go as well as the rush process. I quickly realized that I had nothing in common with my Jewish pledges. My dreams of finally fitting in were crushed. None of my sisters wanted to do anything with me. The inherent kinship that I expected never materialized. Unlike me, they had grown up in communities so full of other Jews that the schools would be closed during the Jewish High Holidays. To them, our Jewish bond wasn't important. The only things they cared about were their Kate Spade diaper bags, Prada wallets, Diesel jeans, Steve Madden shoes, and shiny-but-boring Michael Star shirts. They always said how everything made them naaauuuuseous. They walked in flocks. I felt like an outcast, but hoped that once we all lived together sophomore year, they would accept me.

In preparation for moving into the sorority house, I did everything I could to fit in. I invested in a new purse and wardrobe. I tried to describe everything as "naaauuuuseous," but it was such a limiting characterization. I even tried to develop an eating disorder, but I was just too hungry.

A week before sophomore year started, all of my sorority sisters arrived at the AEΦ house with their designer purses, expensive jeans, brand name shirts, new Lexuses, and Long Island accents. I never had any of those in Minnesota. I realized that no matter how much money I spent, or how much I tried to change my vocabulary, I didn't fit in. But only when the Jewish High Holidays arrived did I realize how out of place I was, despite being surrounded by fellow Jews.

On the eve of Rosh Hashanah, the Jewish New Year, I prepared for synagogue. I put on a nice but fairly modest dress. I pulled my tallis bag out of my drawer, which also held my knitted, feminine kippah. My family always

went to services on holidays—not to see and be seen, but to pray. We were active Jews. My synagogue back home was progressive, spiritual, and observant. I hoped for the same experience at the Hillel service, especially since the rabbi was female.

After getting ready in my room, I walked into the hallway to see my sorority sisters running around wearing more makeup than clowns, straightening their hair with contraptions that looked like torture devices used at Guantanamo, and donning designer outfits. It looked more like preparation for New York fashion week than services on a Midwest campus.

At synagogue, I stood next to my sorority sisters, but in a completely different world. During a prayer for repentance, I thought about how I'd felt at home the last time I visited Israel. I remembered meeting Tzipporah Porath, an elderly American woman who recounted studying abroad at Hebrew University during Israel's War of Independence. She had struggled to get food during the siege on Jerusalem. She had rejoiced during the UN's resolution to create the State of Israel. She survived daily terrorist bombings, smuggled weapons under her skirt, and became a medic in the underground Haganah Force. After a terrorist attack in the middle of Jerusalem, she had pulled out her red lipstick and drew the six-pointed Star of David on a shop window to signal to the injured that she was providing medical help.

With a thump, the congregation sat down. As I took my seat, wishing I had done more this past year, I saw out of the corner of my eye the sorority sister next to me pull out her hand mirror and reapply her bright red lipstick.

In that moment, I knew that I was going to follow in the footsteps of Tzipporah Porath to study in the Holy Land verus the Jimmy Choos of my sorority sisters.

Only a week after deciding to study in Israel, I was finalizing my application process, my living situation, getting my passport ready, and buying my airline tickets.

At the same time, Arafat was leading the Palestinian people into the second Intifada. Jerusalem was suddenly full of stone-throwing terrorists, Molotov cocktails, and exploding buses, but the media blamed Israel. Sitting alone in the sorority cafeteria, I stared in disbelief at the TV as the images of two Israeli soldiers being brutally lynched by a Palestinian mob in a Ramallah police station flashed on the screen. I saw a Palestinian raise his blood-covered hands in victory out a window and heard the crowd below him cheer. The other sorority girls were busy gossiping. When a gaggle of my Jewish sorority sisters—who didn't normally acknowledge my existence—walked in, they accosted me with questions.

"You aren't still going to Israel, are you?" they asked in singsong unison, faking concern for me. They must have heard of my plans through typical sorority gossip.

I rolled my eyes and said, "Yes, of course," knowing that their Jewishness was pulling them to Italy, Spain, and France to worship their gods known as Prada, Louis Vuitton, and Diesel.

Switching subjects like they change fashion, one of the girls asked another girl who was only eating boiled egg whites, "Should I eat another sandwich? I think I'm still hungry, but I don't know . . ."

To her, it was a decision that could change the course of history. After considerable deliberation, she grabbed two pieces of lettuce and a thin slice of turkey, sprayed it with bottled butter, and then ate it without bread.

I was amazed that it took her longer to decide about her two-calorie meal than it took me to decide to go to war-torn Israel.

＊   ＊   ＊

My time in Israel that semester flew by. On its surface, it was just like any other study abroad program—classes during the day and cultural outings in the evening. But there was more to it. I wasn't just discovering a country; I was discovering myself. There was something magnetic about Israel, from the Jewish soldiers in the streets to the bearded religious men, and from the women in their revealing shirts to the history at every corner. The streets are named after famous and historic Jews. The money has pictures of Jewish politicians. The language is the same one used by our ancestors two thousand years ago. Jewish holidays are celebrated where they occurred thousands of years ago. In Israel, I didn't have to tell people that I'm Jewish; instead, the country told me.

But it wasn't all a fairy tale. Terrorism was no longer simply a news item. The *pegu'im*, terrorist attacks, were not daily, they were twice daily. There were terror attacks so close to my Jerusalem dorm room that I had felt the sound boom move through my body. However, just like the Israelis, I and the other students on the program didn't let the terrorism stop us from living. We would go out to dance clubs, malls, and markets. Everything we did was a reminder of the solidarity of the Jewish people—from dressing up for Purim instead of Halloween to the quiet that fell over the entire country on Friday nights. I felt as if I was with my people, but with the semester ending, my time in Israel was about to come to an abrupt close.

At 11:30 p.m. on a typical Saturday night a man wandered through the crowd of laughing teenagers in line for a Tel Aviv night club.

I was supposed to leave Israel in a few days.

"Something is about to happen," the man yelled.

Waiting for the night of fun to begin, everyone in line ignored him.

BOOM! The man blew himself up and everyone around him. The sound was heard throughout Tel Aviv. The entire country felt the blow. Twenty-one teenagers, who just wanted to have fun, were killed. One hundred and thirty-two were injured.

I was safe in my dorm room when I heard the news. I called all the other students to make sure they were safe. I'd just walked past that night club last weekend with a group of friends. We'd almost gone inside.

I was packing to leave, but questions swirled through my head. How could I abandon Israel? Why should I be safe in the US while my fellow Jews risked their lives here? When a country is under attack, most people flee, but it made me want to stay.

I stared at a picture I had taken a few months ago during a trip to Ein Gedi, where King David is said to have sought refuge. In the picture is a typical Israeli man on a hike with his young family. He looks like a modern-day David. On his right shoulder rests the curly-haired head of his two-year old daughter with a pink bottle in her hand, and slung over his left shoulder is a rifle. It's as if the future of the country rests on both of his shoulders.

I looked back at the pile of clothes on my bed and the half-empty suitcase. I didn't want to go. I wanted to stay and . . . do something. Like join the army. But instead, I just returned to packing.

*　　　*　　　*

Starting my senior year back at Indiana University, I decided to live in an off-campus house away from my sorority sisters. I still longed to go back to Israel. I had trouble adjusting back to the US. Walking into stores, I'd open up my purse to show that I was only carrying tampons and not a bomb. I said *slicha* instead of excuse me. And I got scared at the sound of a car backfiring. Things seemed so trivial now. I felt lost. I kept waiting for a sign to tell me what to do, where to go.

But today, I didn't have time for signs. I was late, as usual. As I ran out the door, I grabbed the mail and started scanning through it while walking to class. Bills, more bills, coupons, junk mail. The last envelope had a picture of Israel on it. I quickly turned it over and read:

If you know what you're going to do for the next ten years, put this back where you found it!
About to tear open the envelope, I heard a thick New Jersey accent yell, "OH. MY. GOD! You're alive! Was Israel fun?"

I looked up to see one of my former sorority sisters in the AEΦ uniform: dark jeans and a tight black shirt. For all the concern they had feigned before I left, I never once received an email from them after a terror attack.

I didn't know how to respond. Should I have told her that the Hebrew University cafeteria that I ate at on a daily basis was blown up by a suicide bomber two months after I left? How should I sum up life and death in a short casual conversation?

Before I had a chance to answer, she started rambling about the food she had eaten, the clothes she had bought, and the men she had fucked. As she bragged, I looked down at the envelope with the map of Israel in my hand. I thought back to a few months ago when I celebrated Israel's 53rd Independence Day in the streets of Jerusalem with the rest of the country. Seeing kids, adults, and even senior citizens celebrating in the streets late at night, I had suddenly realized that every generation has to fight for Israel's right to exist. I had noticed an older couple with Holocaust numbers tattooed on their arms, sitting on a bench and watching the celebrations. For the first time, I had understood that when they were kids, Israel didn't exist to protect them. It had been like a punch in the stomach realizing how vulnerable Israel still is. With the firecrackers overhead, I had suddenly felt as if I was a part of that vulnerability and should contribute to the country's protection.

As she pointed to her new Prada bag, I realized that I had to go back to Israel. And just like Israeli movies that cut to intermission mid-sentence, I walked away in the middle of her spiel.

I tore open the envelope and found my plans—a year-long volunteer program in Israel.

No Such Thing as a Coincidence

From the first time I visited the country at thirteen years old, being Jewish took on a new meaning for me. I felt connected to everyone I met, as if we shared a common bond, a common history, a common ancestor. A conversation on the street with a random stranger felt like a family reunion. I could have a screaming match with a store clerk, but we'd still wish each other *shabbat shalom*, a peaceful sabbath, at the end and actually mean it. While I loved being in Israel, unfortunately, I didn't fall in love with my volunteer program. I didn't feel as if we were making a difference. I felt trapped with Americans and desperately searched for a way to integrate myself more with real Israelis, almost as if I knew that I should be making my home in the country.

About two months into the volunteer program, called Otzma, we were about to be assigned Israeli adoptive families for the High Holidays.

Our counselor began listing the names of our host families.

I couldn't wait to hear who my family was. I desperately wanted a place to call home in Israel.

"Jessica, your family is . . ."

My head popped up.

The counselor laughed before he said, "Fuks."

Two days later and with flowers in hand, I knocked on the door of my adoptive family's house. An overweight couple opened the door and invited me inside. As I stepped into the house, I was transported to an Israeli version of Roseanne Barr's house. There were layers of dirt everywhere. Newspapers stacked a foot high. Weird smells in every corner.

The rest of the family introduced themselves. Her kids were just like the kids on Roseanne. The oldest daughter was like Becky, around my age, and an art student. She lived in her room with her boyfriend, whose name was Dudu—a nickname for David. I had a hard time calling him that because I felt like I was insulting him to his face. The middle child, like DJ, was a scrawny teenage boy and kind of creepy. The youngest girl barely said a word, but rolled her eyes a lot, just like Darlene.

At the Rosh Hashanah dinner, there was more food. It looked like they had ordered the entire super-sized menu. Too busy eating, no one talked. I wondered if all Israelis were like this. I was not surprised to learn that Israelis gain weight during the September and October High Holidays, like Americans do during Thanksgiving and Christmas.

As soon as dinner ended, feeling completely alone, I climbed into bed. The sheets hadn't been changed. Instead of a nice little chocolate mint on the pillow, I found a small, curly black hair.

I felt completely fuksed!

After four long days at the Fuks' house, I gave up on finding a home and a family in Israel—something that I longed for, without ever really knowing I was searching for it.

*   *   *

UNKNOWN NUMBER. UNKNOWN NUMBER. UNKNOWN NUMBER. UNKNOWN NUMBER.

My phone ringing was the only thing that broke up the day of volunteering. I stared at the blinking screen on the cell phone. I couldn't imagine who would be calling me. I didn't know anybody in this country.

"Jeeeesssiiiikah? You know who theees is?" a female with an Israeli accent asked.

I could almost see her smile on the other end of the phone.

"Orli!" I shrieked.

My family had hosted Orli two summers ago when she had worked at a Jewish summer camp in Minnesota. When I had picked up Orli for the first time, I had found a cute, compact, spunky, blond-haired, twenty-year old female Israeli. At barely 5'2" and less than a hundred pounds, she had more punch in her than a heavyweight boxer. She had jumped into my car and quickly started jabbering away in her broken English. I had been surprised that such a petite person had such a big mouth.

She screamed back, "Yeeas! Eeet ees mee. How arrr yoooo? How ees Yisrrrael? When deed yoo arrrrrive? Why yooo neverrr wrrrrit mee back?"

"How'd you get my number? How'd you find out that I'm here?" I asked in disbelief. The only possible answer I could think of was that it was written in the stars for us to meet again, or else Oprah was doing a special Middle East version surprise reunion show.

Orli and I had been close friends the summer she spent at my family's house. Every night, we would trade stories about our very different lives. I told her about what it was like growing up and going to college in the US. She wanted to know if college was like in the movies. She told me about her life in the army as a sharp shooter instructor. She told me about the funny pranks they would play on each other as soldiers and what it was like serving with all of the cute Israeli guys. Her stories made me wish that I had joined the army instead of a sorority.

In the evenings, I would take Orli out to dance clubs, the Minnesota State Fair, movies, and house parties. She had promised me that the next time I was in Israel, she would take me out and show me how Israelis party. On the weekends, she would jabber away on the phone to her friends in Israel, telling them about her time in the US, but usually giving them advice. Just like her name, Orli, which means 'my light,' brought warmth and happiness to everyone around her.

"Last weekend, I work at my grocery store and Rachel walk in. She says to me that you look for me and give me your number and now I call you," Orli proclaimed.

A few weeks ago I had called Rachel, an Israeli who had also been a counselor at the Minnesota summer camp, hoping she could put me in touch with Orli. Rachel had coldly told me that she wasn't in contact with Orli and didn't even really like her. When she had dismissed my request so quickly, my dreams of ever finding Orli, escaping from my group, and becoming immersed into Israeli society had been broken. I had given up and conceded the fact that I would always be viewing Israel from the outside, as a tourist.

With the sound of Orli's voice, my hopes and dreams roared back alive. I couldn't believe how small Israel really is—and yet the UN still wants to give away half of the land.

"Why yooo neverrr wrrrrite mee back?" Orli repeated.

She had written me and my family a heartfelt letter after she left. I was too embarrassed to say that I had been busy with school and forgot to respond.

I heard music, yelling, and laughing in the background. Orli explained that she was on her way back from a week of partying in Eilat with all her friends.

"So, when you come to visit my house and family?"

A few days later, I sat on the edge of the bus seat. I wasn't even supposed to be on a bus. The volunteer program forbade it because of all of the terrorist attacks. My eyes nervously darted back and forth as the bus slowly pulled to a stop. Out the window I saw her with a big smile on her face. I jumped out of the bus and practically fell into her arms.

We chattered back and forth about the past year of our lives. Most Israelis didn't have the patience to listen to me trying to formulate a sentence in my beginner-level Hebrew, and the ones who did answer back spoke Hebrew too quickly for me to understand. But

Orli listened carefully trying to understand me while I strung together random words to create a thought.

While leading me to her house, she spoke slowly and explained new words to me with the calmness of a kindergarten teacher. And then she suddenly turned into a drill sergeant and dictated the plans for the night. "We take a nap for two hours. We have dinner with my family. We take two hours to shower, get dressed, put makeup on, and do our hair. By midnight, my two guy friends pick us up and we go out. We stay out until at least four. We sleep all Saturday. We have fun!"

I couldn't wait! I was used to Friday night dinners with my family and then services on Saturday morning. While I had been missing the traditions of my family, this sounded like fun. It was nice to realize that I no longer needed a synagogue to find Jewish community.

She opened the front door to her apartment and I was greeted by the aroma of Friday night dinner. Staring back at me was her family. Before I had a chance to put my bags down or say shalom, they were giving me hugs and offering me something hot to drink, even though it felt like a sauna. Cheerfully and with lots of commotion, we sat down in the small living room and introductions began.

After dinner, Orli and I got ready. I quickly threw on a pair of jeans and a tank top. Orli meticulously put on makeup, curled her already curly hair, and picked out the most revealing tank top and shortest skirt in her closest.

Standing in front of me, looking like an Israeli Playboy bunny, Orli asked, "How I look?"

"I think you forgot your shirt!"

Orli acts and dresses like a typical Israeli. She is tough, yet feminine. She has commanded gun-training classes of hundreds of horny and boisterous eighteen-year-old boys. She does her nails on a weekly basis. Just like most Israeli females, she can be very intimidating, and at the same time very friendly.

RING! RING!

In her high heels, Orli ran to the door and two dark, tall, and handsome Israeli guys entered. They looked like models. They are the friends Orli had mentioned.

"*Shalom, shmi Jessica*," I introduced myself in my best Hebrew.

Insistent on learning the language, I forced myself to speak only Hebrew. If I didn't know how to say something, then I found a way to explain it. It was like a really bad magic trick in which I turned one sentence into three.

"I'm Liel and this is Asaf," said one of Orli's friends. My eyes lingered on Liel's big brown eyes, long eyelashes, and bright smile.

They jabbered among themselves, but afraid that I would embarrass myself, I kept my mouth shut. I watched them laughing together and felt a pang of jealousy seeing how they all seemed to fit in together. It was as if they knew exactly where they belonged. After a few drinks, we headed to a night club. The club was so packed that we barely had room to move. The music was so loud that the walls vibrated. We took shot after shot. The four of us danced until our feet throbbed. Every time Liel touched me, I felt electricity. I never wanted the night to end.

When we got home, just like so many Israelis are willing to give somebody their shirt off their back, Orli insisted that I sleep in her bed while she slept on the trundle. She exemplified the true meaning of *sabra*, a prickly pear—thorny on the outside, sweet on the inside.

I spent the entire Saturday with Orli and her family. I spoke Hebrew. I ate Israeli food. I heard stories about growing up in Israel. It felt like my first real Israeli experience. But more than that, I so quickly and easily fit in. Orli, her family, and her friends welcomed me into their lives. For the first time, things felt natural to me.

It's not like things were perfect in Israel; I was just realizing that I was better suited for the country. As the program continued and I spent more time in the country, Israel became a bigger part of my future. The country's Jewish identity became synonymous with mine. As my future became intertwined with Israel's, I could forget my past, which I was trying to hide from myself and the world. It was finally easy to feel and be Jewish here. I almost couldn't believe that there would be something in this country that would make me feel not Jewish.

2

Little Blue and White Lies

When my volunteer program ends, I make *aliyah* to Israel. Not to be confused with the female R&B star, the term *aliyah* comes from religion and means to ascend, both literally and spiritually. In synagogue, a Jew *has* an *aliyah* when reading from the Torah. But when a Jew *makes aliyah*, this means moving to Israel. The first person to ever make *aliyah* was Abraham, the father of the Jewish people, when God sent him from his birth land to the land that is now known as Israel. Ever since, Jews have considered Israel our homeland, the land of our founding fathers and mothers. It is the land that the Jewish people have returned to throughout history, no matter how many times we were exiled. It is the land where Moses brought the Israelites, where the Maccabees fought the Romans, and where King David ruled. It is the land where our Jewish fate will unfold, and now mine as well.

After spending the past month in the safety of my parents' house preparing for the big move, the day arrives for me to go play in a neighborhood surrounded by Jihadists. I spend my last hour at home sitting, jumping, and pounding on my suitcases, trying to zip the two bags that hold the past twenty-two years of my life. I'm so relieved to get the suitcases closed, that it never occurs to me that they might be overweight. With my family waiting in the car, I walk through my childhood home one last time. I stop to look at the paintings of Jerusalem's Old City that my parents bought during our first family trip to Israel. The ability of the painting's vibrant colors to catch the beauty of the sunset over the city amazes me every time I look at them. I can't believe that tomorrow, I'll call that city my home.

I had been thirteen during our first trip to the Old City. On the way from our hotel, we had rounded a corner and the Old City's huge stone walls towered before us. We all stopped in unison. It was like a fortress right out of the Bible . . . or a fairytale. Afraid that the walls might disappear into history, we quickly approached. Admiring each stone in the road, I wondered what history they would tell if they could talk. My shoes had slipped on the stones, which were slick and smooth as if water had been flowing over them for centuries, but really they were worn by people who had flocked there from all over the world on their path to find God.

Now driving as a family to the airport, we pass our synagogue, where my parents got married, where my family prayed every Saturday morning while I was growing up, where I had my bat mitzvah, and where my rabbi wrote the letter testifying to my Jewishness so I could make *aliyah*. Growing up in a Conservative Jewish family, we went to synagogue every Shabbat. We said prayers before every meal. Just this past weekend our rabbi announced me making *aliyah* during Saturday morning services and the entire congregation wished me *mazal tov*, good luck. I looked around and smiled at everyone, knowing that, even though Israel is full of Jews, I'll miss going to synagogue, hearing my rabbi's insightful sermons, and having this tight-knit community.

I won't go to synagogue. Instead, I'll be going out with Orli. We will get dressed in our high heels, tank tops, and tight jeans for the High Holy Days. I think about how different Judaism can be. In Israel, the

entire country is my Jewish community. I can watch
The Simpsons and after, see the daily Torah portion if
I want. With Judaism part of my daily life, I will have
a better connection to the culture, but less to religion.
There isn't a middle ground in Israel for religion. It's
black or white. It's either ultra-Orthodox or secular.
And I know which side I'm choosing.

Sitting in the backseat of the car, I look into my
carry-on bag to make sure that I've packed all of my
documents: passport, immigration visa, birth certificate, the letter from my rabbi attesting to my Jewish
identity, and my parents' *ketuba*—Jewish marriage
certificate. I smile, relieved that my parents had
agreed to my request to modify their ketuba so that
the rabbinate wouldn't be able to tell that my mom
converted to Judaism. I tense up, thinking back to the
day that I discovered that I wouldn't be considered a
full Jew in Israel.

As part of the volunteer program, once a month,
we had an in-depth educational day with Nouriel, a
Conservative rabbi and lawyer in Israel, who taught us
about the intricacies of the country—from its politics
and social issues to its collective memory and biblical
history. When Nouriel began summarizing one of our
recent sessions, I tuned him out, thinking about all the
preparations for my move to Israel: packing, paperwork, and more. The only thing I still needed was a
letter from my rabbi to prove my Jewishness to get citi-
zenship.

"Today we're discussing the question 'Who is a Jew?'"
he announced. The question pulled me out of my head
and back into Israel's Independence Hall. Proud to be
Jewish, I chuckled and ironically asked out loud, "With
centuries of persecution, why would anyone who isn't
Jewish claim to be?"

Ignoring my sarcasm, Nouriel began his lecture.
"When Israel was established in 1948, David Ben-Gurion,

the first prime minister, envisioned a country that provided a safe haven to any Jew who had been persecuted during the Holocaust. This meant that a person whom the Nazis defined as being Jewish would have the Right of Return to the new Jewish homeland. The Nazi's definition of a Jew was anyone with one Jewish grandparent."

I smiled to myself, thinking how the same definition that once led to Jews being murdered now leads to their salvation. Content with the poetic justice, I returned to planning my *aliyah* in my head.

"However, the ultra-Orthodox rabbis didn't agree with this definition," I heard him explain. "The ultra-Orthodox rabbis believe that the definition of who is a Jew should come from *halacha*, traditional religious law and customs. According to their interpretation, a person is Jewish only if his or her mother is born a Jew. And the ultra-Orthodox believe the only conversions that God accepts are the ones done by their strict, ultra-Orthodox standards."

My head snapped, with the force of a car accident, in Nouriel's direction. The blood rushed through my ears. All I heard were the thoughts streaming through my head. How do the ultra-Orthodox know what God wants? Who made them experts on interpreting God's words? It seemed like dangerous pedagogy, strangely similar to those people announcing every single day that the world would come to an end tomorrow.

I thought back to the past summer when I had been working at the Jewish Community Center's gym, trying to save money before the volunteer program. Sitting at the fitness center desk, I was reading *The Red Tent*, a novel that depicts the biblical story of Dinah from a woman's point of view, when I was interrupted by an Orthodox Jewish woman, who exercised in a long skirt, baggy T-shirt, and a handkerchief covering her head.

"Don't believe any of that book! Nothing in it is true!" she had forcefully said.

I had looked up to respond. But before I had the chance to ask what her proof was that the burning bush was not Moses on shrooms, she had run out.

Thinking about that encounter, I felt the blood drain out of my face, but Nouriel didn't notice. In the US, the woman at the JCC was just expressing her opinion, but here in Israel, people like her have power over my Judaism, over my identity.

"Ben-Gurion was concerned that using the ultra-Orthodox definition would hurt the relations between the international Jewish community and Israel. He didn't want to isolate the Conservative and Reform Jewish movements abroad, nor did he want to cause a rift between the religious and secular Jews in Israel. He considered the long-term prospects of the Jewish state if it only accepted ultra-Orthodox marriages and conversions done abroad. He realized that both of these outcomes could cause the destruction of the small and vulnerable state as much as an Arab attack," Nouriel explained.

I exhaled for the first time since he had said that only ultra-Orthodox conversions are acceptable. I looked over at the Israeli flag with a big blue Star of David and my hand instinctively grabbed the Star of David hanging on my necklace.

Nouriel continued. "Ben-Gurion understood the importance of unity between the secular and religious. So he made a compromise."

I gripped my necklace tighter. The points from the star dug into my palm.

"For the purpose of making *aliyah* to Israel, a person is defined as Jewish if he has one Jewish grandparent. This is called the Right of Return Law. But Ben-Gurion allowed the ultra-Orthodox to use their definition for the important Jewish lifecycles: birth, marriages, death, and more. This means they decide who is Jewish enough to get married or be buried in a Jewish cemetery in

Israel. Basically he gave the ultra-Orthodox a monopoly over Judaism."

I swallowed hard. I couldn't believe that free-thinking people in the democratic State of Israel would actually agree to these outdated and primitive laws. What would this mean for me? I'd have the right to move here, but not to marry? It was far away, but I knew I'd want an Israeli family of my own in the future.

After finding my voice, I hesitantly asked, "Doesn't that sort of create a purgatory for some Jews here? What do the Jews who meet Ben-Gurion's definition, but don't meet the ultra-Orthodox definition, do? How do they get married?" I tried to hide my fear of my identity being erased in Israel.

"It creates exactly that. Many go abroad to Cyprus to get married. There are no civil marriages in Israel, only religious ones. And it is illegal for Reform and Conservative rabbis to perform marriages here."

"But how does the rabbinate know if you're Jewish to their standards or not?" I asked. I had a feeling that I didn't want to know the answer.

"There are many ways. A letter from an Orthodox rabbi whom the rabbinate accepts. A ketuba, a Jewish marriage contract, is another way . . ."

With my heart pounding in my ears, I didn't hear the rest of his answer. I was starting to doubt my decision to move here. I couldn't believe what I was hearing. Was Israel actually a fundamentalist country like its neighbors? No! It couldn't be. I thought about all the secular fun I had in Tel Aviv. There was nothing fundamentalist about the house music in the club. I calmed myself down by convincing myself that this who-is-a-Jew law is probably just like some of the other archaic Jewish laws that no rational person in today's day or age follows, like stoning an adulterer or swinging a chicken around your head to rid yourself of sins. Or sort of like how oral sex is illegal in Texas.

It won't affect me.

When the lecture ended, I approached Nouriel, whom I instinctively trusted. As everyone else left the room to explore the building where a free Jewish nation was declared over fifty years ago, I asked Nouriel what I could do so that I wouldn't be one of the Jews in purgatory. He clarified for me that a letter from a rabbi is enough for making *aliyah*, but that for marriage, a higher standard of proof is needed. After discussing different options, weighing the pros and the cons, the ethical dilemmas, and the legal ones, I decided that I wasn't going to let these anti-Semitic laws change my identity. Nouriel, understanding the importance of my Jewish identity and the absurdity of these laws, agreed to help.

A few months later, I went to his synagogue with a copy of my parents' ketuba. I carefully pulled out the document, a botle of Wite-Out, and a pen. I delicately placed them on the desk. As I looked up at the Ten Commandments hanging in the sanctuary, I opened the Wite-Out bottle and slowly and carefully whited out the name "Abraham," which was written as the name of my mom's father. Abraham, as the father of the Jewish people, is accepted by every convert as their new father after conversion. His name on my parents' ketuba would have been an obvious sign to the rabbinate that my mother had converted.

I gently blew on the Wite-Out to speed up the erasing of my past. With my face next to the paper, the fumes seeped into my nose. Once it dried, Rabbi Nouriel adjusted his kippah, took the pen out of his pocket and carefully wrote my grandfather's real name: Jonathan—Yonatan in Hebrew—making sure that each Hebrew letter matched the original handwriting. It seemed to be fate that my grandfather's name can pass for some Jewish peasant versus a traditional Christian name. As the ink dried, my secret and my family's past began to fade.

With a swipe of the pen, he had changed my future. He had given me his blessing. It made what I was doing kosher and not just an act of defiance. I felt like a young Gloria Steinem. A modern-day Ester. A Jewish Rosa Parks. Looking at this new document, I couldn't see any evidence of my original history. I hoped that it would also pass the rabbinate's scrutiny.

"If they don't accept our Judaism, I'm not going to accept theirs," I said, while staring at the new *ketuba*.

Thoughtfully stroking his beard and nodding, Rabbi Nouriel agreed, knowing that the rabbinate doesn't even accept him as a real rabbi or his teachings as real Judaism.

Now, sitting in the back seat of the car, with our synagogue behind us, I take out the forged document. While I only need the letter from my rabbi to prove I'm Jewish enough to make *aliyah*, I will someday need the forged ketuba to get married in Israel. My thumb caresses my empty ring finger. It feels strange thinking about something in the distant future, but I'm forced to so that I can be accepted in Israel as fully Jewish. I closely inspect the ketuba. I can't even tell that it has been altered. There will be no reason for anyone to doubt my Jewish identity when it's time for me to get married. I think I've secured being able to build my own Israeli family. Content, I tuck it safely away in my bag for future use, wishing that I didn't have to hide the truth, but knowing that I have to so that I can have the full rights of a citizen in Israel. This law doesn't seem fair or just. But I can't fight the law. I'm going to have enough battles to fight as a new immigrant.

As we pull up to the Minnesota airport, I look at my Israeli immigration visa. It is proof that the country has accepted me. I wonder to myself where the greater irony lays, that the homeland of the Jews is the only country that would consider me not Jewish, or that I choose, as my home, the only country in the world that doesn't consider me to be a Jew. Either way, my sarcasm and self-mockery as a survival tool is proof that I'm part of a culture that has been persecuted for thousands of years. And now with my plan to join the IDF, I'll be a part of preventing that persecution.

Jewish Spring Break

My flight to Israel is supposed to be a charter flight full of Jews making *aliyah*. The flight was organized by *Nefesh B'Nefesh*, an organization that provides scholarships and guidance to North Americans who want to fulfill the ultimate Jewish dream of moving to Israel. It's sort of like a Make-A-Wish Foundation for Jews: except that we aren't dying . . . we just have a death wish.

The organization is largely funded by evangelical Christians who want all of the Jews to move back to Israel to bring about the Armageddon and eventually the return of Jesus Christ. It's no wonder we need our own homeland; even people supporting Jews want us killed. I hope they don't expect to get their money back when that plan does not come to fruition.

After my flight from Minnesota, I am now dragging my two oversized suitcases to the check-in desk at JFK. I can already picture this flight being like a Jewish spring-break trip. I'm imagining hundreds of other twenty-somethings, just like me, who packed up their entire lives, left their entire history behind them, in the hopes of beginning a new, more fulfilling life in a strange and foreign country.

When I arrive at the check-in area, instead of seeing a bunch of young adults ready to party, I see little children running around screaming, babies crying, women in long skirts and hair coverings, and religious Jewish men gathered together in one location, praying. The scene reminds me of the first time I visited the Western Wall of the destroyed Temple in Jerusalem. It was the first time I directly felt the control of the ultra-Orthodox in my life. We had spent the evening lost in the Old City and then we had suddenly walked out to a bright, crowded open area. This enormous wall was towering over people who looked like ants in comparison. Each stone was the size of a car. It was magnificent.

But my awe quickly ended when I had noticed that, unlike in our synagogue, where women and men are equal and pray together, in Jerusalem I saw that women were praying on one side and men on another . . . and it seemed like the men had the better side. We had approached the Western Wall as a family, but then my dad had to separate from us. As I had watched my dad veer off to the left to go to the men's section, I remember being upset that he had to be alone during this meaningful family event. We had spent years praying together in the direction of the Western Wall, and now that we are here we can't be together.

At the airport, staring at the men praying separately in one section, I freeze, thinking that this must be a sign from God: "Go back! These zealots will control your life in Israel!" This is a very powerful omen, considering that I don't actually believe in God. Yes, it's true: I'm an Atheist Jewish Zionist making *aliyah*, but that just goes to show that I'm a true intellectual and a deep individual. These multiple personalities have nothing to do with being confused, lost, or disturbed. At least that is what I have been trying to convince rabbis . . . and psychologists. Rabbis have recommended prayer; psychologists have suggested Xanax. I think it is clear now why I would have the tendency to lean towards secularism—they prescribe the good drugs.

Just as I'm doubting my *aliyah* decision a smiling twenty-something woman wearing tight jeans and a tank top appears out of the sea of families.

"Hi, I'm Ester," she introduces herself to me. I can instantly tell that we'll be good friends.

In a short conversation, we find out that we'll be living, interning, and studying Hebrew together. This coincidence reassures me that I'm making the right choice.

So, I decide to leave the signs from God to the men with kippahs, praying in the corner near the baggage carts. I quickly get in line to get my ticket to my new life.

By now I've flown back and forth to Israel a number of times, so I've grown used to the interrogations. While I realize the need to ask these questions to weed out the terrorists, I'm still impatient.

"Where are you coming from?" The security checker greets the passengers ahead of me in Hebrew.

She looks just like the security checker from my first trip to Israel ten years ago. I remember how strange it seemed back then.

"Is this your first time in Israel?" the security checker had asked with a stern face.

"Yes." I beamed. At thirteen years old, I, like every teenager, enjoyed talking about myself.

"For how long you go?" she asked.

"Two weeks. I'm missing summer camp," I said, pouting.

Uninterested in my disappointment, she looked down at her notepad. "Do you go to synagogue? Which one?"

"B'nai Israel, a Conservative synagogue. We walk there every Shabbat. My dad is the president of the synagogue and on the JCC board, and my mom is the president of Hadassah in our city," I said proudly, before I remembered that I was too cool to mention my parents.

She nodded in recognition, as if she personally knew the rabbi at our synagogue. I thought that maybe she had a synagogue list on her clipboard. "Who are you traveling with?" she asked.

Looking over at my family, I rolled my eyes. "My parents and my younger sister."

Glancing at them, her face remained blank. "Do you speak Hebrew?"

"Ummm . . ." Re-adjusting my backpack, I wasn't sure how to answer. My dad had tried to teach me Hebrew when I was younger. "I know how to read Hebrew. I read for my bat mitzvah and we pray in Hebrew at synagogue every Shabbat. At my Jewish day school, Talmud Torah, I took Hebrew lessons and learned how to say a few words. But, no. I don't really speak it."

She perked up following that answer and asked, "Do you keep kasher?" Instead of saying it kosher, like I did, she emphasized the word oddly and rolled her "r."

"Of course!" I said defensively.

She continued with her line of questioning, "You said you went to a Jewish camp. What's its name?"

"Herzl Camp. After the founder of Zionism," I said, not realizing the irony that I preferred to sing songs about Israel while at camp in the Midwest rather than actually be in Israel.

"Do you know anyone in Israel?" she persisted, in accented English.

At my childhood synagogue there was one wild-haired Israeli with a bushy mustache. When his daughter had a temper tantrum during services, he had picked her up, stomped out of the sanctuary, and slammed the door behind him—making more noise than his toddler. "Yes, at our synagogue there is an Israeli. Some of my Hebrew teachers are Israeli. Oh, and we hosted an Israeli for a few weeks during her army service when she worked at a Jewish day camp."

The questioner looked down as if she was trying to think of other questions and I wondered what she was going to ask next—what my favorite prayer was? What my bat bitzvah haftarah portion was? If we lit candles on Shabbat? Irritated, I looked over at my parents and

sister to see what their interviews were like and overheard a young man, wearing the same security outfit,
ask my mom what synagogue she went to as a child.
A quick wave of pain, that only I noticed, flashed over
her face.

"Where are you coming from?"
It takes me a moment to realize I'm not thirteen
anymore when the security guard asks me the same
question in Hebrew.
"Minnesota," I answer, as I proudly hand her my
passport that now has an Israeli visa.
After looking at my passport, she asks me where I'm
going.
"I'm making *aliyah*," I say in Hebrew, enthusiasm
oozing from me. I add, as if I'm a thirteen-year-old
again, "I'm also planning on joining the IDF."
She laughs at my declaration, asks me a few questions that sound like they are out of a high school
yearbook, and then quickly waves me through. Unlike
my first trip here, my Jewish identity is no longer in
question. I'm beginning to think that the amount of
time that I spend in the country is inversely proportional to the amount of questions I'm asked at the
airport.
The security guard moves to the next person in line
who is wearing an IDF T-shirt with a keffiyeh around
her neck. I wonder what her security check is like
and then think to myself that she is an identity crisis
waiting to happen.

Somewhere Over the Rainbow

As I'm boarding the plane, I look at the ticket in my
hands. The free one-way airplane ticket that I got from
the Israeli government feels like a golden ticket.
After pushing through the lines of families, I find my
seat. The middle seat. In between two religious girls in
their twenties. As I sit down, I grumble to myself, why

can't I be sitting next to a cute guy on my *aliyah* flight? Is that really too much to ask?

I arrange my bags and get comfortable. Just after I get my pillow in the exact right position, a religious girl standing in the aisle looks at me oddly and walks away. I figure she doesn't like the fact that I'm wearing a tank top and I lay my head back down.

Two minutes later, there is a tap on my shoulder. I open my eyes to see a flight attendant wanting to check my ticket. This twenty-something-year-old girl tattled on me for being in her seat. It turns out that they had double booked us, so the flight attendant offers me a seat in business class. I quickly gather my belongings and leave her with her long skirt and mouth hanging open. I think it must be a sign.

Running true to Jewish Standard Time, the plane takes off an hour late.

I expected this flight to be one that I'll always remember. But in spite of being bumped up, it is one that I'll always try to forget. The thirteen-hour flight is full of babies crying, children screaming, men praying, and nine cats meowing. Yes, *nine.*

Immediately after we take off, the religious men gather to start their praying and swaying right next to the bathroom. Unfortunately, at the same time, I have to use the bathroom. After getting out of my seat, I nervously approach, hoping that they'll let me use the restroom, but also knowing that they probably won't while they are praying since they believe women and men must be separate during prayers. When I reach the nearest toilet, a religious man says to me, "You can't be here. Us men are praying!"

Ugh! I scream in my head. Isn't it enough that they have control of the Western Wall? Do they need control to my bathroom use in this plane too?

I turn around and head back to my seat, with my bladder still full. I hope this isn't another warning that the religious will control my life in Israel.

I sit back down and take a sleeping pill.

I wake up from my pill-induced coma to the sounds of people singing and frantically dancing in the aisles. Under any other circumstance, these people would have been Tasered for being a security threat.

I go to see how Ester is doing and to ask her what all the commotion is about.

"We received our new Israeli identity cards. Didn't you get one?" she asks. It turns out that Nefesh B'Nefesh performed a modern day miracle by getting an Interior Ministry representative, infamous for always being on strike, to actually do some work and brought this representative on the flight to give out Israeli identity cards.

"No," I say, frantically looking around for the agent. The process of getting an Israeli identity card usually takes months, but everyone on the plane got theirs in hours . . . except me. How did I miss out on getting my Israeli identity? I've been waiting to receive an Israeli identity for a year now. This feels like another bad omen.

"They woke me up for crappy airplane food, but not to give me an ID card!" I exclaim.

I run around the plane looking for the representative, but she somehow was able to disappear mid-flight. I can't believe that even on a plane, a government employee can escape extra work. Disappointed, I slouch back into my seat. While fighting back tears, I pull out my parents' ketuba and quickly inspect it to see if anyone else could catch the forgery. While staring at it, I become afraid that getting my Israeli identity is going to be harder than I thought. I start becoming afraid that my Jewishness will always feel like it is in doubt.

Homecoming Queen

I'm one of the first people to step out into the fresh air of Israel. The doors of the plane open to the sun shining down on hundreds of people singing, high-level politicians clapping, and IDF soldiers waving Israeli flags, celebrating our arrival. I can't wait to be a soldier like all of them. All of my concerns melt away.

I feel like Dorothy when she first stepped out into the Land of Oz—like I'm seeing the world in color for the first time.

Only a few minutes ago, when I felt the landing gear descend, I took a deep breath. The familiar cheering of the passengers as the plane landed charged the stale air in the cabin. I was ready to start my new life.

Walking down the steps of the plane, I can't stop smiling. The crowd is still cheering.

I'm receiving a celebrity's welcome. It's like the entire country is throwing me a surprise party.

More of the plane has de-boarded and people are kissing the ground.

Some of the highest political officials in Israel are thanking me for moving here.

I don't understand why people said this was so hard. This is great!

I shake hands with Ariel Sharon, Benjamin Netanyahu, and Sallai Meridor[5], and then stand in between all of them for a group picture.

It is clear that I made the right decision. My fears wash away.

And then, the welcome ceremony is over.

We're herded to the bowels of the airport to register as citizens. I fill out forms, which seem to require an SAT preparation course. The Interior Ministry agent asks me personal history questions that make me genuinely prefer to be interrogated by the Mossad, but he doesn't give me my identity card. Instead I receive a stamp in my American passport. Before I can voice my concern that I have no identity in the country, he hands me the monthly stipend I get for being a new immigrant and

---

5. Ariel Sharon was the current prime minister, Benjamin Netanyahu was previously prime minister, and Sallai Meridor was president of The Jewish Agency.

sends me away from his desk. I count the cash, which is supposed to cover my monthly living expenses, but is actually enough for the massage and haircut I need and won't be able to afford.

Walking out of the airport with my suitcases, I'm confronted with a mob of taxi drivers trying to gather as many passengers into one car as possible.

The sun is beating down so hard that it is blinding. There are people yelling outside, but I hear nothing.

This is my first time in Israel when I'm not in a program. No one is awaiting my arrival. No one has planned an agenda for me. No one knows I'm here. And I don't even have an identity here. I look around for Ester, but I don't see her. She probably already left with her friend.

I freeze. It suddenly occurs to me that there is a chance that I may not make it here. What if everyone sees me as an imposter and I'm never accepted? Wondering if I can change my mind, I look back to the airport doors that are automatically closing. I want to go home. I don't think I could survive being rejected here.

I think back to the night I decided to make *aliyah*.

Sitting on the beach with Liel, Orli, and the rest of their Israeli friends, I watched as the waves crashed. It was dark outside and the ocean seamlessly melted into the night sky. The fruity smoke from the hookah mixed with the saltiness in the air. Under my bare feet, the sand still emanated warmth from the day. The home-made hummus melted in my mouth. Orli was kneading pita dough in a plastic bowl and threw another pita on the fire. The guitar, Liel's singing, and laughter filled the emptiness of the beach. I thought to myself, this is it. This is what I've been looking for. I've never felt more at peace with myself and with my surroundings.

In the middle of the party on the beach, I decided to move here. I'd join the IDF. Maybe I could find a way to use my English skills, degree in journalism, and American perspective to help improve Israel's image in the world.

Without another thought, I whispered to Orli, "I'm going to move here after my volunteer program." Now that I had said it out loud, I was going to have to do it. All of the sudden I was scared. I realized I didn't know how to survive here.

Orli leaned in to me. "I'll help you with anything you need." Then she jumped up and announced my decision to everyone. They burst into an Israeli song that I was afraid would end up following me: *"Jessie, Jessie, Jessie, Jessicaaaaah! She used to be a complete foreigner, she worked on the kibbutz for two years, but now she is somewhere else."*

After the celebration ended, Liel asked me, "What are you going to do for work?"

"I'm going to join the IDF!" I expected the same celebration at my declaration, but instead I received silence and blank stares.

"Where are you going?"

I'm quickly snapped out of my trance when a taxi driver yells at me.

Before I answer, he's already pushing my luggage cart to his taxi.

As part of the *aliyah* welcome package from the Israeli government, I get a ride from the airport to anywhere in the country.

"Jerusalem," I say. Like any rational person, I state the location of my new home. However, if I had been thinking like a veteran Israeli, I would have taken full advantage of this benefit and traveled to the most southern point in Israel, Eilat, for a week of sun and fun on the government's shekel.

The driver brings me over to his large taxi that already has ten people in it and three times as many suitcases. Another taxi driver grabs my bags and the two of them begin fighting over them. I'm too tired to intervene. Taxi drivers, like a veteran Israelis, know how to take full advantage of being the end receivers of the government's money. They stuff us naïve new immigrants into their cars like sardines so that they can charge for multiple rides, but only have to make and report a single trip.

The taxi driver who won my bags runs around his car, tying the suitcases onto the roof. He tells us exactly how and where to sit as to maximize the amount of room for all the suitcases. I'm surprised he isn't trying to tie us onto the roof.

Once everything is secured, we begin our drive to Jerusalem. It's the middle of July and the air conditioner is broken . . . or at least that is what the driver is claiming. The windows are open, but that doesn't help. The air whacking me in the face is streaming through the sweaty armpit of the man in front of me.

Escaping to my memories, I think back to the first time I made this ascent to the Holy City. I strained my eyes trying to see the rusted tanks on the side of the road that were used to liberate the ancient city only thirty years ago. Now the tanks feel like part of my history. But when I saw them for the first time, Jerusalem had felt like a city in a fairytale land far, far away. I couldn't believe then that we were about to enter the hilltop capital. I remember seeing the Mount of Olives glistening in the sun as the tour guide listed the name of historical Jews buried on the mountain side. It had been proof to me that the childhood stories were true. My history had suddenly come alive, even if it was in a graveyard.

As my family entered the city, the sun had been high in the sky. The narrow streets were packed with cars. People crowded the sidewalks. Stone buildings, bearing satellite dishes, were pushed together. I expected to see David and Goliath or Joseph in his multi-colored coat walking the alleyways, as if they had never left, almost like a biblical-themed Disneyland. I had not expected to see a messy, modern city. The city had not looked holy. With my face pressed to the glass, I still hoped to get a glimpse of Moses and his staff or Noah with animals following him, but instead I was in awe of the guys and girls, only a few years older than me, wearing army uniforms and semi-automatic weapons.

I smiled when I saw ultra-Orthodox Jews wandering the streets, openly and free of discrimination, unlike during the Holocaust when they had been harassed and forced to wear yellow Stars of David. In Minnesota, we didn't have many ultra-Orthodox Jews. I almost never saw one up close. And I certainly never talked to one. I laughed when I saw one smoking and another one talking on a cell phone. I guess because of their clothing, I almost expected them to be more like the Amish. Instantly, I felt connected with them, as if they were my long lost brothers from a previous century.

As the taxi driver swerves the car to avoid a car accident, I'm thrown into the stranger next to me. I spend the next two hours, while every other passenger gets dropped off, wondering if this path will redefine my identity. Then we finally reach the Merkaz Hamagshamim—my new home. When I get out, the taxi driver practically lobs my luggage at me. I don't even have a chance to yell at him. He just takes off, leaving me in his dust. I'm going to have to become a lot quicker with my responses to fit in.

Standing at the gate to the apartment complex, I'm taken back to the chance conversation that brought me here. I had been thinking of living and studying Hebrew at *Ulpan Etzion* in Jerusalem but I didn't really want to live in the capital because it was too religious. However, it was supposed to be the best *ulpan* in Israel. When I mentioned to an American guy who I had met at a house party during my volunteer program, he had recommend that I apply to Merkaz Hamagshamim. He explained it as a commune for English-speaking new immigrants, but without brainwashing or prophets who sleep with children.

"We all help each other out until we are strong enough to be released into Israeli society. We're like a makeshift family," he said. Needing a place to belong, I was instantly convinced and applied. Not only was I accepted to live there, I was also offered a job. I almost couldn't believe that going out for a few drinks one night was all it took to figure out my next year. Everything seemed to fall into place so easily. It felt like the momentum of destiny. It was as if what Herzl had said was really true: "If you will it, it is no dream." Despite what the rabbinate thinks about my Jewishness, I felt like I was getting signs from above that I belonged in Israel.

"Welcome to Merkaz Hamagshamim." Two guys appear at the gates and offer to carry my bags.

On our way up the steps, one of the guys says in an Australian accent, "If you have any questions, this is my room. You can come day or night." He winks to the other guy.

By the second floor they are complaining more than Jewish grandmothers about the heavy load.

I enthusiastically open the door to my room, and am greeted by four bare walls, a cot, a broken shelf, and a closet that is falling apart.

"Thanks for the help guys. I'm going to get settled," I say as I close the door. They look at me like they want a tip.

I lay down on the bed.

Surrounded by silence for the first time, all of a sudden it hits me, stronger than a bomb's sound wave. From now on, everything in my life is going to be hard: learning Hebrew, going to the grocery store, earning a living, and this mattress. Without bothering to make the bed, I turn over and fall asleep, knowing that all of the difficulties will eventually be worth it. Every difficulty that I overcome will make me into a stronger Israeli who will be able survive here, no matter what.

Identity Makeover

The sun is just coming up. I lay awake thinking about the notorious Israeli bureaucracy. It sounds like having diarrhea and not being able to find a bathroom—you run around hoping to find an open office, and once you do, the line is so long that you don't think you'll make it in time.

I roll over and try to fall back asleep.

A rooster crows.

Where am I? Auntie Em's farm?

It doesn't stop.

With a pillow over my head, I'm dreading facing the first day of bureaucracy. I wonder if the reason Israelis are always so stressed is because of the bureaucracy—not the terrorism.

Unable to fall back asleep, I get dressed and head to Ester's room to see if she is up early too. The entire building, full of new immigrants, is silent. I wonder what all of them are doing here in Israel. How long have they been here? What brought them here? Where are they working? How do they support themselves? Will I succeed like them?

When I get to her apartment, I knock on the door and she cheerfully opens it.

"Jet lag or the rooster?" I ask.

"Both," she says and laughs.

"Well, we can get an early start. Do you want to make a list of everything we need to do?" I ask.

If we do things in the wrong order and forget any documents, we will be perpetually stuck in a bureaucratic game of monkey in the middle.

I need to go to the Interior Ministry to get my ID card that I didn't get on the plane and Ester agrees to join me, even though she already received hers. The

veteran immigrants at Merkaz Hamagshamim recommended that we get to the Interior Ministry as early as
possible. Some even suggested camping out in front of
the doors as if we were getting tickets for some rock
concert in the 80's.

Armed with all of our official documents, hydration
packs, power bars, maps, a change of underwear, and
toilet paper, we head out looking more like we are going
on a wilderness survival course than to do paperwork.
We jump on the bus and ask the driver to tell us when
he arrives at the Interior Ministry. He looks at us with
pity, as if we've told him that we've just been diagnosed
with terminal cancer.

Ten minutes later, the bus driver slams on his breaks
and yells, "Interior Ministry stop" in the same tone
that he would announce reaching the gates of hell. We
excitedly jump off the bus and then are stopped dead in
our tracks.

In front of us is a massive mob, as if there is a prison
yard fight going on or people trying to get into the
newest dance club, but really they are just in line for the
ministry. We knew that the process could be emotion-
ally demanding, but we never imagined that it would as
physically challenging as running with the bulls.

Both Ester and I can barely speak Hebrew, much
less yell in Hebrew—which is really the only vernacular
understood in the country. And we are too petite to
push our way through the mob. Looking at each other
in disbelief and defeat, we turn around and go sit at the
bus stop.

"Maybe we should just come back tomorrow," I say
with my face in my hands, not really believing it will be
different any another day.

"Wait! I know someone here," Ester exclaims as if
she just realized she has a super power.

Both of us jump up in excitement, knowing that her super power is one called *protectia*[6], having a connection in a high place.

Ester calls her contact and within a few minutes, we hear our names called out over the noise of the mob by the security guard at the front door. We feel like VIP's again. The mob parts like the Red Sea. When we walk past the security guard, I smile when I hear him humming the tune of the Israeli song called "Jessica."

I think back to the first time Orli and her friends sang me the song. I was at Orli's family's house one Saturday during my volunteer program when her friends called her to say that they would pick us up in five minutes for a picnic. That was when I feel in love with Israeli spontaneity—even though it sometimes seems like they have impulse control problems, but that's what makes them exciting.

We quickly got ready and ran downstairs. I opened the car door and inside Liel welcomed me with an overconfident smile, but with his looks, who wouldn't be conceited? I swooned a little before jumping in the backseat with blankets, a guitar, a *mangel* (grill), and a cooler. I loved hanging out with Orli's group, speaking Hebrew, doing Israeli things, being Jewish without going to synagogue.

As we began to drive, a conversation I'd had with high-school students at my volunteer job earlier that week snuck up on me. I was supposed to be teaching them to read in English, but instead they pounced on

---

6. Another word for *protecia* is Vitamin P. While these are not as cheap as a daily multi-vitamin, they can be bought. Although connections are important in any country, in Israel, nothing is possible without them, from finding a job to finding a husband. The country is so small that the concept of six degrees of separation doesn't apply here. Legend has it that in Israel there are only three degrees of separation. This means that from our bus driver to the prime minister, there is only one person in between.

me with questions. "How old are you?" "Do you have a boyfriend?" "Where are you from?" "Are you Jewish?"

"Of course I'm Jewish. Why else would I be here?" I had exclaimed, surprised at my defensive tone, and then quickly began speaking to them in Hebrew. I thought that if I improved my Hebrew enough, no one would ever doubt my Jewishness again.

When Liel started playing his guitar in the car, he rescued me from having to think about my fears. He started with an upbeat Israeli song and everybody else joined in.

She used to be a complete foreigner
She worked on the kibbutz for two years
But now she is somewhere else.

She said "It hurts
That nobody loves anymore"
She went somewhere else

She always thought that God
Liked to see us play music
Because that is the head of Jessica
Jessie, Jessie, Jessie, Jessi-caaaaah ooh ah ooh ah!
Ahh ooh ah ooh ah!
Now she is far away.

Orli translated the lyrics for me and told me that it was a classic Israeli song by the Ethnix from 1993, the same year as my bat mitzvah, fatefully. She said the girl in the song loved chocolate, just like me. I thought it was weird that it was such a cheerful tune, while the words seemed so depressing. I hoped the song wouldn't jinx me.

When we arrived at the forest, we met up with a dozen other people. Within minutes it looked as if an entire army base was set up, with a full kitchen and living room. It's no wonder how this country was built so quickly out of nothing.

At the picnic table, everyone was chatting, barbecuing, making shakshuka[7], chopping salads, and smoking hookahs. I tried my hardest to understand what they were saying. Orli would turn to me after everyone laughed to explain the jokes. When I got stuck trying to say something, she knew how to finish my sentences. It felt like we had been friends since childhood.

Liel, with his contagious and irresistible laugh, was the life of the party. Every now and then he would look over at me and wink. I tried not to blush. His smile made me feel like I belonged in Israel. I felt like I was getting my first glimpse behind the curtain. I pulled Orli aside and asked her if he was single.

She smiled and said, "Ah, yes. If you like, I can make a *shiduch*!"

I fantasized about having an Israeli boyfriend. I imagined the romance of dating a soldier. I dreamt about having a family to go to for Friday night dinners, someone to speak Hebrew with, and a place to call home. When it started getting dark and chilly, Liel handed me his sweatshirt.

It is much colder in the Interior Ministry than it was in that forest at sunset. As Ester and I walk inside, our eyes have to quickly adjust to the darkness. We both shiver as we head up the stairwell, passing people on the steps who look like they have been waiting in the hallways for days . . . or months. Men's stubble has begun to grow, women's make-up is smeared, and children look like their clothing is ripping at the seams from growth spurts. Ester and I look at each other, scared to see what is upstairs as if we are in a haunted house. There isn't supposed to be a hell in the Jewish faith, but the Israeli

---

7. For a shakshuka recipe, please see see the appendix.

government sure seems to have created a perfect tenth circle for Dante's Inferno.

We walk into a waiting room full of over two hundred people; some have set up tents and others are cooking meals on portable *mangels*. On the wall, we see a sign showing that they have just accepted number 37. We take the next number in the dispenser. It is number 512.

I look down at our number and wonder why the international media always makes a big deal that Palestinians have to wait at checkpoints. Why has there never been any coverage of the Israelis who wait at the Interior Ministry for days on end? Why aren't the NGOs and the UN organizations demonstrating against this suffering?

"What are you going to do? At this pace it is going to take you a year to become Israeli," Ester says, half-jokingly.

Instead of crying, I laugh. I wonder if the reason Jews wandered the desert for forty years is because they didn't want to deal with Israel's immigration bureaucracy.

Overwhelmed, I sink into the seat.

Within the next ten minutes, the number changes once and when it does, twelve different people run up to the open booth claiming to have the same number, but of course all had lost their tickets.

As I see a man trying to pick-pocket another man for his number, Ester's connection pops around the corner with a smile . . . and a halo.

"What are you waiting here for? Come on back," he yells, waving us back.

He whisks us away into what seems like a completely different vortex. The sun shines through the windows of the hall. There is calming music in the background. People are relaxing, drinking coffee, and gossiping.

We walk into a room with thousands of identity cards scattered like they are poker cards. I'm sure that most of the people camping in the waiting room belong to these identity cards, but won't receive them for another few weeks.

I tense up, annoyed at the pointlessness and disorganization. I want to yell at them for hindering all of us from realizing our dreams, but am thankful that at least I'll be getting my Israeli identity today.

"What is your name?" one of the women asks.

"Jessica Fishman," I say, trying to do it with an Israeli accent.

"Like in the song, *Jessie, Jessie, Jessie, Jessicaaaaah!*" She continues singing and nods her head to the pile for us to start looking.

We dive into the pile like children searching for a toy at the bottom of a cereal box. We know better than to expect the cards to be in any sort of order, so we look at every single one.

"Here it is! I found it!" I yell and wave it in the air, feeling as if I've jumped over the first hurdle.

I ask if I need to sign anything or fill out any documents, but they say that it isn't necessary. It's comforting to know that anyone can easily steal my identity—not that I really have one in Israel yet.

As we walk out of the room, I take a closer look at my new ID. Seeing my picture with my name written in Hebrew on an official Israeli document, I almost feel reborn. I examine it to make sure they got my identity correct. I look for the line that says I'm Jewish, but I don't see it listed[8]. Before I have a chance to ask, Ester reminds me that we have to rush to get everything

---

8. Israeli identity cards used to list a person's religion, but in 2002, the Knesset's Constitution, Law and Justice Committee canceled the nationality clause after the High Court ordered the Interior Ministry to classify Reform and Conservative community members as Jewish, in Israel and abroad. At the time, Interior Minister Eli Yishai refused to comply with the ruling because he did not want to put his signature on a document that listed Reform and Conservative converts as Jewish and therefore began leaving the religion section blank on everyone's' ID cards.

done. I quickly stuff my ID into my pocket and push away my fear.

The Friar Society

We run out of the offices, past the people in the waiting room. Number 38 is still showing.

When we get outside, we look around and realize we don't know where to go. I ask a random Israeli on the street, "How do we get to the Absorption Ministry?"

After he responds with the canned Israeli response for directions—"Go straight, straight, straight, until the end, turn right and then when you get there you'll know"—I don't know why I bothered asking. Last year during Yom Kippur while trying to find a synagogue, I followed these same exact directions and nearly ended up in an Arab village in East Jerusalem.

After an hour of being nomads, we decide to grab a taxi. The driver, after hearing that we wanted to go to the Absorption Ministry thought it would be best to teach us a lesson in what it really means to be Israeli and took us on a scenic route. Up until now I have been lucky and only had the nice Israeli taxi drivers. The taxi drivers who argue about five shekels one minute, but then the next minute would invite me over for a Shabbat dinner to meet their son. They would teach me Hebrew during our ride.

Just a few months ago, while I was still on the volunteer program I had an Israeli taxi driver so nice that he should have been a *shaliach*, ambassador. I was on my way to see Liel for the weekend. We had started seeing each other last year when Orli had played matchmaker. After hailing down a taxi, I jumped into the front seat of the cab. Israelis often times sit in front and chat with the driver; after all, the taxi drivers are Jewish too.

"Where to?" the grandfather-like driver asked me.

I gave directions to Liel's house from Orli's.

After hearing my accent, he curiously asked me, "Where are you from? What are you doing here?"

Since not everyone's reaction to my *aliyah* was as positive as Orli and her friends', I hesitantly told him about my volunteer program and my plans to move to Israel.

Family, friends, acquaintances, people that overheard my conversation on the bus (there is no word for eavesdropping in Hebrew since everybody's personal affairs are considered everyone else's business), and quite possibly the Israeli Minister of Immigration and Absorption all thought I was crazy for wanting to move here. In fact, most of them responded with the question, "Really? Why?"

Their responses were getting to me. They were making me doubt that I was making the right decision. I was getting concerned that it was going to be more difficult than I had thought. Maybe this land wouldn't be all milk and honey.

For some reason, I desperately needed this random taxi driver to share in my excitement for Israel. Trying to figure out how to answer this taxi driver's question without getting another negative response, I thought back to all the idealistic tales I had been told about this far, far away country while growing up. It felt like I was fulfilling a dream by moving here and I didn't know how to sum up all these emotions in the little Hebrew I knew. So, I just said with a smile, "I'm a Zionist. I'm a Jew. Of course I want to live in Israel."

But instead of asking me why, the driver inquisitively asked me what everyone back home thought of me moving here.

I thought about when I told most of my friends back home. They also thought I was crazy, but for a completely different reason. Most people pictured me dodging bullets on a daily basis or having to run into bomb shelters during lunch breaks. No matter how much I stated the statistics—that I was more likely to die from a car accident, a heart attack, or second-hand smoke in Israel than be killed in an exploding bus—they didn't relax. When they asked me if I was planning on taking buses, and I responded yes, everyone became very concerned, but nobody volunteered to pay for my taxis or buy me a car.

When old my friends from high school had heard through the grapevine that I was moving to Israel, I had gotten a few emails telling me how great it was that I was going to live in the land where Jesus lived. One person had even asked me if Israel had cars yet or if they still use camels. Just for fun, I had written back, "Only the rich people have camels. Most people can only afford goats."

"All my friends are really excited for me," I lied.

"Well, what about your family? Won't they miss you? What do they think?" the taxi driver asked.

Luckily, and maybe a bit surprisingly, my parents had been tremendously supportive of me wanting to move to a country where I could be killed by terrorists. But they were probably kicking themselves for sending me to synagogue, Jewish day school, on Jewish Agency missions, and for teaching me all of those Zionist values. All my parents really hoped for was to make me into a nice Jewish girl that would find and marry a nice Jewish man, a doctor or lawyer preferably, and provide them with cute Jewish grandchildren. I guess that plan backfired. Instead, I was running off to Israel, and while there were plenty of doctors and lawyers here, I had been finding out that nice Jewish guys were few and far between. "They're happy for me, but they are going to miss me," I finally answered, truthfully.

The driver nodded and then I told him how I was planning on joining the IDF Spokesperson Unit.

When I told Israelis my dream of serving in the IDF Spokesperson Unit, most gave me the same look that they would give a little kid who said that he wanted to be an astronaut when he grew up. Then they would rhetorically ask me, *"At chai b'seret?"* literally asking me if I was living in a movie. I thought this meant that I was a superhero or a superstar, until Orli told me it meant that they thought I was living in a fantasy world. I was beginning to realize that getting into the unit of my choice was not going to be easy, but I refused to give up hope.

After telling the driver about my IDF dreams, I expected to receive that same look. Instead he said, "I'm proud of you. We need more people like you in this country. You must be a very brave young woman to move here alone."

I wanted to tell him how just the other week I had actually met an officer in the IDF Spokesperson Unit. I wanted to tell him how excited I was to sit at the IDF Spokesperson Headquarters and how I had stared at the badge the officer wore, but I didn't, because I didn't want to tell the driver that the officer gave me the same negative response as everyone else. Instead, I just reached over and gave the driver a hug. I was so thrilled to finally receive support for my decision that I thought I should leave him an unaccustomed tip, until I quickly came to my senses and realized that he was probably overcharging me since he had heard my American accent.

I grabbed my overnight bag and headed up to see Liel.

Now, waiting to get to the Absorption Ministry, I realize that I'm going to have to be tougher to survive. Just like I was with that taxi driver and with Liel. I miss Liel. But I had pushed Liel away to protect myself. I was afraid that if I had a boyfriend here, I'd become dependent on him, and if we broke up, then my life in Israel would collapse. I was determined not to end up like all the stereotypical American girls who move back to the US after a breakup here. I was going to be a real Israeli.

I was going to have an Israeli family, not just an Israeli fling.

Ester nudges me to get out of the taxi when we arrive at the Absorption Ministry. Walking in, I realize that the Interior Ministry is methodical and technologically advanced in comparison.

"At least the Absorptions Ministry has slightly improved its absorption process since the state's founding when they would spray new arrivals with asbestos," I joke, trying to cheer us up.

"Who is next in line?" I ask the crowd.

Everyone gives the same response: "Me." No one admits to being last.

A young, tiny, tan South American woman begins screaming in a high-pitched voice at a big, brawly, Russian man who is ahead of her in line. The Russian man actually looks afraid of her.

Since the Absorption Ministry deals with new immigrants from all over the world, and not with native Israelis, everyone here has different cultural backgrounds and speaks different languages. The one thing that everyone has in common is that they are fresh off the boat, barely speak Hebrew, and are eager to prove that they are just as tough as native Israelis.

The man and the woman are yelling at each other in heavily-accented and broken Hebrew. Neither of them can express exactly what they want to say, so they just yell louder and get more frustrated.

It is clear that both the woman and the man are afraid to be called a *friar* or "sucker." In Israel, being a friar is the worst possible fate. Being called a friar is worse than being called a liar, cheater, thief, or terrorist. Because of this most new immigrants, including myself, develop a phobia of getting screwed over. I think that this fear is in the dictionary as friaraphobia or in the medical dictionary as N.I.I.S.—New Israeli Immigrant Syndrome, which is very similar to post traumatic stress disorder.

Ester and I watch the fight, amused that neither of them can understand what the other is saying. As they get more frustrated, they both regress to yelling in their native languages. Other people join the argument, yelling in French, Spanish, English, Russian, Italian, German, and Amharic. With all of the different languages and the inability to find a solution, the room starts sounding like a UN conference, except no one seems to be sanctioning Israel.

As the fight intensifies, Ester and I sneak around everyone into one of the open offices where we are greeted by a woman sitting at her desk, drinking a cup of coffee and smoking a cigarette. Looking like she just woke up from a nap, she motions to the seats in front of her cluttered desk. Her nails look long enough to be weapons.

Ester and I sit down.

Behind the woman is a framed poster with a picture of a thorny cactus in the desert that says, "We didn't promise a rose garden" with a stamp of the Israeli Absorption center. I don't remember seeing this poster displayed in any of the pre-*aliyah* offices. The picture gives me a jolt and my fears of fitting in hit me like a physical wave. I suddenly understand why Dorthy wanted to go home so badly, despite how beautiful the Land of Oz was.

The woman taps her nails rhythmically on the desk to motion for us to start talking.

"Before a day we done *aliyah*. Now need our rights," Esther tries to explain in broken Hebrew.

The woman makes it obvious that she deals with people who do not know Hebrew on a daily basis. She makes it even more obvious that she doesn't have the patience for it. I don't understand why someone would choose to work at an immigration ministry if they don't like new immigrants. It would be like someone who hates children becoming a kindergarten teacher.

I try not to let her cold reception dampen my excitement. I remind myself that I'm doing all of this so I can get into the army and really make a difference.

With an exasperated look, she starts pulling out papers and pointing to dotted lines for us to sign. In a monotonous, quick-paced voice, she explains our rights. Our eyes glaze over and we slip into a trance like Buddhist monks, but she keeps talking.

It makes me think that maybe Israel should use paperwork as a strategy against its enemies, like Iran—"Oh, no, you can't nuke us until you fill out this form, take it to this ministry, and then get it stamped at another ministry." I think Iran would realize that it isn't really worth all of the paperwork to wipe us off the map.

We begin to sign the documents, but of course none of her pens work—more proof of the inefficiency that embodies the Israeli government. How does anyone expect the Israeli government to find a solution for Middle East peace when they can't even successfully manage to supply working pens to its ministries?

Once we finish signing with the pens that we had in our bags, she asks us for our bank account numbers so she can start an automatic deposit of our monthly allowance.

By the look of desperation in our faces, she realizes that we have yet to open an account. Looking at her watch she says, "You have thirty minutes until the bank closes. If you run, you can make it." That was the first word of encouragement that we got from her all day. I savored it like a piece of chocolate in my mouth.

"When you come back, go to a different person," she yells to us as we run out her door.

Show Me the Money

Despite the fact that we get to the bank fifteen minutes before closing time, it's already closed for its siesta. Which is surprising because the country typically runs on "Jewish standard time"— at least fifteen minutes late. People are always late, nothing starts on time, including movies. However, when it comes to closing the banks, the post office, and grocery stores, then the country runs like the Swiss Army.

In order to speed up getting drafted into the army, I want to get as much done as quickly as possible. I don't want to lose even one day, so Ester and I decide to convince the security guard at the front door of the bank to let us in. First we try making him feel sorry for us. He doesn't.

Then we moved to the next stage of negotiating: arguing. Arguing in Israel almost always works. It's often the only way to accomplish anything; however, this method proves to be unsuccessful at persuading the guard.

We then resort to the lowest, but most fool-proof of all tactics: flirting. I offer him one of our snack bars. I ask where all the good places to go out are. I ask him questions about his army service. I swoon at his big gun. I bat my eyelashes and smile. Parts of me feel guilty for using this tactic, but I figure any guy dumb enough to fall for it, deserves it. I turn on my full charm and use my American accent to our advantage. After a few minutes of flirting with him, the doors fly open. (Flirting with Israeli men should only be reserved as the last tactic. It often backfires, resulting in non-stop phone calls and being called *mami*, darling.)

Running into the bank, we feel invigorated. So far, we have accomplished more on the first day than most people do in their first week. I feel like I'm closer to getting into the IDF with each step.

When choosing a bank, I had asked around to find the best one, since opening up a bank account in Israel is like a marriage under the rabbinate: you get screwed and death is the easiest way out. During my inquiry, I found out that all the banks have the same bad service, equally rip off their clients, and each has higher charges than the next. I was told not to be surprised if I see a charge on my statement for breathing the bank's air while waiting in line.

With no other customers in the bank, I'm hoping this will be a quick stop. Ester approaches one teller as I sit down with another.

"How can I help you," the teller asks without looking up.

"I need to open a bank account," I say.

"Okay, give me your Israeli ID card," she says. I hand it over with pride. She looks at it and then at me.

She then hands me documents to fill out.

Being foolishly stubborn, I'm determined to speak only Hebrew. Unfortunately being able to state all the colors and count to one hundred is not very useful when signing a financial contract. After failing to understand the legal and financial mumbo jumbo, I decide to just go ahead and sign everything. The teller keeps pointing to dotted lines and I keep signing. For all I know, I'm signing away my organs or making a deal with the devil.

After signing everything, I'm given an account. And even though the balance is zero, I feel like a millionaire.

As I'm about to leave, she says, "You know there is a song about you," and starts singing, "*Jessie, Jessie, Jessie, Jessicaaaaah!*" I roll my eyes and wonder if someone singing this song to me will be a daily occurrence in my life. Is it prophetic? Will I, like the girl in the song, someday be far away too?

We head back to the Absorption Ministry. Sneaking around the crowds again, we enter the same woman's office. She looks surprised to see us back already, but also somewhat proud. With a nod of her head towards the seats, she tells us to sit down.

We begin talking to her, but she is on the phone. She gestures for us to hold on. Instead of putting up her index finger to say one second, she uses the Israeli hand gesture for "hold on" which is the same as the Italian motion for "Fuck you"—and no, I don't think that it is a coincidence.

It's going to take me a while not to be offended by that gesture.

She makes a hook motion with her finger to signal to us to give her our bank account numbers and our new Immigrant Identity Booklets, which resemble cheap autograph pamphlets that they give out at Universal Studios. And I value this booklet as much as eight-year-old me treasured that pamphlet.

"It is 120 NIS charge to receive your rent subsidy," she says while still on the phone.

Already getting used to the bureaucracy, we are not shocked that we have to pay the government in order to get our money from the government. I should have known that the airline ticket to move here was the last and only free thing I'd ever receive from the country.

Without saying a word, she stamps both of the pamphlets. The slam of the rubber stamp sounds like the gavel of a judge sentencing us to life in prison. We jump with joy.

While walking out, I turn around to ask her if she knows how I can get drafted into the IDF Spokesperson Unit, but she is already busy lighting a new cigarette and laughing on the phone. I figure it is probably better that I didn't ask her anyway. I had asked everyone else we met today and was only greeted with laughter.

Road Rage

"Drive!" was the only instruction my driving instructor gave me a few minutes ago and now cars are coming at me from all directions.

I've barely been in Israel for a week, but I'm almost finished with all the logistics. To get my Israeli driver's license, I only need to take a road test and not the written test since I already have an American license. I don't know any of the rules of the road, and yet I'm supposed to take my driving test right after this one-time, twenty-minute drive with the instructor. Based on the drivers already on the road, I shouldn't be surprised that getting a driving license requires barely any knowledge of the driving laws[9].

Gripping the wheel, I'm confused by the traffic lights. When the light shows both green and yellow lights, I slow down, even though everyone else is speeding up. When it is green, I yield to turn left and everyone behind me furiously honks at me to turn. And when the light is red, I turn right, even though it is illegal in Israel. Driving is so counterintuitive here that they call the roundabouts "squares."

Now, safely stopped at the traffic light, I take a deep breath to calm down. I look to my instructor for guidance, but he is busy reading the newspaper, clearly not caring that I'm about to crash his car.

My first experience with Israeli drivers was at thirteen, right after my family got off our long flight to the country. Our tour guide, a short, curly-haired man wearing leather sandals, thin-rimmed glasses, and a wide smile, had eagerly greeted us at the Israeli airport and enthusiastically welcomed us to our homeland. Lightly tossing our heavy bags over his shoulder, he led us to a van and explained that we had an hour-long drive to Jerusalem.

We all piled into the van, excited to arrive in the holy city. But after the long flight, we all began to fall asleep. Just as our eyelids got heavy, the driver slammed on the brakes. The back of the car in front of us got uncomfortably close to our front windshield. We shrieked simultaneously.

"*Ha'kol beseder*, all okay, noh waurries," he said with a thick Israeli accent, while chuckling.

---

9. For a list of Israeli driving rules, please see the appendix.

BEEEEEEP! I'm surrounded by a swarm of motorbikes that look like they are coming at me from all directions. Scared that I'm going to be hit, I cover my eyes. Annoyed, the instructor looks over at me and demands that I drive. He rolls his eyes and then goes back to reading his newspaper.

After another ten minutes the driver points to a parking spot and tells me to park.

I pull to the side of the road and a car nearly sideswipes me. I wonder if most Israelis drive like they are driving a tank because they actually learn to drive a tank before they learn to drive a car.

Finally, the driving lesson ends. But without a chance to catch my breath, my driving test begins.

"Drive!" The tester says when he gets in the car.

My hands are shaking on the steering wheel. At this point I'm more afraid of being killed by the Israeli drivers than not passing the test. If all these other people on the road have licenses, then I'll undoubtedly receive mine.

A pedestrian jumps out in front of me to cross the street. I slam on my brakes, while the car next to me speeds up and honks his horn. I think to myself that Jesus might have been able to walk on water, but he'd have a hard time getting across a street in Jerusalem today without being run over.

After the longest ten minutes of driving, my test is over.

I receive my license . . . now all I need is a car. And with my finances, I don't see that happening anytime soon.

Screwed in Translation

COOKAROOKA! COOKAROOKA! Even the roosters speak Hebrew here.

The rooster wakes me up again at sunrise.

It's Thursday, the last day of the Israeli work week. The last bureaucratic task I have to do is sign up for *ulpan*. It would have been helpful to have had Hebrew classes before all the bureaucracy, but leave it to Israel to do things backwards.

I get out of bed and get ready to take a short work through the alleyways of Jerusalem to *ulpan*. When I arrive, I'm checked by the guard and walk through the tall gates of the Absorption Center. I'm not sure if the gates keep the immigrants in or terrorists out.

I'm more nervous for this than I was for all the other bureaucracy. My placement in *ulpan* can determine the rest of my absorption. Learning how to speak Hebrew is really important to me. There are so many Americans who move here and never bother learning the language. They are outsiders in the country. They can't watch the news. They never get the jokes. They don't fully understand the culture. I'm determined to be an insider. I want my Hebrew to be as good as possible for the army so I can fit in. I have only five months of *ulpan* to get it right.

Last year, when I started *ulpan* during my volunteer program, all I could say was, "yes," "please," and "excuse me." Never mind that I had no idea what I was agreeing to when I said "yes" . . . which explains some of those awkward situations I got myself into. But now I know that the word *b'vakasha* (please) is nowhere near as useful as *akshav* (now). And that *slicha* (excuse me), is more of an "Excuse me! What the hell are you doing?" than a "Pardon me."

I sit down in front of three older women to start the placement test. After spending all of last year teaching Hebrew to myself, I'm confident that I will be in one of the higher, if not the highest level.

"Can you please explain to us what you did this past year?" ask the examiners in Hebrew, who look like sweet little old ladies, but would probably knock someone over at the *shuk* on a Friday morning for getting in their way.

Yes! I've explained my past year to people hundreds of times in Hebrew. I'll do great on this!

"I was on a volunteer program. I volunteered with Ethiopian kids for three months. I volunteered with kids in a day care center in a city up north for three months. I volunteered with one kid who had problems learning. I volunteered with high school kids and taught them English. I volunteered with kids who had social problems and lived in a state-run youth village. I love volunteering. I even want to volunteer in the army."

Whenever I told this story I was always surprised by peoples' reactions: it was shock, which I always attributed to Israelis being surprised that I would work for free. Some would laugh too, which I attributed to Israeli cynicism. However, these ladies have a look of pure horror on their faces.

"Have you told this story to anybody?"

"Many people! I'm very proud of my volunteering," I reply with a smile.

One of the teachers shudders. With a look of embarrassment on her face, she says in Hebrew "Jessica, I think you have been confusing your verbs, the word you have been using for 'to volunteer' actually means . . . 'to fuck.'"

My stare goes blank as I repeat what I just said in my head. I'm having a *Sixth Sense* moment, like when Bruce Willis' character realized that he was dead . . . it makes me wish that I was dead. Instantly all of the laughing and shocked expressions for the past year make sense. How long have I been doing this? How in the world did no one ever correct me? How did they just let me continue on presenting myself as a child molester? Do Israelis get their kicks by letting immigrants make fools of themselves?

I walk out of that room completely humiliated and even more insecure about my Hebrew and my future.

On my way back to Merkaz Hamagshamim, I console myself by thinking that at least I have another "war" story to tell.

Now at the end of my week, I crawl into my bed. Staring at my walls that now have pictures on them, I take stock of my past week. I've accomplished a lot, but I still have so much more to do. Especially if I want to be in the army.

Even though I'm technically a citizen, I still don't feel like I'm an Israeli yet. I'm realizing that being Israeli is more than just receiving an identity card. I'll have to learn how to be an Israeli, from eating off of other peoples' plates, cutting in lines, and offering hot drinks on a hot summer day, to aggressive driving and calling everyone *achi*, my brother.

As I drift off to sleep, I wonder how much longer it will take for me to describe Israelis as a "we" instead of a "them." Will it be when I speak Hebrew fluently? Join the army? Make more Israeli friends? Or marry an Israeli?

3

It's a world of laughter. A world of tears.

Gathered in the classroom before the lesson starts on the first day of *ulpan*, the only way for us to communicate is with our broken Hebrew. Our varying languages and accents make us unintelligible to one another. Instead we use hand gestures, but luckily that is the universal language of Jews. With our hands wildly flailing around and our conversations probably being about totally different subjects, the classroom could be the Knesset, Israeli Parliament, minus the personal insults and water-throwing.

"Shalom. Hello. *Boker tov*, good morning. Welcome to *ulpan*," our teacher says in the same sing-song tone as a kindergarten teacher. "We have a lot of work today." She seems understanding, patient, and sympathetic— possibly the only Israeli with these characteristics. "I'd like everyone to introduce themselves in Hebrew."

Somehow I ended up in the highest level, which says more about other people having much lower Hebrew levels than me having good Hebrew. But maybe the hard work that I put into learning Hebrew is paying off. Early on I realized that the key to getting a real Israeli experience was learning the language. The realization came to me on my way to my study-abroad program when the cute security guard from El Al[10] had asked me if I knew Hebrew. Wanting to impress him, I told him in Hebrew that I did. He then laughed at me when I said I knew a "small" instead of a "little" bit of Hebrew.

We go around the room to introduce ourselves. There are people from all around the world, from France, Uzbekistan (yes, there are Jews there, or should I say there *was* a Jew there until now), England, and Australia. There is an Argentinean couple expecting a baby who will probably have better Hebrew than me in a few years; a Brit who has come to class barefoot and has incomprehensible English and Hebrew; a young, religious French girl wearing a long-sleeve turtleneck and a long skirt that are both so tight that there is nothing modest about her dress.

The teacher continues by introducing the semester's itinerary, from grammar to tenses and from Israeli culture to history and field trips. One of the students asks where we will be going and the teacher mentions Masada, the Supreme Court, and the Golan Heights. When I hear the Golan Heights, I instantly smell the air there. It was in the Golan at only thirteen years old that I fell in love with the legacy of Israel.

It was while I bounced around in the back of a Jeep surrounded by the lush hills. At that age, I was more interested in our new, strong, and handsome tour guide. I had checked my reflection in the rearview mirror as he was driving the Jeep like it was a tank. When he pointed at something with his rugged hands, it was like

8. El Al is Israel's flag carrier airline. It is known to have the tightest and best security. After September 11, 2001, El Al was the first airliner to resume flights to the US. Its security starts with an intense screening process before the ticket counter, includes air marshals on board every flight, and equips every plane with a missile defense system, which was implemented after an Israeli charter jet came under attack following takeoff in Kenya.

a command for my family to look. When he stopped the Jeep to get out, my parents, sister, and I followed.

He stood in front of us, nearly six feet tall, with flowing, curly hair, wearing a T-shirt with ripped-off sleeves. I couldn't tell if his skin was tanned or caked with dirt. Like a little child, he had turned in a circle with his arms stretched out and yelled, "This is the Golan Heights. The Golan Heights has an incredible story."

Standing still, he had told us the story in an irresistible Israeli accent, "Against all odds, we won the land we are standing on only twenty-six years ago in the Six Day War. We were attacked simultaneously by all of our neighbors, on all of our borders, by Egypt, Jordan, and Syria. But we, our small country, which was only twenty-eight years old, won in only six days! And not only did we win, we tripled our country's size in those six days."

As he told us the details of the war, it sounded like a modern-day miracle. A story that could have come right out of the Torah. I was almost able to hear the echoes of the fighting, the gun shots, and the tanks on the hillsides and in the valleys.

I wanted to ask him if he had fought in any wars, but he was so cute and I was too shy. Instead, I just tucked my hair back behind my ear.

He pointed to a valley and we all turned to look. "You see that road right there? On the sixth day, the IDF drove south to make the Syrian army believe that we were retreating. Then at night, we drove back up with our headlights turned off and surprise attacked the Syrian forces." As the guide continued to tell us every detail of the six days as if he was recounting from his own experience, I imagined him in the trenches. Then he laughed and said, "And on the seventh day, we rested, just like God commanded."

"Break time," the *ulpan* teacher commands, and I realize I missed the first half of class.

When we get back from break, the teacher starts the class by saying, "We're going to review body parts."

Oh, good: sex ed in Hebrew.

The teacher asks two people to volunteer. No one does, so she picks the religious girl with the tight clothes and the guy from Uzbekistan. The teacher begins pointing to different body parts and we yell out the names.

"Good. Now I'm going to point to a body part and first you have to say the name and then you have to tell me if it's masculine or feminine." She points to the teeth of the Uzbekistani guy.

"Masculine," we guess.

"Wrong, it is feminine."

We go through almost every body part. Then she points to the religious girl's large breasts protruding from beneath her turtleneck.

Clearly liking the attention, the religious girl smiles and blushes.

That is obvious. "Feminine!" We call out, trying to out-yell the next person as if we are in kindergarten.

"Wrong!" our teacher says, pleased that she tricked us again. "I have a great trick to help you remember. All of the singular body parts are masculine, like, nose, mouth, and forehead. All of the multiple body parts and paired body parts are feminine, like legs, toes, eyes, etc. The two pair of body parts that are masculine are breasts and testicles. That is because men think that both are theirs!"

On that high note, the teacher sends us on another break. While I've learned a cute mnemonic device, I feel like I have a lot more Hebrew to learn if I really want to be able to fit into Israeli society and effectively serve in the army. Even though *ulpan* is intensive—five hours a day, five days a week, for five months—based on all the games we play, the songs we sing, and the pictures we draw, we might be ready for second grade when our classes are over, but none of us will be productive members of society.

A Grim Forecast

The teacher is setting up a radio with a tape player. There are only six students in class today. Most of the students are dropping out of *ulpan* for various reasons, they found a job or a boyfriend. Some are just too tired to come. The shoeless Brit stumbles into class half-drunk. "Why are you late?" the formerly calm teacher now screeches at him. He responds, but no one understands him through his thick accent.

Despite all the obstacles, I force myself to make it to *ulpan* every day. I'm even more determined to learn Hebrew now, since I learned that nearly everyone at Merkaz Hamagshamim works at an English-speaking answering service that has been outsourced from the US. If I wanted to stay in an American bubble, I would have stayed in the Midwest.

"Listen carefully to the words. We're going to discuss the recording afterwards," our *ulpan* teacher states.

She pushes play.

BEEP. BEEP. BEEP.

To Israelis, those three beeps signify the start of a news broadcast on the radio and are like the ringing of an ice cream truck miles away for kids. No matter how far away or how quiet the beeps are, Israelis stop what they are doing and tune into the news. If Israelis don't listen to the news every hour, on the hour, then they might miss the toppling of a government coalition, a failed peace deal, or an entire war.

The announcer begins broadcasting. He's talking so fast that I barely understand him. How am I going to be able to do a good job in the IDF Spokesperson Unit if I can't understand the news?

The teacher stops the tape. Rewinds it and plays it again. "Who can tell me what the headlines are today?"

One student summarizes the news about another terrorist shooting in the West Bank, another Kassam rocket falling in the city of Sderot, another corrupt politician, and another traffic accident. Despite Israel being in the global news every day, the news never seems to change.

As I'm taking notes about Israel's security situation, I think back to when I first decided that I wanted to join the army.

I had gone out again with Orli and some of her friends to a club. Pushed around by the thumping music and pulsating crowd, I became separated from the group. I looked around for Orli, but couldn't find her.

"Hi," some guy said to me in unaccented English.

"Hi," I yelled back, thinking that I must really stick out as an American.

After introducing himself as Daniel, he asked, "What are you doing in Israel?" The club was so dark that I only caught a glimpse of him when the flashing colored lights hit his face.

I told him in English that I was on a volunteer program. "What about you?" I asked.

"I moved here from the States with my parents about five years ago. I'm in the Israeli army now."

The loud boom of the music in the night club transported me back to the day that I had fired an M-16 for the first time. I had served in the Israeli army for four days during my six-week teen tour to Israel. Our officers, who had been only a few years older than us, were responsible for our lives and safety, while our parents didn't even think we were responsible enough to take care of the family pet fish. We had followed everything they said like a life-or-death game of Simon Says.

"Silence!" our officer had yelled.

No one dared to move.

"Lie down on your stomach."

We did. No one had complained about the scratchy blanket on the desert ground.

"Put your legs straight back behind you."

We assumed the position.

"Move your right leg to a 45-degree angle."

We moved our legs so that they looked like a lop-sided V.

"A commander will come around to put the gun in your hands."

We had all held our breath.

Our commander came to me. She put the gun in my hand. It felt dead. It was cold and hard.

"Switch your gun from safety to semi."

I had been too afraid to move, but I flipped the switch.

"*Aish!* Fire!"

BOOM! BOOM! BOOM! We pulled the trigger three times.

I felt the kick back of the gun through my entire body. The gun felt alive.

I set it down and stopped moving. As I lay on my stomach, the smoke from the barrel and the dryness of the desert filled my lungs.

I stood up and slowly backed away from the gun, like I had backed away from the Western Wall the first time I had visited it.

When handing in my army uniform the next day, I thought about all the Israeli girls and boys who had to join the army at eighteen and give two or three years of their lives for the country's security. If I had grown up in Israel, I too would have been joining the army at eighteen. But instead, I went to college, and while I was deciding between a beer or a shot of vodka, my Israeli peers were deciding whether or not to take life or death shots.

"Can I get you another shot?" Daniel, the guy from the bar, asked me. I suddenly realized how much I admired him for being in the army.

"Yeah, thanks. By the way, what do you do in the army?" I asked, trying to play it cool.

"I serve in the IDF Spokesperson Unit. It's sort of like doing media relations for the army," he said.

"Wow!" I said out loud, with envy. The famous picture at the beginning of the Intifada that showed an Israeli policeman with a baton standing behind a bloodied teenage boy popped into my head. The New York Times had plastered it on the front page of its paper with the caption "An Israeli policeman and a Palestinian on the Temple Mount." The world assumed the soldier had just beaten the boy. But the bloodied boy was actually a Jewish boy from Chicago, who had just been dragged from a taxi and beaten by Palestinians. The policeman was rescuing him. It was as if the media intentionally wanted to make Israel look bad. I thought to myself, if I could learn Hebrew, I could serve in that unit too. Suddenly, the party experience in Israel was no longer fulfilling enough for me. As I slammed my empty shot glass down on the bar, I decided that I would join the IDF's Spokesperson Unit.

The *ulpan* teacher knocks on my desk. "Jessica, are you with us? What was the headline?" she asks me, supposedly for the third time.

I don't know the answer. I can't even try to fake one. I'm too busy thinking that when I join the army, I'll change those headlines.

When I think about the Israeli soldiers who were kidnapped and lynched at the start of the Intifada, I get angry. I had learned that the next day, the international media apologized to Arafat for airing the bloodshed and condemned Israel for defending itself. I wanted to change that dynamic. I worked so hard during my volunteer program trying to get drafted into the IDF Spokesperson Unit. I mentioned to anyone I talked to: random people on the bus, at the grocery store, and in coffee shops, that I wanted to join the unit to see if maybe they had a connection. Just by doing this, I found somebody who had been in the unit a few years earlier, another person who had served about ten years earlier, and even an officer who was currently in the unit. While all of these people had plenty of advice, such as "You don't know what you are getting yourself into," and "Don't get your hopes up," no one was able to help me get in.

Everyone in the class starts gathering up their note-books and homework assignments when the teacher dismisses us. On my walk home, I realize that *ulpan* will be over in a few months and I still don't have any plans for what I am going to do afterwards. I haven't made any progress on the army front. I've been trying, unsuc-cessfully, to get drafted for nearly a year. I had meet-ings with soldiers in the unit who told me not to even bother trying because only people with *protecia* get in. I talked to people in the unit's reserves and they basically laughed at me. I called the drafting office, but they just hung up on me.I feel as if I'm at a dead end and I don't know where to turn. This dream may not come true. To get in, I might need a miracle.

The Not-So-Merry Virgin

It's a Friday afternoon. Everyone's in a rush to get their errands done before Shabbat starts and everything closes down.

I'm in the post office to pick up a package. I'm staring at the clock. I know that as soon as it hits 12:00, the tellers will simply close their windows, gather their things together, and get up and leave, no matter how many people are still in line.

I've now been a citizen of Israel for nearly two months.

As *ulpan* continued, I got braver about using my Hebrew out in public. I started preparing for upcoming conversations by practicing them in my head. I prepared on the bus, in the street, while sitting by myself in a café.

People would look at me strangely because I probably looked crazy, talking to myself.

While still learning, I got myself into situations so awkward that I would have preferred getting on a bus behind someone who had sweat dripping from his brow, a suspicious bulk in his stomach area, and was yelling "*Allahu akbar.*" There was the time that I meant to ask a waitress for *cos mayim*, a glass of water, and instead asked for *koos mayim*, pussy water. Another time, I tried to ask shop owners if I could put a flier on their *knisa*, entrance, but instead said *kinisia*, church—not the best mistake to make in Israel. Or there was the time that I meant to ask a sales person if I had to wash a shirt by hand, but instead asked if I could masturbate it. And most embarrassing was the time that I told a date that I would *l'redet lo*, go down on him, when I meant to *l'redet alav*, make fun of him.

Besides vocabulary, I've also been working on improving my accent, since my Hebrew teacher told me that it really bothered her. She had told me to change it as if it was as easy as changing my shirt or my hair color. My biggest problem seems to be pronouncing the letter *resh*, a guttural r that is rolled. I had asked Orli for help and she had suggested that I gargle water while trying to say a *resh*. All I ended up doing was getting saliva all over my face.

Despite these embarrassing mistakes, my Hebrew is improving.

Impatiently, I look at the post office slip. Why can't it at least be easy to get mail in this country?

After thirty minutes of waiting, I'm finally at the front of the line. I look up at the clock. The minute hand is quickly approaching the number twelve.

I squeeze the postal notice in my hand. I'm excited to see what is in the package. I hope it is a care package from my parents.

I used to be very timid while in line in Israel. During my first trip to the grocery store on my volunteer program, a woman started screaming at me while I was waiting in line at the register. I was busy reading a special weekly newspaper called *Gate for Beginners* when someone tried to sneak in front of me. At the same time, someone pushed me from behind. Not sure where to address my first complaint, I looked behind me.

"Why push me?" I asked in broken and hesitant Hebrew.

"You give her *la'akof*. You need to put heart," the woman behind me said in Hebrew.

"What?" I asked, translating her words in my head literally.

"You give her *la'akof*. You need to put heart," the woman repeated loudly, as if I had a hearing problem instead of a comprehension problem.

"You no to need to push me," I said.

"You no *l'tzricha l'kroa b'tor. Yesh harbeh anashim . . .*" she kept yelling at me, but too fast for me to understand.

Back then I wasn't prepared for the grocery store on a Friday in Israel, which feels like a looting scene. Since grocery stores are closed on Saturdays, people are in a rush to buy food for the weekend. Trying to pull food off the shelves, especially the tomatoes and cucumbers, can prove to be a violent, if not life-threatening task. It feels as if a war has been declared and people are going mad, trying to stock up on necessities for the next month. Forget the terrorists! I needed to be more aggressive at the supermarket to survive in this country—or else I may starve. The woman ahead of me in line turned around and began yelling at the woman behind me. I felt helpless. I hoped that she was sticking up for me, but now that I know Israelis, I know that they argue just for the sake of arguing—as if it were an Olympic sport.

Back in the post office, I notice a teller chit-chatting with some tourist. "Can I come to the window?" I ask her.

As if she is a judge, she snaps, "I'm not done with my current customer. I'll call you when I'm ready."

Without thinking, I quickly yell back at her, "You *are* done. You're just chatting with this tourist and *that* doesn't count."

And with that, my yelling virginity pops. I initiated my first argument in Hebrew. And it looks like I might win!

I hear my *ulpan* teacher's voice in my head, "The Israeli spirit is to question authority, to speak up and out, and to look at things in a different way. Israelis don't just do something because they are told to, they want to know the reason why and if they don't agree with it, they will say so. For instance, Israeli students often don't even bother to raise their hands when they want to argue with the professor."

Then the tourist yells in English that it is none of my business. But I refuse to talk to him in English, since I can now yell in Hebrew.

"It *is* her business. In fact, it is *everybody's* business," a man behind me yells, as he motions to everyone still in line.

Then everyone joins in the yelling. A woman behind me starts telling the teller how she should be doing her job and the teller says that she does not need a lecture.

I look around, almost proud that I started a commotion. I no longer care about my package. I stand a little taller and straighter, thinking to myself that I am becoming an Israeli. I'm becoming stubborn, rude, obnoxious, and straightforward. Even though my innocent American appearance makes me look like Dorothy wandering around the Land of Oz, I've learned to hold my own in this country. A sweet, innocent Midwestern girl could never survive in Israel, much less its army, without *chutzpah*!

The Man Pulling the Levers

After a few months of *ulpan*, out of the blue, my counselor from my volunteer program calls.

"I just remembered that Nachman Shai, the current director of United Jewish Communities (UJC) in Israel, which is connected to *Otzma*, was the former IDF spokesperson. I've already talked to his secretary and he's expecting your call to set up an appointment," he says.

My old counselor goes on to explains that Nachman Shai is an Israeli legend. He was the IDF spokesperson during the First Gulf War and is nicknamed "The Calmer." It's not by mistake that this sounds like the name of a superhero. When Scud missiles were being fired into the middle of Tel Aviv from Iraq, he was responsible for calming down an entire country, a nation full of Jewish mothers and grandmothers. As any married Jewish man knows, calming down one Jewish wife is hard enough, and Nachman Shai did it for an entire nation of Jewish mothers. Now if that doesn't qualify as a superhero skill, I don't know what does.

Now, walking through the florescent-lit hallways of the UJC building in the middle of downtown Jerusalem, I feel like I'm following the yellow brick road—minus the tacky, red-sequin slippers of course. This is my door to my Jewish destiny. This is my opportunity to prove wrong all the Israelis who doubted me joining the IDF Spokesperson Unit.

Their voices continually haunt me: "You're how old? Twenty-two? Oh, no! You're way too old to join the IDF!" or "There's no way you will get into the IDF Spokesperson Unit. You'll end up wasting two years as a secretary."

The echo of these voices makes me think that stubbornness is more useful than Zionism in Israel.

When I find Mr. Shai's office, his secretary tells me to take a seat. As I wait outside the office, I feel like I'm waiting for the wizard to grant my wish.

This man holds all of my dreams in his hands.

In my head, I review all the new vocabulary, questions, and answers that my *ulpan* teacher gave me to help prepare me for this meeting. I look down at my clothes, hoping that I picked the right outfit to wear. I was so nervous about what to wear since attire is very tricky in Israel. Men wear torn jeans to work, a wedding, or a bar, while women will look like over-priced call girls in all the same locations. Nobody wears a suit—anywhere—except the ultra-Orthodox, and they, of course, are the only ones who don't participate in the workforce.

With a smile, Mr. Shai calls me into his office.

"Can I get you something to drink?" he humbly asks.

Sitting down with Mr. Shai is not nearly as intimidating as I expected.

"How can I help you?" He asks, genuinely interested.

Since I'm speaking in Hebrew and not English, I nervously tell him an abbreviated version of my personal story. Being especially careful to use the correct word for volunteer, I tell him about my experience in Israel and my dreams for the future. "I volunteered on *Otzma*. I have a marketing and journalism background. I just made *aliyah* by myself, without any family. I'm in *ulpan* now. I want to use my skills to help the army and serve in the IDF Spokesperson Unit."

With English as my mother tongue and my journalism degree, I'd change the world's perception of Israel. I'd show the world that Israeli soldiers aren't vicious killing machines, but eighteen-year-old boys and girls who handle a lot of responsibility with the utmost maturity. I'd change the narrative.

"I love you. We need more people like you. I want to help," he responds from the bottom of his heart, and not because he works at an *aliyah* organization.

"I'll organize a meeting between you and the deputy spokesperson of the IDF Spokesperson Unit. Expect a call from her within the next few days," he says.

Using all my effort to not jump over his desk and hug him, I calmly thank him.

While I walk out of his office and skip down the yellow hallway, I quickly call Orli to tell her the good news.

"I knew you could do it, Jessica!" Orli says and tells her mom. I hear her mom get excited at the mention of Nachman Shay and then yell to me, "Look at you. Just running into the fire!"

"You are celebrating Rosh Hashanah with my family, right?" Orli tells me, more than asks me.

Happy to have a place to call home for the holiday, I say, "Of course."

Pretty in Pink

With sweat dripping down my face, neck, chest, and back, I wonder if there is a term for "swass" in Hebrew. I'm going to make a terrible first impression. I don't want to disappoint Nachman Shai in my first interview with an IDF officer. It's been a month since I met with him and now I've been walking up and down this busy and crowded Tel Aviv street for the past thirty minutes, trying to find the IDF Spokesperson offices.

Soldiers pass me from every direction. I longingly stare at their uniforms, too embarrassed of my *ulpan*-level Hebrew to ask for help. Close to giving up on my dream, I collapse on some steps leading up to a dilapidated building and think back to a week ago when the secretary of the deputy of the IDF Spokesperson Unit called me to schedule an appointment. I was surprised to hear from the army before my thirtieth birthday since everybody told me that army bureaucracy moves slower than the building of the light rail in Jerusalem[11].

Out of the corner of my eye, I see the sun glimmering off of a small sign that says "IDF Spokesperson Offices." I look up at the building again and can't believe, that from this shack, communication decisions are made about the most publicized army in the world.

I jump to my feet.

Five minutes later, I'm sitting with the deputy IDF spokeswoman and another officer. Intimidated by the ranks on their shoulders, I quickly rattle through my resume: "I was the marketing VP for a fundraiser. I interned in the media relations department for a major US company. I answered media relations inquiries. I wrote key messages for . . ."

Interrupting me, she says something in Hebrew to the officer next to her, but it's too fast for me to understand. As they nod their heads and smile, I picture myself being interviewed by CNN, FOX, and BBC, changing the world's opinion of the IDF.

She turns to me and says in slow Hebrew, "We'll try to make this work. Expect a call from the drafting office. Call me the day you are drafted so I can pull you into the unit. I make no promises."

Not paying attention to the last sentence, I repeatedly thank her on my way out.

I walk back down the same street, but this time I feel a few inches taller. I head to the mall that is conveniently and oddly located next to the army base. After walking through a metal detector and getting my bag checked for bombs and weapons by the armed security guard outside the mall, I walk inside.

In the food court, there is a group of officers sipping on coffee and joking around. I walk past a store and see a

---

11. The light rail in Jerusalem, which is only 8.6 miles long, took nearly nine years to be constructed. The construction faced many problems and the inauguration was delayed four times.

girl in her army uniform trying on a pair of red platform shoes. In another store, a girl pulls a yellow sweater over her army shirt. I love how they look in their uniforms. I hope the uniform will look as good on me.

I walk into a store that has a cute pink, lace dress in the window. I haven't bought anything for myself since I moved to Israel. I don't have the money. I'm saving all of my Nefesh B'Nefesh *aliyah* scholarship money for when I join the army so I can afford to feed myself.

Unable to resist, I try on the dress. It fits perfectly. Standing in front of the mirror, I feel like I deserve to treat myself for all my recent accomplishments.

Walking out of the store, wearing the pink dress surrounded by a sea of army green, I feel like I'm on my way to becoming Israeli. Just like after a good first date, I wonder how long it will be before I hear from the army.

Aaloo

I look down at my phone for the tenth time in the last thirty minutes.

Ever since I had my meeting with the IDF spokesperson deputy a few weeks ago, I leave my phone on my desk while at *ulpan* so that I won't miss a call from the army. So far a month has passed and I've heard nothing. It's starting to feel like the army is an ex-boyfriend I can't get over.

Suddenly my desk vibrates. I look at my phone. It's flashing with a blocked number.

I run out of the classroom.

"Aaloo?" I say, trying to answer the phone like an Israeli, but sounding more like a lame pirate.

"Are you Jessica Sara Fishman, daughter of Eliezer?"

Who is Eliezer? Confused, I flash back to my bat mitzvah when I was called to the Torah. My rabbi had called me up using my Hebrew name and my father's Hebrew name—Eliezer.

"Are you Jessica Sara Fishman, daughter of Eliezer?" the prepubescent voice on the other end of the blocked number asks again.

"Yeah. I guess that is me."

The guy must think that I'm a complete idiot.

"On Sunday, at 8:00 A.M. you need to come to the IDF drafting office for testing and interviews."

"I'm supposed to be going to the IDF Spokesperson Unit. But I can't come in at that time. I have *ulpan*."

Uninterested in my dreams or problems, he repeats the time and hangs up.

I don't have anywhere to address my complaints since I can't just look up the IDF in the yellow pages.

The next Sunday, I spend the entire day in interviews, IQ tests, background screenings, Hebrew tests, and giving my medical and socioeconomic history to the army. The tester explains to me that if I get drafted into the army, I'll be a lone soldier since I don't have any family here. He says that as a lone soldier, I'll have some benefits, like instead of being paid $100 a month like all the other soldiers risking their lives, I'll be paid $1000, plus I'll get days off to do errands, and vacation time to visit my parents.

After the tests and interviews are over, I get on a bus to Merkaz Hamagshamim. As I sit down, I think about how painful that was and hope the worst part of my army experience is now over. However I have a feeling it's just begun. When I had mentioned that I was supposed to be drafted into the spokesperson unit, one of the officers stared back at me blankly and said, "You really don't get how the army works."

The bus stops and an ultra-Orthodox man gets on the bus. He looks for an open seat that is not next to a woman. Even though there is an open seat next to me, he turns to the guy across the row and asks him to get up so that he can sit in his spot.

"No! Sit there! That seat is open, next to that girl," the guy says, pointing to me.

Great! Thanks, I think sarcastically.

The ultra-Orthodox man makes a face and goes to stand at the front of the bus. Even though I didn't want to sit by him, I'm still slightly offended that he refused to sit by me.

The guy turns to me and says in Hebrew, "I can't stand them. Thinking that they can tell everyone what to do."

"You know what drives me crazy? The fact that they dress like it's the middle of winter when it's boiling hot outside. How do they think that makes them more religious?" I say, excited to have a real Hebrew conversation. "Abraham, Noah, and Moses definitely didn't wear that garb in the desert."

"Oh, that penguin suit! I like it. It makes me happy to know they are suffering," he says, laughing.

"But who is suffering more? Them in their sweaty, unwashed clothes or the people who smell them?" I ask half-jokingly while trying out my Hebrew.

Trying to make myself feel better after being rejected as his seat neighbor, I remind myself that I won't be seeing any of them during my army service since they believe they protect the country by studying Torah and don't serve in the IDF. Looking at the ultra-Orthodox man with disdain, I smile, knowing that unlike me, he has never even visited the IDF drafting office. I think to myself, *I'm more Jewish than he will ever be.*

Phone Call 3

Another blocked phone call. It must be the army.

I quickly answer. I'm probably the only person in all of Israel not screening calls from the army.

"We want to draft you in two weeks."

I nearly drop my phone from excitement, but quickly realize that I won't be ready for the army in fourteen days. "Oh, no! That won't work. I'm still in *ulpan*."

I open up my calendar and start picking out dates.

"What do you think you are scheduling here? A date with some guy?" the officer on the other end of the phone yells and laughs at the same time. "This is the army! You have the date in two weeks or in November. You're lucky you're even getting a choice!"

Two weeks later, as I'm checking my mailbox at Merkaz Hamagshamim, I see an official army envelope.

I open it. It is my draft date and just like the Ten Commandments, now that it's written, it's set in stone.

I want to frame it.

I jump with anticipation.

I look at the date more closely. It is in less than a month, the day after I finish *ulpan*.

4

disOrientation

BZZZZZZZZZZZ! BZZZZZZZZZZZ! BZZZZZZZZZZZ!

The snooze button in Hebrew is called a *nudnik*, which also means an annoying person. I push the annoying person three separate times. The sun has yet to rise. On the fourth buzz, I get up and look in the mirror. With dark circles under my eyes, I look like I've already been to boot camp. Today is the final test in *ulpan*, but I won't be going to class. I have a far more significant Hebrew test.

Yesterday was the first night of Hanukkah. I celebrated the victory of the Maccabees with Orli's family. We lit the candles and ate fried food. That is the summary of every Jewish holiday: they tried to kill us, we won, let's eat.

In Orli's tiny childhood bedroom, we talked all night. She explained what I should and should not expect in the army. Before I went to sleep, I made my first journal entry. I filled the first two pages with words of idealism, passion, and optimism that could have rivaled Chaim Bialik's Zionistic poetry.

This is the last morning I'll wake up as just an Israeli citizen. In a few hours, I'll be an Israeli soldier. Not knowing what the day has in store for me, I throw on some clothes and gather my things into an oversized backpack. I've packed enough stuff for the next three weeks, since I don't know when I'll be returning.

Last week, one of the Israeli girls from the Merkaz Hamagshamim who had been in the army took me "army shopping." We went to a place right on the border of Meah Sharim, the ultra-Orthodox neighborhood, to get some gear, which is ironic, considering that the ultra-Orthodox don't join the army.

When we were shopping, it hit me that instead of prom shopping, this is the shopping that Israeli seniors do. And shopping for the army was not as fun as prom shopping. Instead of buying heels, I bought ugly black Reebok tennis shoes; instead of a lacy bra, I bought ugly long-sleeve olive-green, black, and white shirts, and white tank tops to put under my uniform; instead of a necklace, I bought a cover for my dog tag; and instead of a cute little clutch purse, I inherited a backpack that I could fit into. The actual prom dress—my army uniform—will only be issued on my draft date. Not that I can say that my prom dress was very flattering. I'm hoping my army uniform will look better.

Now at Orli's house, she and I quickly eat a nutritious piece of processed cake and a cup of *nes* coffee. (*Nes* is a popular type of instant coffee in Israel. *Nes* also means miracle in Hebrew.) Just in case I don't have any real miracles today to get into the spokesperson unit, I figure I should at least drink one. Ready to leave, I struggle to put on my backpack. If I fall over with it, I'll look like a turtle that is stuck on its back with arms and legs flailing. I wonder if there will be a baggage weight limit on the army bus.

After a long bus ride, we get to *Bakum*, the IDF's drafting and processing office. We walk into a huge outdoor courtyard. Everything is concrete: the walls, the ground, the buildings. Orli and I are greeted by a sea of young girls and their families. They're all taking pictures as if it is prom night, but without the updos. Their faces are filled with excitement. But with anxiety showing in their eyes, it is obvious that this will be the first time they are leaving their parents' homes. I, on the other hand, left my childhood home six years ago. They are all eighteen years old and are being drafted into the army. I, on the other hand, am twenty-three and volunteered to be here.

With no family by my side, I cling to Orli. I thought I'd be more excited for this day, but for some reason I'm terrified. I'm suddenly wishing that I could wake up in the tornado-torn Midwest in the safety of my parents' homes. It has taken me a year and a half of fighting, begging, pleading, and making the right connections to get to this point, and now I'm scared that it won't be what I've been expecting or that I will fail.

Orli and I barely talk. Neither of us is a morning person and I'm too nervous to form complete sentences in Hebrew.

It's cold in the courtyard. The sun doesn't seem to shine here.

It's nothing like when my parents dropped me off at college. The sun was shining brightly. There was pride mixed with sadness in their eyes. My dad's advice to me as a freshman, "work hard and party hard," probably won't apply here. I don't have fraternity parties to look forward to. Instead I'll have kitchen duty, target practice, and military drills.

After anxiously waiting outside in the cold for hours, which Orli tells me is the norm in the army, Orli says, "It's your turn. There's your name. Let's go, I'll take you to the bus."

I can't believe that I'm actually going to be an IDF soldier. Today I'll finally receive my puke-green, polyester uniform with pride.

I look up and see my name lit up by red bulbs on a board. All of the sudden those previous hours seem too short. As I begin walking to the bus, the memories of playing on the beach on our first family trip to Israel ten years ago, to my IDF Gadna training experience during my subsequent high school trip, to making pita on the beach with Orli and Liel, to the prayers I said at synagogue every weekend asking for the safety and security of Israel and her soldiers come rushing back to me.

Despite my previous excitement to give my life to the country, I want to be the last one on the bus. Unfortunately, it seems as if all the other girls feel the same way. This must be the only bus in Israel that people push others in front of them instead of cutting them off. When I finally board the bus, I turn on the stairs to see Orli snapping a picture, which will soon be hanging on my parents' fridge, of me with wide eyes, a hesitant smile, and a larger-than-life backpack.

I turn back around to see the crowded bus. My eyes dart back and forth searching for a seat. I feel like the loser in junior high that no one wants to sit next to on the school bus. The bus seems so big and the girls, even though they are five years my younger, are intimidating. I find a small empty section of a seat. Without saying a word, I squeeze into it and place my backpack on my lap.

As my bag becomes heavier and heavier on my lap, I think about my sorority pledgeship. Having to wear baseball hats for a week, put on green nail polish, mash creamy peanut butter into our hair, and fill our mouths up with marshmallows doesn't seem so worthy of our complaints. I wonder how all of the JAPs from my sorority would deal with boot camp. How would they fare with an M-16 on their shoulder instead of a Kate Spade? Would they bring their Louis Vuitton trunks and expect someone to carry them? Or would they try to wear their Manolo Blahnik high heels with their uniforms?

After only five minutes of driving, the bus stops. A young female soldier gets on to the bus, yells something that is too fast for me to understand and then everyone starts getting off the bus. I follow everyone else. I've learned that the best thing to do when I don't understand something is to smile and follow what everybody else is doing. I'm unsure why we had to board a bus for such a short trip, but since no one else is asking, I decide not to either.

As we single file into a lecture hall, we're handed purple toiletry bags. I sit down and start looking through the bag. There are tampons and pads in it.

An older male officer walks to the front of the room and welcomes us to the IDF. Since I just finished my "high-level" ulpan class, I'm feeling particularly confident about my Hebrew comprehension. Then the speaker begins his second sentence and I have no idea what he is saying.

Based on the purple toiletry bag with the Always logo on it, the lecture might be about makeup tips and how to deal with our first periods. It becomes apparent to me that the meanings of high-level in ulpan and high-level in the real world are very different. This obvious language difficulty makes me start wondering about my ability to serve effectively . . . and safely. Will I be running into the shooting field when we are supposed to start firing?

I don't have much time to continue contemplating my fears, since the lecture quickly ends and we begin our trip down the endless, dreary hallways of the drafting office. It looks nothing like the yellow brick road that Dorothy skipped down. Instead of feeling like I'm realizing some Zionistic dream of mine, I feel like I'm entering a prison. Like a bunch of cattle, we're herded through the long concrete hallways, from one door to the next, with each stop being a different, unfriendly station that processes us into the army.

Exactly like in a prison, the first station is finger printing, which is manned by apathetic teenage soldiers who obviously prefer to be anywhere else. One of the soldiers dips all ten of my fingers into ink and individually rolls each of them on a piece of paper.

At the next station, I receive my dog tags. Females only receive one dog tag, but the male soldiers receive two—the second one goes in their boot. This is not in case they misplace their boot.

The next step is getting my picture taken for my army ID. Unlike a passport photo, this photo op does not offer any do-overs.

"Pull your hair back into a pony tail," the faceless soldier tells me.

I do. Without any warning, the flash blinds me. Less than a minute later, the soldier hands me my new *choger*, IDF ID card.

In the picture, my eyes are not shining with joy in anticipation for a trip to some exotic island or someone about to fulfill a dream. Instead this picture resembles a mug shot, with the look of panic showing in my eyes.

Everything moves along quickly and efficiently. Like from a scene in *Brave New World*, we walk through the hallways, which seem to have an invisible current pushing us in one direction. Things come to a screeching halt when I enter a large hall with a few chairs and a lot of bored teenage girls sitting on the floor waiting around. Everyone is waiting to be called into one of the rooms for some type of interview . . . or interrogation. I find a spot on the cold concrete floor and call the IDF deputy spokesperson to let her know I've been drafted today. She thanks me and again reminds me no promises.

I look around the room and realize that I'm no longer an individual. I am being processed.

Two hours of girls coming in and out pass until my name is called. I enter a small, plain room with a table and two chairs. One of the chairs is occupied by an officer sitting across the table. I look around to see where the two-sided mirror is, but don't find it. The officer asks me questions about myself, my family, my education, and my history. The only thing he does not ask me is where I was at a certain date and time. He also does not ask me where I want to serve in the army, so I decide to tell him.

Like a person orders pizza and expects to get exactly what he orders, I say, "I want to be in the IDF Spokesperson Unit."

He does not respond. Instead, he smiles to himself, writes something down, and tells me that we are done. I walk out of the room to see that there are even more girls waiting outside than when I entered.

I'm beginning to realize that my decision to join the IDF Spokesperson Unit has no real significance. It is sort of like the Florida voters voting for Gore.

The windowless building makes it impossible to see how late it is. It feels like time stands still here. I look at a clock on the wall and it seems like it is melting off the wall. This day may never end.

Then I reach the last station: IDF uniforms, which I secretly think are sexy in a tough kind of way. I remember when I had spent those four days in the army at sixteen, how excited we were to wear the IDF uniform. Instead of handing them to us high-schoolers, they had dumped them in a big pile. Frantically diving through the pile of green army uniforms, we had looked like we were at an after-Christmas sale at Macy's. Hoping to find a size that would make us look like sexy Israeli soldiers, we had tried on uniforms over our clothes. I felt like I was playing dress up. None of us looked like we had hoped. We had wanted tight fitting pants that would make us look bootylicious, but instead our pants were baggy and saggy. We walked with accidental swaggers, hiking up our pants every few feet so that we wouldn't trip.

"Quiet! Attention!" a young Israeli soldier, with her hair tightly pulled into a ponytail that reached her lower back, had yelled at us high-schoolers. Despite her petite figure, she demanded respect. "Get in line."

Not knowing what to do, we had looked at one another. We had made a single file line, one behind the other, as if waiting in line for school lunch.

Pretending to be mad, the female soldier tried not to laugh at us. "No, not like that. Like this," she said, as she gently moved us so that we were standing shoulder to shoulder in three lines.

After we had been rearranged like a chess set, she said, "I know your pants are too big, but if you put on your belts, then they will stay up." The IDF had refused to provide us tourists belts since previous high school groups had stolen them as souvenirs. After putting on our shiny and sparkly belts that we fished out of our suitcases, we looked like an army of JAPs.

This time around I don't have a sparkly belt with me.

"What is your size?" a female soldier, who looks at least five years younger than me, yells at me. She hands me three pairs of pants, two shirts, and a sweater in the size that I tell her.

I try to find a quiet place to try on my uniform. With everyone changing and rushing to get different sized pants, the room feels like an overcrowded H&M, but with no selection or dressing rooms. After putting on my uniform, I look in the mirror to see high-waisted green pants from the 80s, a bulky button-down shirt, and a sweater that looks like it came from Big and Tall, even though I'm small and short. My black Reebok tennis shoes do not help improve the reflection in the mirror.

When I look around and see some more experienced soldiers with uniforms that look cute on them, I gullibly wonder if my uniform just needs a wash and a dry. I go back up to the soldier who is handing out the uniforms and, as if she is a dressing room attendant at Bloomingdales, I say, "Mine don't look right. Maybe I need another size."

"You should take at least one that is a size or two too big for you. All girls gain weight in the army."

I look over when I hear a new recruit saying to a friend that she is going to take her uniforms to a tailor to fix the shirt and bring down the waist in the pants. I do not know whether to be more surprised that I actually understood this or that the army gives us such unflattering uniforms.

I look at myself in the mirror again. I'm going to have to spend more money tailoring my army uniforms than I did my prom dress.

Now that we received our uniforms, I assume that we will now finally be told which unit we'll end up in. It's not that I would mind being on the front lines, but I of course, expect to hear that I am going to the IDF Spokesperson Unit since that is where I can make the most difference. After all, I am a young Zionistic American who moved to Israel and volunteered to join the army so that I can help them improve its international image. They do realize that *I* am here to help *them*, right?

They should be begging me. But I'm slowly realizing, like Hezbollah and Hamas, that the IDF does not beg anybody for anything.

The day ends and I am not told where I will be serving. Instead I'm bunched in with a lot of young girls who are starting to look like real soldiers. We board another army bus, but this time we are in uniforms and not in our civilian clothes. Hours or possibly even days have passed since I first entered the drafting building and it is now dark and cold outside. We are not told where we are going or how long it will take to get there.

I look around the bus and see a bunch of girls who look exactly the same. We do not look like the modern day Biblical heroes that I had envisioned. We look kind of dorky. When I look into the window on the bus and see my reflection, the realization finally sinks in that I too am another faceless soldier. I am no longer Jessica Fishman, American immigrant. I am 7063618. The words of my educational director from *Otzma* echo in my head: "Even IDF soldiers who are killed while protecting the country cannot be buried in a Jewish or a military cemetery if the Orthodox rabbinate does not consider them Jewish."

The bus comes to a screeching stop. The lights go on and my reflection disappears. A twenty-year-old boy with an acne problem stands up at the front of the bus and begins yelling, "You are being sent home for the weekend. We will start boot camp at 8:00 A.M. Sunday morning. Being late is not an option."

We jump out of the bus looking like a bad scene from an 80's movie with our pants' waistlines coming to a rest right below our boobs. Wandering around the bus station, our shiny Styrofoam uniforms and fuzzy berets that look like dead cats propped on our shoulders make us stick out as the army freshmen. We look like such losers that I'm not worried about being a terrorist target. I'm more concerned about being picked on.

After my long day of becoming an Israeli soldier, I jump on a bus back home to Jerusalem. It is thrilling flashing my army ID card instead of having to pay for the bus ride. Thankfully the government figures that since it is going to send its kids off to the army, it should at least pay for the carpooling.

On the bus, I run into one of the religious girls from *ulpan*. I thought I would be proud to show off my new uniform, but I'm not. Embarrassed to be seen in my wannabe G.I. Jane outfit, I try, unsuccessfully, to hide behind my backpack. She chats with me about the final *ulpan* test. The test seems insignificant now.

The bus reaches my stop and I head up the hill to Merkaz Hamagshamim, backpack and all.

The doors swing open. I'm greeted by smiling faces and the wonderful ring of the English language. Today was the first day that I have not heard one single English word, and my head is hurting from all the Hebrew. After telling everyone about my day, I quickly get into bed so that I can get up early the next morning and take my cardboard uniform to the Russian tailor on the corner and have it taken apart and put back together like a patchwork quilt. I will have to get the waist lowered, the seat and thighs taken in on the pants, and the shirt will require pleats in both the back and the front to make it a bit more flattering. I'm hoping that by the time they are done it will look more like a Britney Spears' outfit than a Cindy Lauper costume, so that I will be able to defend Israel's reputation with pride.

IDF Pledgeship

I try to keep my eyes from closing, but the lull of the train makes it hard. My eyelids are heavy. The sun has just risen, but the train is already packed with soldiers on their way to their bases to report for duty. I'm afraid if I fall asleep I'll miss my stop and be late for my first day of boot camp. I can hear two girls behind me speculating about what boot camp will be like. They sound like news analysts trying to predict the elections on a twenty-four-hour news station—everybody has something to say, but nobody knows anything.

When we get to the base, we are greeted by the same scrawny acne-covered boy who yelled at us Thursday night and two new commanders: a chubby tomboy and a girl who looks like she has stepped out of an Abercrombie and Fitch catalog.

By 8:00 A.M. a group of us are huddled together on something that resembles an old basketball court. One of the commanders yells at us to stand in the formation of a chet—ח, a Hebrew letter that looks like a square with a side missing. If we were in the US, these twenty-year-olds would be hazed, but here in Israel they are commanding me.

Running around and bumping into each other, trying to get into formation, we look like a bunch of really bad cheerleaders, minus the pompoms. One side of the chet is twice as long as the other two and another side is slanted inwards. After nearly five minutes, the forty of us finally prove that we have passed fifth-grade geometry class. Our commander, the pimply-faced kid does not look amused, but the chubby, tomboy commander is trying not to laugh.

Our commander begins taking roll call, "Miriam Avraham"

"Yes," a girl mutters, obviously intimidated.

"Yes, what?" the officer yells back at her.

"Ehhh . . . Yes, I'm here?"

"Yes, *mifaked*!" he screams back at her.

It's ironic how much that sounds like McFuckhead, I think to myself.

"Yes, officer," she says, near tears.

He continues along the roll call. Everyone answers with the mandatory *mifaked*.

I look around at the girls. They all look alike at first glance. They look so much younger than me. I wonder if I'll be friends with any of them. Their uniforms make them blend into one another. Only when I take a closer look do I notice the differences in their hair, make up, nails, and even their postures.

"Did I say you could move?" the oily-faced commander yells at someone.

"Ehhh, no, but I only wanted to take my coat off," says an innocent-looking eighteen-year-old.

"You mean, you only wanted to take your coat off, officer," he snarls at her. Then he turns to the rest of us and says, "You are in the IDF now. You are soldiers. You do not do anything without asking permission. You don't scratch, you don't breathe, you don't take a shit without first asking permission. Do you all understand?"

We are too afraid to say, "Yes, *mifaked*."

After roll call, the commander takes us on an all-day expedition to get our new army equipment. We receive our kit bags, our *medai bet*—work uniforms, sleeping bags that have probably not been washed since the Israelites wandered across the Sinai for forty years, and blankets that are as rough as a cactus.

Our cotton work uniforms are unlike our formal uniforms that we received at the drafting office. The baggy pants look like Justin Bieber's drop-crotch pants. We receive a canteen water bottle that looks like it carries herpes. Our commander tells us to put rocks and toothpaste in our canteens to get rid of the smell, but all this does is give us chalky water with dirt taste.

Throughout the day, our commander commands us to run everywhere, but then once we get there, we have to wait for over an hour until something happens. I guess that is why everybody told me that the IDF's motto is "hurry up and wait."

The entire day I am anticipating getting our semi-automatic weapons, but we never get them. As the sun starts setting, we are taken to a Hanukkah ceremony on a large concrete field. We are set up in line formations and the head of the base is leading the lighting ceremony. I'm so far away, I could be in the nosebleed section of a really boring concert.

With the sun going down, it starts to get cold and the wind picks up. Without our coats, we are all trying to fold ourselves into our thin, cardboard uniforms to stay warm. Unlike combat soldiers, who refuse to wear their coats and walk around with their sleeves rolled up when it is freezing outside to prove how tough they are, I'm fine showing that I'm a wimp. I miss The North Face coat I got back in college so that I could fit in with all the sorority girls. Since it is the fourth night of Hanukkah, the ceremony luckily doesn't take too long. I can see the high-ranking officer joking up front, filling his pot belly with jelly-filled donuts to stay warm. It is so cold that if I could have any miracle for Hanukkah this year, it wouldn't be for the spokesperson unit. It would be for a coat. Instead the only miracle I get is another cup of *nes* coffee, since all that is served at dinner is a soggy salad and a burnt slab of *tivol*—breaded, tasteless tofu.

After dinner, we are taken to our tents, which make the cold sorority dorms sound cozy. I feel like a toddler going to bed right after dinner. In my bed, I hear the other girls talking. I haven't said a word to anyone today except, "Yes, *mifaked*" when my name was called at roll call this morning.

The girls with whom I am bunking are totally different than my AEΦ sisters. Unlike the JAP mold that all my fellow sorority sisters came in, these soldiers are as diverse as the ice cream at Ben & Jerry's, but not as sweet.

As I quietly crawl into my sleeping bag, the others start talking. Many pull out their phones, as this is the first time all day we can use them.

"Mom, I miss you. This is horrible. It is so cold. The food is awful. The commanders are so mean. I want to come home," one girl sobs on her phone.

"Does anyone know when we have to get up tomorrow?"

"When do you think that we are going to get our guns?"

"I need enough time to do my hair and my makeup."

"When do you think we will get our first weekend off? My boyfriend is in the paratroopers and I haven't seen him in a month. He is supposed to get next weekend off."

Crackle, crackle, crunch. Another girl is opening up a bag of Bamba, which is basically peanut butter Cheetos. "My mom sent some homemade brownies with me. Does anybody want?" offers the chubby girl who seems to think she is at sleep-away camp and not the IDF.

"I want to be a female combat soldier. My whole family is in the army. My dad is a really high-ranking officer. I'll be the first female chief of staff. What do you want to do?"

"I want to get done with my service as easily and quickly as possible. I'm actually thinking of joining a women's yeshiva and pretending to be religious to get out of it."

"Did anyone notice that the showers don't have doors or curtains? I'm not going to shower during all of boot camp. How many weeks do you think we will be here?"

I am so tired from the day that I fall asleep before the girls stop talking. I guess being five years their senior, I can't keep up with them. I was too worn out to write another page in my army diary. I wonder if I'll have the time in the next two years to write another page.

Before I even realize that I'm sleeping, I am rudely awakened by our commander yelling, "In fifteen minutes you were dressed and ready."

Lessons in Etiquette

It is still dark and cold outside. The thought of getting out of my sleeping bag seems like the most painful thing in the world, so I try switching out of my pajamas and into my uniform while still under my covers as if I'm a junior-high-school student in the locker room, ashamed of my developing body. After getting dressed, I rush to the bathroom, which is already filled with girls.

The entire unit shares the same bathroom. These facilities make bathroom rest stops seem as sterile as operating rooms. Instead of sinks, there is a big trough, the toilets do not have seats on them, and the showers have no curtains. The drains of the showers look like Cousin It is trapped inside and all the toilets are clogged, which is odd, since we are not provided with toilet paper.

It might have felt like summer camp with us all brushing our teeth together, if it were not for the commanders outside with guns on their backs yelling at us, "You have nine minutes and twenty-three seconds and then you were in the *chet* formation."

Some of the girls are rushed and stressed, worried that they won't make it on time. Other girls mumble under their breath for the officers to shut up. They are still teenagers. They are still in their rebellious stage. I have already accepted that for the next three weeks I will have to do what these teenage commanders are asking . . . or demanding. I choose to obey. After all, I'm a volunteer. It makes it easier, thinking that I actually have a choice.

"You have nine minutes and fifteen seconds and then you were in the *chet* formation," the officer yells again. It feels like I'm on a bad *Sesame Street* episode in which they are teaching counting backwards.

No matter what we do, we are timed. And we are usually given a ridiculously small amount of time to perform a task, like build a tent in three seconds or make dinner for the entire unit in three minutes. It is like they are purposely trying to make us fail.

We are always counting backwards, like Cinderella reaching midnight, or a countdown to a bomb explosion.

"You have five minutes and thirty-five seconds until you were in the *chet* formation"

The commander keeps using the past tense to explain something in the future, which keeps confusing for me, since I'm still working on mastering my tenses.

We are now all standing in a shape that resembles a chet and a few stragglers are running towards us with only five seconds to spare. I look at our commanders. It almost looks as if our commanders are hoping that the soldiers won't make it so that they can yell at us.

We spend the next twenty minutes trying to yell *hakshev*, attention, in the right manner. There is a correct way to greet a commander, and it is not, "Ladies and gentlemen, please welcome the commander." The actual salute is much more complicated and must be said at lightning speed. The soldier at the right end of the *chet* is responsible for addressing the commander, so I resolve to never be in that spot.

After learning army greeting etiquette, we are then given a lesson in bed-making. There are more ways to fold, roll, and hang a sleeping bag than I had ever imagined. It reminds me of my days working women's retail.

Bed-making takes more than two hours and it is still not even 8:00 A.M. Since I had barely eaten anything last night, my stomach keeps grumbling and I'm worried that I'll be yelled at for making noises without asking permission.

We are finally marched over to the mess hall. As we are waiting in our single-file lines, a commander walks between our lines and rows and inspects our uniforms.

He scrutinizes us more than movie stars are criticized at the Oscars for their outfits. Since we are all starving, it feels like we are about to go out on the runway, minus the makeup and the heroin, of course.

"Your appearances are sloppy. You are not up to code. Your work pants have to be tucked into your boots. For those of you who aren't wearing boots, tuck your pants into your army-issued gray socks," orders our commander.

Wearing black Reebok tennis shoes, I bend over and tuck my pants into my thick, scrunched down, tube socks. I turn to the girl next to me and whisper, "I feel like I belong in the movie *Flashdance*."

With her forehead crinkled up and a zit on her nose, she looks at me like she has no idea what I'm talking about. I think to myself, "*Wow, I am old!*" She had not yet been born when I was wearing hair scrunchies and bright pink eye shadow.

After our uniforms are approved one by one, we are allowed to enter the mess hall. But once I see the food, I lose my appetite. The food from last night was laid out buffet style in cold metal serving trays. I had been told that many girls gain weight in the army, but with this food I don't understand how. After drinking some chalky liquid that is labeled juice, I sneak back to my tent to take a much-needed fifteen-minute nap.

Would You Like Whipped Cream With That?

My eyelids feel as heavy as lead. I feel like I haven't slept in years. I've only been here three days. I'm trying to keep them open because an extra-long blink will get me yelled at in front of two hundred girls. The punishment for sleeping is standing for the rest of the lesson.

It is hard to pay attention to a lecture when I only understand one out of every four words. It is hard not to zone out and fall asleep. I'm sure the information is important, but there is no way I can understand it, no matter how hard I try. I can concentrate until I have a migraine, but then the only result will be my head hurting. I try asking people next to me what things mean, but I get yelled at for talking. I accept that I will understand less than thirty percent of the lecture.

Every day we have a different lesson. We have been taught Israeli history, IDF history, IDF rules and regulations, different ranks and units, CPR and first aid, radio communications, dieting skills (so we won't gain weight), and other necessary information that most of them will never use as secretaries in some office.

Most of the girls in this type of bootcamp—except for me of course—will be glorified secretaries. If the IDF really wants to prepare them for army positions, then they should teach them how to answer phones, use Outlook, and serve coffee. But there is no way that I'll end up making coffee for someone. I certainly am no Starbuck's barista, considering the fact that the last time I made coffee, I made it for Orli and she went running to the sink to spit it out, since I accidentally used salt instead of sugar.

I force my eyes open as they begin to droop again. I wish I had some coffee now, even with salt.

Boot camp is wearing me down. I've showered once in three days. My hair is greasy enough to fry food. I've stopped having bowel movements. I've eaten maybe a total of two full meals. And I still have yet to get my gun.

"You'll be tested on this information so you better pay attention. The next lesson is on gun parts. After you successfully label all the pieces of an M-16, you'll receive your weapons."

Knowing that I'll never learn all those Hebrew words in time, I wonder if I'll get a plastic gun instead.

Shopping Spree

We are about to get our guns. There is electricity in the air. We know that we will never need to use them, nor do we ever really want to have to use them, but there is still something thrilling about holding a semi-automatic weapon.

My commander hands me the gun and shows me how to attach the strap to it. After connecting it, I hang it over my shoulder.

"What do you think you are carrying? A purse? Put it around your shoulder and carry it behind your back!"

Embarrassed that this is something my AEΦ sorority sisters would do, I quickly put the strap over my head and lay it between my boobs. My gun is hanging behind my back. The *kaneh*, barrel, hits my calves.

The next girl receives her gun. She used to be a gymnast and is so short she could easily date Gary Coleman and still wear heels. When she hangs the M-16 over her back it nearly drags on the ground.

By the time everyone receives their guns, my shoulder hurts from the weight and a bruise is forming on my calf. These new accessories are not very comfortable. I'm already beginning to feel like the Hunchback of Notre Dame. The only person that this gun is going to injure is me.

"You have five seconds and you were in the *chet* formation!" our commander declares.

Even after nearly a week, we still can't get the *chet* formation down. It takes us nearly two minutes to get into configuration, and yet North Korea can arrange more people in a dance routine than we have in our entire country in ten seconds flat.

As the commander is yelling at us, I remember how excited I was at sixteen to shoot an M-16 for the first time when I was a pretend soldier in the IDF. When we first got our guns then, we didn't even really get to hold them. Instead, we sat in classes for hours while the guns sat on the other side of the room, leaning against the wall. We were forbidden to touch them, get near them, or even look at them for too long.

Now, the commander grabs my hand and stuffs a rag into it. He tells all of us to sit down in our *chet* formation. Demonstrating how to strip a gun, he tells us to follow. We take the gun apart into little pieces. It doesn't seem so intimidating lying on the ground in multiple parts that could just as easily be used in a car, a lamp, or a toy.

"Start wiping it down. Use up and down motions, like this!" orders our commander.

We spend the next two hours jerking off our guns with a rag. After having shared such an intimate experience with it, the gun feels like it's mine, more than just a random piece of metal, like it had when I was sixteen. I have a feeling that whenever we have some spare time during our boot camp, our officers will tell us to start cleaning our guns.

During the next few days I wipe my gun more times than I wipe my ass. The worst part is that we won't even get clips or bullets for our guns until our first shooting practice. We walk around with our guns, but without a clip, for nearly a week. It is like my sorority sisters walking around with Prada purses, but without any of Daddy's credit cards—we can't really do any damage.

A Not-So-Imaginary Friend

We have to carry our guns with us everywhere. M-16's become the newest, must-have fashion trend on our base, but unlike the accessories that Paris Hilton carries around, this one cannot be encrusted with diamonds.

I eat with my gun on my lap. I sleep with my gun as a pillow. I share a bathroom stall with it. I stare at it when I shower. It becomes my shadow except I can always feel its weight on my back. I wonder if this is what it's like to have a baby.

If we ever forget our guns, we are yelled at by our commanders. It feels like it would be worse if we left our guns somewhere than if we accidentally left our kids in the car . . . on a hot day . . . with the windows rolled up.

The worst part is that I have this weapon on my back and the only thing I know to do with it is hold it in different positions during our morning inspections.

"Stand at attention," a commander yells to the entire platoon.

CLOMP, STAMP, BANG, BANG, THUD.

In sync, hundreds of us move our guns from their positions on the ground to holding the butt in the palm of our hands and standing straight with our feet together and heads up.

"Stand at ease," the commander yells.

THUD, BANG, BANG, STAMP, CLOMP.

Vastly improved from not being able to make the *chet* formation, we still sound like a bad version of *Stomp* as we put the butts of our guns back on the ground, move our legs apart, and slam the barrels of our guns into our hands.

We do this another fifteen times.

"Break into your classes. Your commanders will check your guns."

It is 8:30 A.M., we have not eaten yet, and this is the fifth time today that our commander is checking our guns.

We line up in a single file line. We follow every instruction that the commander says.

"Angle your weapons up to sixty degrees," our officer commands.

"Weapon at sixty degrees," we say simultaneously, while also raising our guns to point to the sky.

"Turn the switch to semi."

"Switch turned to semi."

"Check for a bullet in the chamber."

"No bullet in the chamber."

"Pull the trigger."

Click.

Not surprisingly, nothing shoots out.

Then the pimply-faced commander goes through the entire line and looks in the bullet chamber to make sure that there is no bullet in the chamber.

A terrorist is more likely to find 72 virgins in heaven than our commander is to find a bullet in our gun chambers.

At the other side of the line he yells, "Is your gun *parok*, *badok*, and *nazor*?"

Like a pep squad, we reply, "The gun is disarmed, checked, and on safety."

They seem to worry a lot about impossible things. I guess you can't take the Jewish grandmother out of the Israeli army.

Would You Like Ketchup With That?

This morning our officers told us that we were going to the *mitvach*. I was surprised when all the girls got excited, because I thought that this meant we had kitchen duty. It turned out that I was wrong. *Mitbach* is kitchen. *Mitvach* is the shooting range.

We left for the shooting range around dawn. It is now lunchtime and we have yet to even hear a loud noise.

While sitting on the sandy ground with the wind hitting my back, I'm watching two girls scraping something called *loof* out of a can and spreading it on a stale piece of bread with a primitive can opener. It looks like pinkish dog food for humans, and smells worse. It is guess-from-what-part-of-the-animal-is-this canned meat.

Our lunch is *manot krav*, battle rations. It looks and tastes nothing like the packed lunch that includes a little "love you" card that I got as a kid at Hebrew day school.

After sitting around like a bunch of prisoners, we are called into the outdoor shooting range, which is a pure concrete building with three walls, a ceiling, and a floor.

We look out to the field and see cardboard cut-outs of terrorists, like those of actors at movie theaters.

Every precaution is taken. We're given reflectors to put on our shoulders so that we will be seen in the dark. We are given ear plugs so that our ears don't ring. We are given exact instructions on what to do. But the most important instruction is that we are not allowed to do anything unless we are told to do it.

Everyone is on edge. No one talks. Our commander seems more tense than normal. The army seems so much more real to me today than it did yesterday. It feels like we are about to go on a mission.

We stand in a row with our guns by our sides. I look down the row. Everyone looks identical. I look exactly like them, but I still don't feel like them. I feel like an outsider, but my uniform makes me blend in.

Facing forward, I'm staring at the terrorist "movie star" cut-outs that we are supposed to shoot. One of our commanders walks down the line and hands us each a clip filled with ten bullets. We are not to put the magazines in until we are specifically given the command to do so. Baby steps.

This time feels different than my time at Gadna when I was sixteen years old. This time it is my gun. This time I won't be giving my uniform back the next day. We are told to go down on one knee. To put in our magazines. And before I know if I'm supposed to shoot or propose to the cut-outs in front of me, the commander yells, "Fire!"

Everyone starts firing, but my gun gets stuck. I raise up my arm, since I am not allowed to talk, turn, or move any other body part.

"*Hadal!*" the officer yells.

What does mustard have to do with shooting? I wonder.

Everyone stops shooting and stares at me. I feel like a complete foreigner.

While the commander fixes my gun, I quietly wonder to myself, *Doesn't* hadal *mean mustard?*

After my gun is fixed, we begin shooting again. I shoot ten rounds.

Then we each go down to check out our targets. I would have done better playing darts drunk. But I'm not worried; I won't need shooting skills in the spokesperson unit.

By the end of the day, we have two more shooting sessions and my aim improves. The third and last session is after night falls, so we can learn how to shoot in the dark. Each time we shoot in a different position: once on our stomach, once on a bended knee, and once in the *tramp* position, which is not sexist; it is the word for hitchhiker in Hebrew.

Now in the darkness, we are all working on cleaning up the shooting range. We are putting all of the equipment back into the trucks, collecting the garbage, and getting things in order. Somehow, I and another girl end up being the last soldiers at the range.

As I'm sitting on the cold concrete, waiting for a ride back, it pops into my mind: *hardal*, not *hadal*, is mustard!

The next morning, I'm allowed to sleep in an extra fifteen minutes for staying an extra two hours at the shooting range. It doesn't seem proportionate, but if someone would have offered me a million dollars or an additional quarter hour of sleep, I'd have chosen the latter. The other soldier who was with me told me that the extra sleep was a *chupar*. She explained to me that *chupar* means a reward—for both dogs and soldiers.

As everyone gets up for roll call, I pull my sleeping bag over my head so I can continue sleeping in the tent. Five minutes later, when everyone is in the *chet* formation outside, I hear the commander instructing them how to make their beds for that day. Everyone runs into the tent and noisily begins making their beds. Realizing that I won't be able to get any more sleep with this commotion, I drag myself out of bed. As everyone runs back outside to get the next set of commands, I pull off my pajamas.

"You have thirty-five seconds to roll up the sides of your tents for inspection," yells the commander, like he does daily.

As I'm standing with my underwear in my hands, I hear my bunkmates marching towards me like a herd of elephants. I quickly put them on, right before all the walls of the tent are rolled up like window blinds. Furious that I almost gave the entire base a strip show, I put on my shoes without bothering to lace them up and march over to my commander as if I think I'm in charge.

"What are you doing? I'm still getting dressed! Is there no communication between any of you? How did you not know that I was given an extra fifteen minutes of sleep? What is wrong with this army? How does this army function during real operations?" I scream in my heavy American accent and broken Hebrew. It certainly doesn't have the right effect with my toddler-level vocabulary.

He stares at me, probably trying not to laugh at what sounds like the temper tantrum of a three-year-old.

Once I stop yelling, he calmly asks me as if he knows he was won, "Where is your gun?"

The cardinal rule: Always have your gun with you.

I freeze. My face turns white. I realize that I left it on my cot.

Without saying anything, I turn around with my head hung low. Defeated, I go back to the tent.

Bathroom Break

At 6:00 A.M. I'm jolted from my sleep. Afraid I overslept, I look around. Instead of seeing darkness, a leaking tent, and a dozen other girls hidden in their sleeping bags, I see the four walls of my bedroom.

I lay back down. My bed, which once felt hard, now seems like a bed in the Hilton's presidential suite. My head is resting on a real pillow and not a hard chunk of metal.

Yesterday we received leave for the weekend for the first time since boot camp started. I have to be back on the base tomorrow morning. I'm not quite sure what to do with an entire day. It has been so long since I've had more than fifteen minutes to myself.

I close my eyes and try to go back to sleep, but I can't. My body is used to getting up at sunrise.

What should I do now? I didn't have time to go grocery shopping. I have no food in the house. Unlike all the other girls at boot camp, I don't have a family or a fridge full of food to go home to. Everybody else in Merkaz Hamagashamim is still sleeping.

As I'm thinking of what I'm going to eat and how I'm going to fill my day, my bowels begin to move for the first time since I started boot camp. I run to the bathroom.

Sitting on the toilet, I think back to yesterday when we were getting ready for our first weekend by getting safety instructions, cleaning and organizing our tents, and being briefed on how to securely store our guns off base. I was so excited to have the weekend off. Now, I kind of miss being around everyone. I feel so alone and lonely here. I don't really know the girls that I'm in boot camp with. I barely even talk to them, so I shouldn't miss them. But, somehow I got used to always having them around. It feels strange to be alone with only my thoughts . . . and my gun.

I flush the toilet and get back into bed. I have nothing else to do. I don't have to clean my weapon, clean the bathroom, endlessly shovel dirt from one pile to another like some Sisyphean task, make a thousand chocolate-spread sandwiches out of starched white bread (I'm still not sure what food group that fits into), hide under my bed on the cold, dirty, concrete floor for some drill, or get into a *chet* formation.

My bowels begin to move again. I'm making up for a week's worth of constipation. I have a feeling that my butt is going to be chafed by the end of the day.

It is 8:00 A.M. Still no one is going to be up. They all went out last night. I decide sleeping will be more fun, even though I slept during the entire bus ride. I never used to be able to sleep on buses. Learning to sleep anywhere is the best skill I've gotten from my army service so far.

9:00. I can't wait any longer. I text a few people in Merkaz Hamagshamim to see if they are up.

9:10. Still no response from anyone.

9:12. I run to the bathroom again. It is nice having toilet seats. I wonder if this is how Tom Hank's character in *Cast Away* felt after returning to civilization.

10:47. I get a text message: *I'm up. Do you want to come over and watch movies? I'll make you an omelet.*

10:50. I'm already curled up in Uri's apartment, waiting for breakfast.

11:13. I'm in the bathroom, again.

12:33. I get a text message from Ester: *Do you want me to make you lunch? I want to hear all about boot camp.*

12:47. I'm eating a scrumptious breakfast with Ester and five other people from Merkaz Hamagshamim.

Looking around, I realize these people really have become my family. We may be the rejects of society. We may be the foster kids that no one wants to take in. But we have one another. In the short time that I have lived here, we have shared birthdays, weddings, births, anniversaries, and break-ups. We cheer each other forward and when we get depressed we offer one another a shoulder to cry on.

14:22. I'm in the bathroom again.

15:54. I'm in the bathroom again.

17:37. I'm in the bathroom again.

I can't believe that the day is almost over. I have spent most of my weekend in the bathroom.

*   *   *

I can't be late. I can't be late. I can't be late. I can't be late. I can't be late.

I woke up extra early this morning to make sure that I would not be late getting back to base. On the bus, I fell asleep and set an alarm so that I wouldn't miss my stop. Now the bus has been sitting in traffic for over a half an hour. Everybody on the bus is antsy and frustrated.

People start getting off the bus to see what the problem is, all of them thinking that they would be able to solve whatever problem there may be, or at the very least yell about it.

Up ahead we see a police barricade in front of a gas station.

"What is going on?" yells one of the passengers to someone closer to the scene.

"*Chefetz chashod*," the guy yells back.

A suspicious object has been found and we are waiting for the bomb squad.

One of the passengers turns to me and says, "Well, at least you can protect us until the police arrive."

Forgetting that I am in uniform and have a gun, I give him a bewildered look.

I look down and see my uniform and my gun. *Wow!* I think to myself. *He has no idea I'm American. He thinks I'm a normal Israeli soldier.* I decide to only smile and nod my head, knowing that the second I open my mouth, I will be outed.

Luckily, he also doesn't know that if I were to shoot in the direction of the gas station with my aim, there is a greater likelihood that I—and not a terrorist—would set the whole place on fire.

More Doodies

With the same food, people, and schedule, I feel trapped in the movie *Groundhog Day*. Every day is the same. Every night the rain pours down as if it is the flood of Noah's Ark. Every morning we wake up to a wet tent and cold air. Every meal is soggy. Every hour we have to get our guns checked for bullets in the chamber. Every few hours we have to get in the *chet* formation. We don't have anything to look forward to. We will have one more day at the shooting range, but it isn't as exciting as the first time. We are used to our guns. We are used to asking permission.

The days are filled with pointless duties, as if they are keeping us busy until boot camp ends.

Every night I have guard duty. At 3:00 A.M. I put my uniform over my pajamas—so that I'll stay warm and so that I can get back into bed more quickly when I'm done. I aimlessly walk back and forth in front of the rows of tents, guarding the sleeping girls from a threat that does not seem relevant, even though I know it is. We're in the middle of a desert. There is nothing around us. I can't imagine a terrorist coming to this camp and killing us. We are so irrelevant to the conflict. We're so far from anything that I can see all the stars in the sky. There isn't even a noise to be heard for miles.

All these eighteen-year-old girls who I hear nightly on the phone crying to their parents about being homesick shouldn't be a part of the war on terror. Besides, Palestinian terrorists seem more interested in blowing up nightclubs and civilians than soldiers.

I see my breath. I feel like a zombie. This is nothing like Jewish summer camp where middle-of-the-night bathroom protocol was, "Go in twos, wear your shoes, and be good Jews."

My guard duty is fifteen minutes long, but I'm so tired and bored, it feels like two hours. Most Israelis start smoking in the army due to boredom, unlike in the US where it was thanks to child advertising. My boredom and the cold make me think about taking up that habit too.

I'm shivering. I can't aim a gun at a terrorist with my hands shaking. I put on my gloves. I'm not supposed to be wearing them since they are gray. I got yelled at this morning for wearing them. Soldiers are only allowed to wear black gloves. But as a lone soldier, I don't have money to buy another pair. These are the only gloves I have.

Another soldier comes out to take over the guard duty. My shift is over. I crawl back into bed. It feels like it was all a dream.

When Nature Calls

We have less than a week of boot camp left, but I don't know if I'm going to make it. The yelling is getting to me. The pointlessness of everything is wearing me down. My body is tired from not sleeping. My head hurts from translating everything. I want to talk to my parents, but the timing never works out. I haven't seen or talked to Orli or anyone at Merkaz Hamagshamim since my leave.

Everyone else talks to their parents, their friends, and their boyfriends nightly. When we get back from dinner, I look at my phone and see no missed calls. I truly feel like a *chaylet bodadah*, a lone soldier.

It doesn't seem as if it can get any worse.

*　　　*　　　*

I have ten minutes of free time now. Every second is precious. I run to the bathroom but find it blocked by four girls who spent the past hour cleaning it.

I've had to pee for the past two hours. I tried to go in the mess hall, but it was closed. I thought I would have time after breakfast, but we had to go straight to a class. In class, I couldn't concentrate on what the lecturer was saying because I was focused on not peeing my pants. Since my accent sticks out like an Arab at a TSA check, I was too self-conscious to ask to be excused.

"No! You can't go in!" says a girl young enough that I could babysit her. "We are waiting to show the company commander what a good job we did cleaning." It is clear that they have not had time to accomplish much in their short lives if they want credit for cleaning a bathroom.

"But I have to go to the bathroom and this is a bathroom," I try to convince her in my broken Hebrew. It sucks that she has the upper hand in an argument that I could easily win in my native language. She is blocking the entrance with her hands on each side of the doorframe. She is acting like she is expecting some plunger insignia medal of honor.

I don't have time for talking. I'm about to pee on myself. I duck under her arms.

She runs in front of me and blocks the stalls.

"If you don't let me use the toilet, I'll pee in the shower."

Testing me, she does not budge.

I walk to the shower drain and pull down my pants. (Oh admit it! You've peed in the shower. You know you've done it. Don't deny it. Everybody does it.)

She, along with a crowd of fifteen girls, stares at me wide-eyed. The girl runs out of the bathroom in tears. I pull up my pants and walk to the toilet. With everyone looking at me, I got stage fright.

Five minutes later I walk out of the bathroom building, buttoning my pants in satisfaction, and am greeted by an angry commander. The girl, even though she had instigated, ran and tattled on me, just like the girl from my *aliyah* flight.

I don't know why, but with the commander staring at me and the absurdity of the situation, I burst into tears.

Later that night I finally reach my family. It is the first time since I started boot camp. Wearing only my army pants and a long-sleeve white shirt, I'm sitting on the steps of the bathroom. My gun, as usual, is strapped around my back. My shoes are untied. As I'm talking to them, my gun starts to feel lighter on my shoulder and

I begin to regain my energy. So much has happened in the past few weeks, I don't know where to start.

"Why aren't you in full uniform?" a commander yells.

Pretending I don't understand Hebrew, I ignore her. I need to talk to my parents.

"Why aren't you in full uniform?"

I stare at her and then return to my conversation.

"Why aren't you in uniform!" she demands. This time it is no longer a question.

I'm not going to let this commander who is younger than my little sister ruin my first conversation with my parents.

"I'm talking to my parents from abroad and it's costing a lot of money. Do you mind?" Then, for sympathy purposes, I throw in that I'm a lone soldier. Needing to be a tough officer, she stares at me, but then her Israeli side feels sorry for me and she simply walks away. Relieved, I burst out crying the second she turns around.

"What happened? Are you okay? What were you saying?" my parents ask simultaneously. Even though they are thousands of miles away and have no idea what I'm going through, I'm glad to have my parents on the other line to comfort me. I don't have to pretend to be someone else or hide who I am. They will always accept me and love me.

Senior Slide

We are nameless, faceless soldiers standing in perfect rows of ten. The lines seem to stretch as far as the eyes can see to both horizons.

The head officer of the base is standing facing us. There are hundreds of civilians in bleachers behind him. I don't know even one of them.

We have been standing in these rows for the past two hours. We also stood in these same rows this morning for two hours when the officer of the base held a dress rehearsal and walked among us, looking at each one of us to make sure that our uniforms met army code.

Today is our graduation ceremony. Tomorrow we leave boot camp and will be told in which unit we will serve. I'm still worried that I could spend the next two years of my life being a secretary in uniform and serving coffee and pastries to an overweight officer.

My row begins to run toward our platoon commander, a red-headed girl who was always particularly tough on us.

She smiles at me and hands me a book—the *Tanakh*, the Hebrew Bible—on which I swear to protect and defend Israel with my life. Then she whispers in my ear, "I'm really proud of you, Jessica. It takes great courage to move to Israel all by yourself and join the IDF. If you ever need anything, let me know."

I smile at her. I run back to my spot in line and wait for everyone else to be individually sworn in to the IDF.

Like a high school graduation, at the end, we throw our berets up in the air and everyone rushes off to see, hug, and take pictures with their families. I wander around the picnics that families have brought for their soldiers. I figure that I will sit in my tent until all the commotion is over. I begin walking through the crowd. People are setting up meals on picnic tables. Families are sitting on blankets. Moms are passing out plates of food. Dads are hugging their daughters and sons. Little kids are jumping on their older siblings, who are now soldiers. Everyone looks so happy.

As I head to my tent, I hear somebody with an American accent yell my name. I turn around and see Ester and five other people, including a newborn baby, from Merkaz Hamagshamim. I hadn't invited anyone. Having tried to toughen up and prevent any disappointment, I preferred to not invite them versus asking them to come and then them not arriving.

I feel the first smile appear on my face since I began boot camp. I run to them with open arms. Each of them hugs me in congratulations. Looking at their smiling faces, I'm sad that my real family can't be here. I know they would be so proud of me, but I feel blessed to have these friends here. They hand me treats and anxiously, almost jealously, ask me all about my boot camp experience. Only one of them has served; the rest of them are all immigrants and won't ever be in the army.

"So . . . are you in the IDF Spokesperson Unit?" Ester asks excitedly.

"I'll know tomorrow," I say.

Trying to hide my fear, I look down and start fiddling with my gun.

The next morning it is pouring rain. We're supposed to be cleaning, but we are all hiding in our tents to stay dry. Everyone knows that we're done with boot camp, so there is no chance that we will have to stay on the base for the weekend as punishment.

For the past few days it has been *avirat sof ha'kors*, end-of-the-course atmosphere—the army version of senior slide. We have been slacking off, getting into the *chet* formation more slowly, and forgetting to salute. Last night, I saw the pimply-faced commander sneak off the base on sick leave without saying goodbye to us. Watching him with his bag on his back, trying to get an extra day at home with his parents, his girlfriend, or his friends, made me realize that despite all of his yelling at us that he, like all our other commanders, was a young kid trying to get through his mandatory army service. They became less scary after that.

By nine in the morning, we have already returned our work uniforms, sleeping bags, and cots. Last night I packed up my bag. When packing, I saw my diary for the first time since I had been drafted. Only the first two pages were filled. If I were to begin writing again, I don't think I would be using the same enthusiastic tone that I used the night before being drafted. I'm slowly becoming a hardened Israeli.

Now standing outside the tent, there are soldiers telling us which unit we are going to be joining. I keep shifting my weight from one foot to the other and squeezing my hands. This is it. I will finally know my fate. I will finally know if it has all been worth it.

My name is called.

I walk up to the soldiers.

"You will go to The Campus," says one of the soldiers. The Campus is a base in Tel Aviv. There are no sororities or fraternities there.

"Am I in the IDF Spokesperson Unit?" I ask expectantly.

"You will find out what unit you are serving in once you get there. Next!" she screams, not caring about my dreams.

I go home both disappointed and optimistic. I still don't know if all of this is going to be worth it, but I try to believe that the Israeli phrase will also apply to the army: *Yihyeh b'seder!* Everything will be okay!

5

The Emerald City

A dozen other identical soldiers and I are sitting
on benches waiting to hear our names called. It feels
like we are waiting outside the principal's office, about
to get detention. Everyone is silent. My puffy winter
army jacket is zipped up all the way. We aren't really
sitting outside, but we are definitely not inside either.
The building, if it can be called that, looks more like a
shipping container with a sukkah connected to it than
a structure at the Israeli Pentagon where the defense
minister and the chief of staff are stationed.

"When is my name going to be called?" I scream in my
head. My stomach is cramping from nerves.

This morning, I woke up extra early. It took three
buses and two hours to get to The Campus on time.
When the gates to the base opened and I saw everyone
walking around in green uniforms, I felt like I was
walking into a dreary version of the Emerald City. Now
I have been sitting in this same spot on this bench for
nearly an hour. Hurry up and wait.

I'm still worried that I'll end up answering phones for
the next two years. Since everyone at Merkaz Hamagshamim works at a call center in Jerusalem fielding calls
from the US, they think that it would be funny if I end
up doing the same thing in the army for ninety percent
less pay. I don't see the humor in that.

"Jessica Fishman and Chen Shapirah," a guy calls authoritatively from behind his desk and through the open door. He doesn't even look like he can legally drink in the US.

The two of us solemnly walk in together. Sentencing is about to begin. I want to make a plea for mercy as he is shuffling through the papers on his desk. Without looking up, he hands us both a form and unenthusiastically states, "You will be serving the next two years in *Dover Tzahal*. Go get these forms filled out and signed." He said it like Ben Stein would announce the winner of Best Movie at the Oscars.

I did it! I want to smile, to scream, to jump up and down. But I can't. I'm in the army. Instead I stare at him, blank faced.

He sends us out of his office without even a nod. As I look to Chen and want to share my excitement with her, I can't find the words to express myself in Hebrew. It suddenly dawns on me that I'll be serving in the IDF *Spokes*person Unit and I can still barely even *speak* Hebrew.

Chen starts chattering to me. "Where are you supposed to be in the IDF Spokesperson Unit? I'm supposed to be a photographer. If I'm in the wrong department, I'm going to have a fit. I'll have to call my dad to get him to fix this for me. How did you get into the unit? Are you in the logistical part of the unit or are you going to be doing a real job? Here, we have to go here. Just follow me."

Despite the fact that she kind of sounds like the girls at AEϕ, I'm happy to have an Israeli help me through this maze of bureaucracy and logistics.

We are greeted by the smiling faces of two female soldiers and the evil stare of a male officer with a unibrow. If dirty looks could be part of Israel's weapons arsenal, then this officer definitely would have been a combat soldier and not a *jobnik*, a desk jockey.

"Welcome to the IDF Spokesperson Unit. You have officially arrived. You are part of us now. We like to call ourselves the commandos of the *jobnikim*. This is the logistics officer, Nimrod," the two female soldiers chirp like munchkins and point to the male officer next to them.

"Wait outside while I figure out where you are supposed to be serving," demands Officer Nimrod.

Another hour passes. Just as my fingers are beginning to turn numb from the cold, Officer Nimrod calls us in.

"Chen you are going to the photography department. Jessica, I should know tomorrow where you will be serving in the unit. In the meantime, go do your *tofes tiyulim*."

The phrase *tofes tiyulim* is deceiving. It sounds fun, since *tiyulim* means trips and is usually used when going on a fun vacation with friends—like after the army, Israelis go on a *tiyul* to India, Thailand, or South America. However, the word *tofes*, means a form, so it turns the phrase into an oxymoron. Chen and I spend the next five hours getting our forms signed and filled out by soldiers all over The Campus. The whole day feels like a really bad scavenger hunt, where we receive badges, pins, tags, and our security clearance.

But at the end of the day, I get my shoulder tags. Proof that I'm a part of the unit. I feel so proud putting on my new IDF Spokesperson tags that all I can do is stare at myself in the darkened windows of the bus on the ride home.

The next morning Officer Nimrod tells me to hurry up to meet Dan at the "S" House.

When I arrive, I'm greeted by a soldier who is supposed to be guarding the building but is more interested in reading the newspaper than keeping the building free of terrorists. But between the building looking like a low-income-housing project and unit's ineffectiveness, I doubt any terrorist would waste his time or life blowing up the office of the army's public relations.

I wander around the building looking for Dan, whose name is uttered around the unit as if he holds magical powers. When I finally find his *pikedah*, secretary, sitting at her desk in a small nook that isn't even big enough to be a cupboard, she is too busy trying to avoid work to help me. She gets up and goes downstairs to smoke a cigarette.

Even though I want to yell at her like I think a native Israeli would, I've been warned to never get on the bad side of army secretaries. They hold the keys to everything and know more than anybody. If you want to know when and how Israel is going to bomb Iran, all you have to do is ask a secretary. So I force myself to wait patiently on a broken chair in the hallway.

More than an hour later, I'm still waiting to meet with Dan. But fortunately boot camp prepared me to wait.

Bored, I wander around the small, messy, stuffy halls. Looking into different rooms, I see that they are cramped, cluttered, and noisy. I notice papers marked "top secret" thrown about, televisions blaring CNN, and phones ringing off the hook. As I walk past one room, a soldier picks up a phone and slams it down before even saying hello.

"I don't have time to field calls from Christiane Amanpour; besides you know what her agenda is," she says to an officer in fluent, unaccented English.

The officer just shrugs his shoulders.

When I'm about to peek into the next room, Dan's secretary calls me into his office.

I walk into Dan's room. He has two *falaflim* on his shoulders signifying that he is a lieutenant colonel. I freeze. As a soldier, I have never been so close to such a high-ranking officer. Having just finished boot camp, where we salute everyone more senior than us—even the dog that has been on base longer than us—I pause to salute, but something tells me not to. I remember Orli telling me that our real army service is nothing like boot camp. She told me that there is not as much *distance* between soldiers and officers.

In army slang[12], *distance* is the degree of remoteness between a soldier and his superior. Pronounced *deestance* with an Israeli accent, it comes from the English word, since Hebrew does not lend itself to such formalities. In boot camp, the *distance* between a soldier and a commander made my family—more than six thousand miles away—seem close. In the US Army, soldiers continue to salute their superiors through their entire service—stopping to salute whenever there is a superior within eyesight—but in Israel, after boot camp is over, soldiers either ignore their officers, give them a nod of the head like they are in the same gang, or run up to them and give them a pat on the back and say, "What's going on, my brother?"

I don't think Dan would know what to do if I saluted. And he probably wouldn't want me running up to him to give him a hug. So I just freeze in the doorway.

He motions for me to come in and sit down.

"What's your name?" he asks.

I tell him my name and he starts humming the chorus of *Jessie, Jessie, Jessie, Jessicaaaaah!* I'm not sure if I should start humming with him, but then he stops and asks me in very slow Hebrew how I am.

"I'm good. Thank you. Happy to be here," I respond nervously, but with a smile.

"Good. Tell me about yourself," he says in the simplest Hebrew possible.

I'm thankful that he is speaking slowly for me. I give him the short summary of my life that I have memorized in perfect Hebrew.

---

12. For a list of army slang and terminology, please see the appendix.

During my explanation, he answers a number of phone calls. I don't mind, because I'm excited to possibly overhear some behind-the-scenes information about the spokesperson unit, but instead, he is talking to his wife about who will be picking up their daughter from kindergarten today.

I look around his room. I see pictures of his family. There is a large map of Israel hanging on the wall. There are a number of different plaques. There are pictures of him shaking hands with famous Israeli politicians. I squint my eyes to get a better look at one picture. Is that the king of Jordan?

He hangs up and asks me a few more questions.

After my short interview, Dan welcomes me into a department called *tzevet t'guvot*. Not knowing the translation, I hope that this is the department that liaisons with the international press so that I can prove to the BBC that Palestinians are not throwing flowers, but rocks, and that they are using schools as weapon arsenals, and ambulances to transport missiles.

As I try to say the department's name out loud to test it out, Dan chuckles at my pronunciation.

Dan stands up and hitches his pants up around his waist. It looks like he has a few falafels in his stomach too.

Tzevet t'guvot, tzevet t'guvot, tzevet t'guvot, tzevet t'guvot . . . I keep trying to say the name of the department in my head as I follow Dan out into the hallway. No matter how hard I try, I can't say the short "tz" and form the guttural "g" and "oo" in my throat. I can't say either of the words. They are like a specially-designed-for-American-immigrants tongue twister. How am I going to tell people what I do in the army?

Dan opens the door to a small room.

There is a chubby female soldier stenciling purple flowers and red hearts onto the wall. There is a tall and skinny fake-red-headed girl reading a book. There is an officer with the rank of a major haphazardly shoveling through piles of classified documents. Looking around, I can't believe that this is the Israeli army—the pride of the Jewish people!

"Shmuel, Shmuel! I have a new soldier for you," Dan says, visibly annoyed. "This is Jessica."

Shmuel, bewildered, looks up from the documents scattered on his desk and says, "Ehh . . . Aalo. How's you do?" in an Israeli-British accent.

English! Does everyone here speak English? Am I not going to be as special as I thought?

He smiles at me and I see that one of his front teeth is missing.

"Welcome to the Rapid Response Team," he says, but when he says the letter "s," he whistles. He then fishes for something in his pocket and shoves a tooth into the gap in his mouth.

"*That is what it means*," I think to myself. Based on my boot camp experience of hurry-up-and-wait, I'm surprised to hear that there is anything called rapid in this army.

"So," he says without whistling, "you are the new soldier. Well, we don't really have any extra room and we only have three computers for the four of us. And you will have to find a chair."

I had an IDF t-shirt showing my pride for this army.

"Shmuel will be your direct officer," Dan explains. "If you need anything, ask him. He used to be the head of something called the explanation department, but that got dismantled because it wasn't working." Only a Jewish army could come up with a department that sounds like a religious philosophy class.

I walk into the office as Dan shuts the door behind me. With the noise from the rest of the unit sealed off, the room feels like a vacuum. I look around and begin to feel trapped. I wonder how I'll be able to make any impact while stuck in this small room.

"I'm being released in four months and then I'm going to the Galapagos Islands." Shmuel perks up, smiles, and then his front tooth falls back out of his mouth onto the desk.

Like Clockwork

My days become routine.

6:30 Hit the *nudnik* button.

6:35 Force myself out from under my comforter and feel the cold Jerusalem air. Put on my uniform.

6:40 Go to bathroom, wash my face, and brush my teeth.

6:45 Pull my hair back into a ponytail.

6:47 Cut up vegetables for my lunch.

6:55 Cut up fruit to eat with yogurt on the bus.

7:00 Walk downstairs.

7:01 Walk back upstairs to get my umbrella.

7:02 Run back downstairs.

7:05 Run down the hill and to the bus stop to catch the bus to the Jerusalem bus station. I'm not too worried about being late. I don't have anything to do in the office. If I miss this bus and Shmuel is mad, I can always claim that there was a bomb scare at the bus station. Always having a bomb scare as an excuse for being late is just one of the perks of living in Jerusalem.

7:07 Get soaked by the cars that are driving through puddles on the road and splashing me, even though I have brought my umbrella specifically to hold it out to the side to block the spray. By looking at my soaking uniform, no one would ever know there is a drought in this country.

7:10 Get on the bus.

7:17 Curse the Jerusalem traffic.

7:25 Run through the Jerusalem bus station like a madwoman trying to catch the next bus. Luckily, I can bypass security by flashing my army ID.

7:30 Board the bus just as it is pulling away. Find the last seat.

7:32 Eat my breakfast and fall asleep.

8:40 Wake up to see that we are, as usual, stuck in traffic at the entrance to Tel Aviv. My clothes are nearly dry. I go back to sleep.

8:55 Wake up again to the bus stopping at the Tel Aviv bus station. Get off the bus and get soaked in the Tel Aviv rain. Step into a puddle with my right foot. Now it is soaked.

8:57 Board the bus that will take me to the "S" house.

9:12 Walk into my office. Both Shmuel and the two other soldiers are already there. I have nowhere to sit, nowhere to work, and really nothing to do.

10:14 Ask hopefully, "Shmuel, is there any work that I can do?"

"No."

11:28 Wander over to the international news desk, where everyone is so busy that no one has any time to talk. Go back to my office and stare at what the other girls are doing on the computer: one is deleting emails and the other is playing solitaire.

12:17 "Shmuel, I'm going for lunch."

"Okay"

14:12 Return from lunch.

15: 32 My sock is still wet.

15:46 "Shmuel, is there any work that I can do?" I ask doubtfully.

"No."

16:57 "Shmuel, can I go home now?"

He looks at the clock, "Wait another half an hour."

17:27 "Shmuel, can I go home now?"

"Okay."

17:45 Catch the bus back to the Tel Aviv bus station.

18:00 Board the bus back to Jerusalem and fall asleep.

19:25 Get to the Jerusalem bus station.

19:40 Catch the bus back to Merkaz Hamagshamim.

20:27 Walk into the doors of Merkaz Hamagshamim.

20:40 Wash my Tupperware, but am too tired to eat dinner.

20:43 Shower.

21:17 In bed with the lights out.

I would feel more useful if I actually was making coffee for someone.

No Glass Slippers

The entire unit is gathered on the first floor of the building. All the high-ranking officers of the unit are gathered in front of us. The three head officers are staring at us, waiting for the last stragglers to file in. I wonder what is happening. Is a war about to start?

"*Maybe I'll get to do something important,*" I think to myself.

"This entire building is *j'ifa,*" Liveah, one of the unit's head officers, says to us with a scolding tone.

"What is *j'fa?*" I turn to a female American who speaks better Hebrew than me. I wonder if it means in danger.

"It is Arabic for filthy," whispers the fellow soldier.

All this excitement is about cleaning? I thought there was going to be a big operation. Sadly, this has been the most action I have seen since I arrived to the unit a few months ago.

"Don't you people care about the cleanliness of the place where you work?" Liveah roars. With her pants so tight and high up on her waist, she looks like Debbie Gibson. It is hard to take her seriously while imagining her singing.

As we are all listening to their lecture about how filthy the building is, the building's cleaning lady walks through with a squeegee, a rag, and a bucket full of water. Pushing a dirty puddle of water through our meeting with a squegee, she is complaining to herself and to anyone else within shouting distance about how dirty the building is, and how much her back hurts from squeegee-ing.

"Why should our cleaning lady have to clean up after you every day? She is old, frail, and it is hard work for her," Dan says, thinking that he is making a good point, but obviously forgetting that she is a cleaning lady and unlike us, she is employed at will and paid a salary above poverty level.

"You all have the next hour to show us that you know how to clean. Both Dan and I will come around to each department to check the cleanliness. Every single one of you needs to be cleaning," Liveah says as if she is a stereotypical stepmom in some fairytale.

"How often does this happen?" I ask the same American girl next to me.

"Oh, usually once a week," she says solemnly, having succumbed to the fact that the IDF Spokesperson Unit is obviously run by people without any media training, but with severe OCD complexes.

I can't believe that this is the army. That I gave up my life for this. This was not my dream. I could be doing this in any army. I came here to be a part of the Jewish army. To make a difference. Instead, I feel useless. Cleaning and sitting bored in a closed-off room doesn't make me feel any more connected to Israel or my Jewish heritage. The thought of doing this for nearly two more years makes me sick to my stomach. But if I throw up here, they'll just make me clean it up. I swallow hard, trying to keep the acid from rising.

One girl raises her hand and, without being called on, says, "I have to set up for a *live* interview with CNN."

"Cleaning takes priority," Dan says emotionlessly.

After being dismissed, I'm now pushing dirty water back and forth on the floor with my full-size squeegee. Becoming disillusioned, I'm starting to understand how we are losing the war on the media front, but at least we will have a clean workspace.

"How is your army service going?" Ester asks me later that night, back at Merkaz Hamagshamim.

"Yeah, we haven't seen you in ages. How have you been?" Ephraim asks. "You seem so busy with top secret army stuff."

"So, do you still think that your worst experience in the army was at the drafting office?" Uri says sarcastically and laughs.

"Come sit down and have dinner with us. We just started," says Jackie, the openly gay rabbinical student.

I collapse on a chair.

What am I supposed to tell them? That I ride buses for four hours a day, shred papers that I didn't even write, and the only time that anything exciting goes on is when we have to clean the building?

"It's good, thanks. I'm exhausted. The army wears me out. How is everything with you guys?" I ask, trying to change the subject and avoid thinking about how I've failed at both becoming more Israeli in the army and at achieving my dream.

The IDF Fashion Police

Surrounded by old, squat buildings and with the sun beating down, I'm wandering around The Campus trying to figure out where I'm supposed to show up for guard duty. Nimrod, our logistics officer, asked me a few hours ago if I could fill in for one of the girls in my department. He told me that I wouldn't actually be guarding, I would just be an understudy. He didn't give me any other instructions. He didn't tell me where to go, when to get there, or what to wear.

I have never guarded on The Campus before, but I assume that it will be like guarding at "S" House, which is also guarded 24/7 to protect the top-secret information of how the IDF Spokesperson Unit is so clean. The guard duty at the "S" House is as easy and mindless as my job at the JCC when I let people into the locker rooms, except for here I have an M-16—even though I do have serious doubts regarding the gun's usefulness for anything other than a paperweight. We all use the same gun for guard duty and I don't know the last time the gun has been fired or cleaned. If a terrorist comes in, I'd probably do more damage throwing the gun at the terrorist than actually shooting him.

I walk past a fenced-in basketball court where there are more than a hundred girls lined up, being yelled at by a boy who looks like he should be practicing his bar mitzvah portion.

"You are not allowed to eat. You are not allowed to chew gum. You are not allowed to read. You are not allowed to sit. You are not allowed to talk on the phone. You are not allowed to listen to music. You are not allowed to text. You are not allowed to play games on your phone. You are not allowed to drink anything except for water from your canteen. You are not allowed to go to the bathroom."

This sounds worse than Yom Kippur. If we could have gotten through guard duty without breathing, they would have forbidden that too.

The soldier continues shouting. "If you see a suspicious person, you first yell '*Ahztur!* Stop!' two times. If the person does not stop you shoot a warning shot at sixty degrees in the air. If the person still does not stop, aim for the legs to stop them." I could barely hit a non-moving cardboard cutout at boot camp a few months ago; I certainly can't hit a moving terrorist in the legs.

Hearing these instructions, I know that I'm in the correct place, but I'm too scared to go inside. This seems more serious than my typical guard duty. I'll probably be yelled at for being late. Instead, I decide to play the only card I have—the I'm-a-poor-lone-soldier-who-is-a-dumb-American-and-can-still-barely-speak-Hebrew card.

When the bar mitzvah boy finally finishes screaming and the female soldiers scatter, I walk up to him and ask him in as broken and accented Hebrew as I can manage, "I here for guard. Here I be, yes?"

He looks me up and down, stares at me, and then starts yelling at me: "Look at you! You're not even dressed for guard duty!"

"Ehh . . . I no . . ." I try to respond, but can't form any words. I'm no longer faking.

"What is this? You're in sandals for guard duty!"

I look down at my feet.

"And they aren't even army-sanctioned sandals!" He is yelling at me like showing up for guard duty in sandals is worse than wearing a black purse with brown shoes.

"But . . . shoes . . ." I say as my bottom lip trembles. I'd prefer Joan Rivers tell the entire world that I have no fashion sense instead of being yelled at by this short teenager with grease-backed hair. I feel like a failure as a soldier. I'm having no impact on Israel's media image. My lack of Hebrew is holding me back. I can't stop crying when a kid yells at me. How would I ever be able to stand up to a BBC reporter, or much less a terrorist? I wish I could just run away. Give up on this dream to have a meaningful part of our collective Jewish history.

"Why didn't you arrive on time?"

He doesn't care about my lack of Hebrew skill. I'm just another soldier for him to yell at. Tears stream down my cheeks. This is not my proudest moment. Here I am, a grown woman with a college degree, crying because a boy, whose mom still folds his underwear, is yelling at me.

Ignoring my distress, he continues yelling, "You and the entire spokesperson unit think you're too good for guard duty! And what is this? You are wearing a dark-navy hair binder instead of black! Oh, this is unbelievable! And your nail polish! That is brown nail polish! You are only allowed pink nail polish!"

Now he has gone too far! Offending my nail polish color! I'm wearing OPI's shade called Not So Bora-Bora-ing Pink—it even has pink in the name! It is AEφ-approved! As much as I can't stand my AEφ 'sisters,' there is no way he understands fashion better than them. Besides, the IDF doesn't give us swatch samples to let us know what is considered the right tone of pink.

"It's black . . . pink . . . I just . . . but . . . lost . . . sorry," I sob. I try explaining through my tears that the terrorists would win if I was ever wearing brown toenail polish.

He keeps screaming. My tears keep flowing. But at some point he begins to feel sorry for me.

"Who is your logistics officer?"

"Officer Nimrod. He never told me the rules—where to go, how to dress, or what to do," I respond, trying to choke back my tears and regain some self-respect. Officer Nimrod and his laziness has already cost me being able to go to officers' course and caused me to be court martialed, for telling me the wrong time for a meeting. I only had to pay a small fine then, but if this guy court martials me, I might be sent to some deep, dark hole.

A look of gleeful disgust spreads across the bar mitzvah boy's face. He turns to a female soldier next to him and says, "We have to do something about him. That Officer Nimrod never does his job. He has a small head." (Small head does not refer to the size of a man's hat or condom; it is an attitude of intentionally avoiding responsibility. It is one of the worst insults in Israel.)

The bar mitzvah boy turns to me. "I see that you're a good soldier. You didn't mean to make the mistake. Come back tomorrow in proper dress and we'll forget this happened. I'll take care of Officer Nimrod."

The next day I showed up in a newly-ironed uniform—even though synthetics don't need to be ironed. The bar mitzvah boy from yesterday says not to worry about a thing. He reassures me that I won't be court martialed and while Nimrod will be reprimanded, he will never know that I was the one who caused the commotion. The bar mitzvah boy then winks at me and tells me to stop by anytime.

While I want to laugh, I smile back, as I'm not too proud to do a little flirting in the hopes of getting out of guard duty next time.

Hell's Kitchen

The humidity inside is higher than outside. My stick-straight hair has turned into curly pubic hair. Sweat is dripping from every part of my body. My uniform is so un-breathable that a plastic bag would be more comfortable. This place is proof that hell exists.

It is my first day of kitchen duty.

When I was being drafted and even throughout boot camp, I naïvely or optimistically thought that the army would exempt me from the grunt work since I am older and have a degree. I thought the army would have made better use of its resources than have a person with an $80,000 degree wash pots and pans. Since I never had to do kitchen duty or bathroom clean up during boot camp, I thought it was an unspoken, unwritten sign of respect for me: but really, they had just somehow over-looked me. Or maybe I just misunderstood them.

I am sticking my hands in pots that are as big as a washing machine. The cheap, plastic dish gloves that I bought a few hours earlier are already full of holes and my OPI nail polish is chipping.

Elbow deep in food, grease, and soap, I see my college education going down the drain with the brown and sudsy water. I had tried to get out of the worst kitchen duty job by flirting with the soldier in charge, but I was not the only one trying that trick. Besides, by his standards, I, at twenty-four years old, am already a cougar.

I could deal with doing this grunt work, if only I was also doing real work on my other days. I keep scrubbing away for the next few hours until all the pots and pans are clean. I look at the pile of clean dishes and think to myself, at least I accomplished something today.

After my kitchen duty is over, I head back to my department. Shmuel lets me leave early. I think he is being nice, but it is probably because I stink and he doesn't want to share the small, airless office with me.

When I get home, I see that my roommates have left their food out, their dishes in the sink, and a mess on the stove.

I walk into my room and slam the door.

Wordsmithing

After a few months of being in the *tzevet t'guvot* department, we are given one of our first tasks. We are asked to suggest names for the structure being built to keep West Bank suicide bombers from reaching buses, night clubs, and cafés in Tel Aviv, Netanya, and Jerusalem. It sort of feels like someone is asking us to name a dog after it already has a tag. The media has already, *unbiasedly*, named it the "separation barrier" and is pounding the country with criticism of being apartheid. No media has or will bother to report the declining amount of terrorism. Before the construction of the fence, there had been two suicide bombings in my neighborhood in Jerusalem—one at café I frequented and the other on the bus line that I take every day. Since the construction of the fence, I feel safer. As far as I'm concerned, the media can call it a *mechitza*. Besides I'm doubtful that the media will ever hear our suggestions, much less use them. I've given up on this unit. But as part of another lesson in futility, we, confined to our small room, suggest such names as the "security fence," "anti-terrorist fence," or "seam zone."

It's as useless as when the chief of staff, three years into the current conflict, suggested that we need to come up with a catchy name for the on-going violence. The Palestinians already branded it: the Intifada. The army's operational name for it is Ebb and Flow. The Israeli population affectionately refers to it as *ha'matzav*, The Situation. Yep, one of the deadliest cycles of violent suicide bombings that Israel has ever experienced has the same name as some guy who is known for his spray-tanned six-pack from *Jersey Shore*. And I thought I would be making a difference here.

Today the two other girls in the department are playing games on their cell phones while I am reading a book—since I grew bored of staring at the clock. The door suddenly opens and Dan walks into the office. We freeze and stare at him. I'm afraid I'm going to get yelled at. We get yelled at for everything in the army.

Dan takes another step into the office and closes the door behind him. I and the other two girls in the office sit at attention and continue to stare at him. Shmuel slowly finishes a text message.

Dan stares at Shmuel until he finally puts down his phone, then says, "There is a top secret operation coming up. It will be your job to prepare the press material beforehand. Your door needs to remain closed at all times while working on this subject."

I try to keep a professional, soldier-like face, but inside, I'm screaming with excitement to finally be doing something besides cleaning, guarding, or kitchen duty. This could be my big break.

Dan continues, "In a week, the IDF will raid a bank in the West Bank to capture the funds from a Hamas account used to finance terrorist operations. This department is in charge of preparing all of the press material before the operation."

The next day I'm the earliest person in the office. I spend the entire bus ride thinking of what needs to be prepared. I start working on all of the press material. That night I stay extra late. I think back to the last big operation that the IDF performed in Nablus, Operation Defensive Shield. During that operation the media reported that the IDF was carrying out a massacre, but that was about as real as the "dead" child, who was being carried to his "funeral" on a body board, fell off the stretcher, and climbed back on by himself.

I spend the rest of the week helping to prepare material such as talking points and official army announcements to prevent the same media disaster. The next week, I go into the office every day hoping to hear news about when the operation will take place.

In the evenings at Merkaz Hamagshamim, when everyone asks me how the army is going, I pretend everything is the same, but I smile to myself, knowing I'm actually making a difference.

By the second week, the operation still hasn't taken place. I'm beginning to feel disappointed and left out again.

Then, one morning a few weeks later, as I'm putting on my uniform, I see on CNN a one-minute newscast about the bank operation for which I helped prepare media material. I freeze, with my shirt half on and my pants, unzipped, nearly falling off my hips. I don't know how to feel. I'm frustrated that the rest of the world heard about the operation before me. I'm disappointed that all the work that I did only led to a minute of coverage. But I'm also relieved that all the material we prepared was used by the media. It was the first time I felt as if I had made an impact. It gives me hope that maybe I will be able to fulfill my dreams in the IDF if I am persistent.

Operation Rainbow

"I'm sorry, but I have to interrupt this class. I have some bad news," says a female officer who is usually in the Spokesperson War Room, but has been teaching our class for the past few days.

After finally getting a taste of what it was like to be a part of media preparations for an operation, I begged Dan to let me take a supplemental IDF Spokesperson course in the hopes of being able to make more of a contribution.

"Terrorists have hit and destroyed IDF's APCs (Armored Personnel Carrier) by the Rafiach Crossing in Gaza. Thirteen soldiers are dead," she announces. The air is sucked out of the room. Our faces turn pale. My stomach clenches up. It feels like she has just told us that our brothers have been killed. She turns on the TV.

On the screen, I see IDF soldiers crawling on their hands and knees looking for the mutilated body parts of their comrades from the explosion.

The room is silent. I choke back tears.

Six days later, the IDF launches Operation Rainbow to prevent continued weapon smuggling from Egypt to Gaza through underground tunnels.

Flipping between CNN, FOX, and BBC on the TV in the office, I watch reports about Israel's operation. But instead of mentioning that Israel is trying to protect its citizens, or explaining that Israel launched a defensive operation to prevent weapons smuggling following the attack, the media is slamming Israel for destroying homes. Every reporter forgets to mention that these are homes that terrorists use as cover for weapons-smuggling tunnels. Reporters don't even mention the Kassam rockets that are being fired at homes in Sderot, Israel. I know reporters want to be unbiased, but not every side has a legitimate or valid message. Not every side should be treated equally. An army blowing up a terrorist arsenal should not get the same type of coverage as a terrorist intentionally launching rockets into a kindergarten.

My skin goes cold when I think about the mothers of the soldiers who were killed last week. Like I'm playing a game of Ouija, my hand instinctively moves the mouse to open up PowerPoint. Sitting at my desk, I stare at the blank slide and start typing. I add pictures of the Kassam rockets, of the weapons-smuggling tunnels. I add colors and titles. I want to show the world that Israel is defending itself. I want the world to see that it is not Israel, but the terrorists themselves that are harming the Palestinian population. The terrorists use the homes of the Palestinian civilians as cover for their weapons smuggling; the terrorists strap suicide bombs to their kids at summer camps like they are flotation devices. I want to show the connection between the terrorist activity and the IDF response.

Hoping that I can actually make a difference with my presentation, I work all day. I don't get up to eat or to use the bathroom. I show Dan the presentation and, after he reviews it, he looks at me as if he sees my potential for the first time. I think to myself that maybe there is still a chance that I can make a difference in the IDF in the next year and half I still have left to serve.

On the bus ride home that night, when a fellow Israeli passenger strikes up a conversation with me, I'm not too shy to answer. I'm not embarrassed about my accent. I'm proud of my Hebrew. I speak confidently, as if I have nothing to hide.

6

Changing the Status Quo

If Jerusalem is the religious capital of the monotheistic religions, then Tel Aviv is its antithesis. It is the city that makes sinning fun. During the Gay Pride Parade in Tel Aviv, men dress up in pink, orange, and green neon-colored G-strings, knee-high boots, religious top hats and long, curly sidelocks, and they dance on floats. It is hard to find a kosher restaurant in Tel Aviv, but every doorframe of every building has a *mezuzah*[13] on it. Tel Aviv is young. Fun. Liberal. Full of energy. The city is always bustling, whether with cockroaches or people in cafés. I always wanted to move to Tel Aviv. I never planned on staying in Jerusalem.

I step out of the air-conditioned van that the army loaned to me with a driver for a day as one of my lone soldier benefits. The humidity sticks to my skin, but I prefer the sweat of the secular in their swimsuits on the beach to that of the religious in their never-washed wool suits.

---

13. A mezuzah is a piece of parchment, contained in a decorative case, inscribed with specified biblical Hebrew verses. These verses comprise the Jewish prayer "Shema Yisrael," beginning with the phrase, "Hear, O Israel, the LORD our God, the LORD is one." A mezuzah is affixed to the doorframe in Jewish homes to fulfill the biblical commandment to inscribe the words of the Shema "on the doorposts of your house."

Opening the door to my new apartment and seeing the dark-wood arch, I realize that it is even better than I remember.

I found the apartment after a particularly long and exhausting night of searching. It was the last apartment on my list. All the other apartments that I saw that night made me miss the tents from boot camp. Out of exhaustion I nearly didn't go to see this one.

I walked up and down Ben-Gurion Boulevard for twenty minutes, trying to find the apartment. I didn't want to call because I was embarrassed to admit I was lost. While wandering the boulevard, I found myself passing the café where my family had eaten ten years ago, during our first trip to Israel. I paused, surprised by my reflection in the café window. I perfectly blended into my surroundings.

During that two-week family vacation, we had experienced everything Israel had to offer. We swam with the dolphins in Eilat. We hiked in the enormous Maktesh Ramon crater. We climbed Masada and were amazed by the story of the Jewish fighters who fought the Romans. We floated in the Dead Sea. In the north, we stayed at a *kibbutz* and bathed in the Sea of Galilee. We spent our last days in the country swimming and sunbathing on the Tel Aviv beaches. On our last night, we ate at this very café on the street named for the first prime minister of Israel, David Ben-Gurion.

While I was staring out the open windows of the café at a group of young, strong and handsome Israeli soldiers in uniform who were laughing and carrying their M-16's and Uzis through the middle of this peaceful and touristy city, my dad interrupted my concentration. "Jessica, for the third time, what was your favorite part of Israel?"

I gazed back at the modern-day biblical heroes with their semi-automatic weapons. "Jerusalem," I lied, but it seemed like the right answer at the time. It was really the soldiers. It was the story of the Six Day War in the Golan Heights. It was the Tel Aviv beaches.

"Do you want to come back?" my dad asked.

"Yes."

I had told the truth.

Back then, I had no idea that I might actually end up living on Ben-Gurion Boulevard, as an Israeli soldier, or that one of Ben-Gurion's decisions while forming the State would soon seal my fate.

I now stared at myself in the windows. Wearing my uniform, I looked just like the soldiers that I saw passing the café fifteen years ago. Newly determined to find the apartment, I pulled out my phone to get directions.

"Hi. I'm looking for the apartment. I'm on Ben-Gurion and Dizengoff, right next to the juice stand and the sandwich shop," I said when a guy answered the phone.

"You're only two blocks away. Just head east and it is on the right side. I'll see you in less than five minutes," he said.

The apartment is located close enough to Kikar Rabin, the square where all of Israel's biggest rallies are held and the same square where Rabin was tragically shot by a religious fanatic for signing the Oslo Accords. I can walk to the beach in less than ten minutes. On every corner there is a café. It has huge windows that look out onto Ben-Gurion Boulevard.

After unloading all of my boxes in the living room, I begin cleaning my new room. With all of the cleaning, it feels like a normal day in the army except that no one is yelling at me in the background to clean harder or faster.

While I'm cleaning, my new roommate finally comes home. Excited to finally be living with an Israeli, I walk out of my room to say hi.

"When are you going to be moving your stuff out of the living room?" my new roommate, Alon, pronounced *ah-lone*, asks as he turns his head from the living room to me, with a perturbed look on his face.

"Uhh, I hope soon. I'm just cleaning first," I say with a smile.

He walks into his room and shuts the door. I go back into my room hoping that he just had a bad day. "I'm sure we will be friends," I say to no one.

I spend the next few hours cleaning, organizing, and decorating. For nearly a year and a half now I have been moving to a new place every few months—from Oshkalon to Migdal Ha'Emek and then from Jerusalem to the Youth Village and then back to Jerusalem for a few months of *ulpan*. I have begun to feel like a nomad, a fugitive, a wandering Jew. I need this new apartment to feel like home.

After organizing all of my belongings and decorating the room with Zionistic posters and pictures of my friends and family, I go into the living room, put my feet up on the coffee table with satisfaction and turn on the TV. This is going to be the beginning of a new life. Even though the army has not lived up to my expectations, I'm sure that Tel Aviv will.

Alon's door opens. He walks past the living room. He then walks back into his room.

Ten minutes later he walks out again. He walks past the living room and then returns.

He does this five other times in the next hour. It is like watching a really slow game of tennis. He keeps heading in the direction of the bathroom. I wonder if he has diarrhea.

By 9:00 p.m., I'm tired. I have to go back to making those all-powerful PowerPoint presentations in the army tomorrow, although I'm beginning to feel that they are not having as much influence as I'd originally hoped.

The second that I shut my bedroom door, Alon's opens. I hear him walk into the living room, sit down on the couch, and turn on the TV. I guess his name is also his preferred state of being—alone.

As I crawl into bed, I'm already disappointed by my first day in the new apartment. I expected that with this step I would be emerging into Israeli society, but I feel lonelier now. As if to emphasize my loneliness, there is moaning and the pounding of a bed board being repeatedly banged against the wall. I don't have a radio or TV in my room to drown out the noise. I try to cover my head with my pillow. When the moaning turns into screaming, I put in the army-issued earplugs that I used at the firing range so I could drown out the noise . . . and a bit of my jealousy.

Knee Deep

"Can you *li'kfotz li?*" I ask Orli over the phone as we are trying to make plans for going out tonight.

In the army today, I found out that all of my Power-Point presentations were never used. The real bullets that the terrorists use in real guns to kidnap journalists are more convincing than the PowerPoint bullets I was using.

Fed up, I want to go out and forget the army.

Through her laughter she says, "You mean 'Can I *l'hakpitz otach?*' It is the same root, but instead of asking me to come pick you up. You basically told me to fuck off." Used to my mistakes, Orli always knows what I'm actually trying to say. I'm glad I made the mistake with her and not someone else. She can finish my sentences for me . . . and usually does. It's nice to be closer to her now that I'm in Tel Aviv.

"We are going to the usual dance club," she says. Every Friday night we go to drink, dance, and flirt at Zamir. It is the only time that I can forget about the army and my disappointments. Unlike Jerusalem, which shuts down on the weekends, Tel Aviv comes alive. Instead of singing in synagogue, we are singing the words to one of Beyonce's songs. Our Sabbath clothes are black tank tops, high-heels, and tight jeans. Our dancing is much more provocative than the *hora*, which actually sounds more scandalous than pole dancing, if you think about it. We drink more than the customary sip during Kiddush—in fact, we usually drink the entire bottle, not leaving even a drop for Elijah. But then again, I doubt Elijah drinks Red Bull and vodka.

"So, what time should we meet?" I ask, after we decide to meet at the club.

"Around 11:30. I'll give you a call when we leave."

Luckily I don't have to go to the army tomorrow, but if I did, I've learned, just like every other soldier, how to perform my duties without sleep and with a hangover. It makes going to Friday classes after a frat party seem easy.

"Okay, see you all then," I say.

As I walk up to the club, I see Orli and everyone else in line. When they see me, they leave the line and we walk to the front door. They push me forward.

"How long is the wait?" I ask in perfect English.

"How many people you with?" asks the bouncer in thickly-accented English.

"Four other girls," I say. He waves us through. My English works every time. It is the only time I don't mind standing out.

The pounding music, the flashing lights, the young, hot bodies, the smell of alcohol. Everything is so much more tempting in the Holy Land.

"So, where were you last weekend? Why didn't you come out?" one of Orli's girlfriends yells to me over the music.

"I had guard duty at The Campus." I roll my eyes.

"That sucks," she says, having finished her army service four years ago.

Yeah, it does suck! I think to myself. It really does suck that I left all my friends and family, that I moved to this country, that I volunteered for this army in hopes of making a difference, and all I'm doing is wasting my time.

"I need a drink," I tell everyone. "Who's with me?"

While I'm ordering a drink at the bar, a guy comes over and starts talking to me. I decide to play my "I'm an American tourist" game. This has become an old-time favorite of mine. In the game I pretend that I'm visiting Israel for a short time, don't understand any Hebrew, and am awestruck by anything having to do with the IDF.

"So, how long you here for?" the guy asks

"A few weeks," I say while twirling my hair. "I love Israel. This is my first time here."

He smiles at his friend. "This is going to be easy." I hear him say to his friend in Hebrew and then he offers to buy me a drink.

I accept. After all, I am a poor, lone soldier, even if he thinks I'm a rich American tourist. Just yesterday I had to eat my cereal with water because I did not have any milk.

"So, are you a soldier?" I ask with fake excitement in my eyes.

"Oh, yes. I'm a soldier. You come over and see me in my uniform?" He asks me in broken English and then again turns to his friend and says in Hebrew, "I'm going to bang this American tonight."

While I sometimes feel guilty playing this game, it is a good way to weed out the douche bags.

I lean into him and whisper in Hebrew in his ear, "You'd have a better chance with Hezbollah than you do with me."

I walk away with the drink he bought me. I'm not interested in finding a boyfriend now. I want to make it here on my own before I rely on a boyfriend. There are just too many tales of girls falling in love, breaking up, and leaving the country. And I'm determined to make this country my home.

As the night gets later, we continue drinking and dancing. The club gets busier. The music gets louder. The people get drunker.

We take one shot after another. With each shot, I forget about another PowerPoint that I made that went to waste.

A popular Israeli song comes on and we all get excited. We jump up and down in excitement. We dance with abandon. We move to the beat. We don't care what we look like. We don't care about the security situation. We are having too much fun.

Right as the beat picks up, I feel a crunch in my left knee. But I don't feel any pain so I keep dancing and drinking.

*   *   *

My head hurts. My ears are ringing. My mouth is dry. My knee is throbbing.

It is 1:00 p.m., but my bedroom is still dark. The best thing about Israeli apartments are the *trisim*, blinds. Unlike American blinds, the Israeli *trisim* completely block out light, as if the world has been cast into eternal darkness. With my *trisim* closed, I could sleep through an atomic bomb, which might actually be necessary soon.

I'm supposed to meet Orli and her friends at the beach. I look at my phone. Three missed calls.

I swing my legs out of bed. As I stand up, I fall back into bed. Not only am I dizzy, but I can't put any weight on my left leg.

I sit in bed, not knowing what to do. It is my ritual to go to the beach on weekends—even though it is forbidden for soldiers to tan during the high-sun hours. Not because the IDF is worried about skin cancer, but because, just like a tank, an aircraft or a shirt, my body is army property and they don't want me damaging army property by getting a sunburn. The army would be just as upset if I lost my IDF shirt as if I got hit by a car.

I call Orli.

"Aaaloo! Where are you? I've been calling you. Come to the beach."

DOINK, DOINK, DOINK, DOINK.

I hear the *matkot*, paddle ball games in the background. Using the word *doink* to explain the noise that it makes is much too gentle for a sport that can be so vicious. The entire Tel Aviv shoreline is lined with *matkot* players. Trying to get through them and walk into the water is like trying to dodge the bullets of a firing squad.

"I'm not feeling well. I think I hurt my knee last night," I say.

"You should go to the army doctor and get *gimelim*."

"What are *gimelim*?"

"It's sick leave from the army. Just tell him that you can't walk. It's that easy! I had *gimelim* for a few months when I broke my ribs in a car accident."

An Apple a Day

"So, tell me what happened?" the doctor asks.

"I hurt my knee while serving in the Israeli army."

When I arrived in Minnesota on my *meuchedat*, the one-month vacation I get as a lone soldier, my dad saw me limping and instantly made an appointment for me.

"How'd you hurt it?" asks my dad's friend, the orthopedic surgeon. He couldn't just leave it at that explanation. He wanted specifics.

"Uh . . . dancing drunk in high heels," I fessed up.

He looks disappointed. He probably wanted to hear some superwoman story about fighting terrorists even more than I wanted to tell it. I just hope he doesn't ask what I do in the army; I don't think I could confess that I do nothing.

"Okay. Let's take a look."

It is nice hearing and speaking English. It is even nicer having a doctor that actually wants to help me.

I have been limping for the past two months. Getting *gimelim* had not been as easy as Orli said. In fact, just getting quality medical attention was difficult. Unlike civilian doctors who focus on making a good diagnosis, army doctors focus on trying to filter out the people who are actually sick from the fakers—and Israeli males are not good at telling when a woman is faking. Many soldiers will go to great lengths to get *gimelim*, from putting a potato on their skin for a week to cause frail bones to putting blood in their urine.

When I went to the army doctor to seek help, I was greeted by a doctor who yelled at me more than my boot camp commanders had. He didn't believe that I was really in pain. He must have thought I'd be willing to go through unnecessary surgery just to avoid the army food. So like a settler in the West Bank, I refused to leave, and after some complaining, he finally gave me a referral for an ultrasound on my knee and a full body scan that pumped me so full of radiation that I could have been strapped on a missile and sent to blow up Iran's nuclear facilities. However, when I showed him the results of the tests, (which I later learned were completely diagnostically worthless), he kicked me out. Limping out of his office, I didn't know where else to turn.

This new doctor begins manipulating my knee.

"AHHHHHH!" I scream in pain. I don't think even a healthy knee is supposed to move that way.

"I'm sending you to get an MRI."

This is the type of diagnostic test I should have been given from the beginning, but I didn't because it is too expensive for the army.

"But, I don't have medical insurance here."

"That is okay. This one is on the house, as a thank you for your service to Israel."

I try not to laugh. But it is nice being back in Minnesota where I have my family to take care of me. I feel as if I can finally put my guard down. I don't feel like I always have to be ready for some type of battle. I know that if I fall here, my parents are here to pick up the pieces. Here, I'm important to someone and not just another faceless soldier.

As I lay in the MRI tube, I think about how, because I'm a lone soldier in the army, the IDF social worker is supposed to make sure that I'm okay, but she doesn't even bother answering her phone. As the machine bangs around me, I begin wondering, "How am I going to get through another year in the army? How am I going to get my knee fixed?" I lay still, almost hoping that if I don't move that I can stay in the safety of this tube forever.

The MRI reveals that my meniscus is torn. Realizing that without proof of the injury, the only way I'll get medical attention in the army is if I shoot myself in the knee, I ask for a copy of the film.

When the month is over, I head back to Israel wearing a knee brace and carrying an MRI picture, newly determined to get the surgery that I need.

Remote Control

I don't know why the E.R. is called the emergency room; it really should be called a waiting room. I have been sitting here for three hours now. Even while sitting, I cry from the pain in my knee.

My new commanding officer sent me to the doctor on the base to have my knee looked at again. Since I got back from the US two months ago, I still have yet to receive medical attention. I have almost become resigned to the fact that I'll be disabled for the rest of my life. When I showed my MRI film to the grumpy army doctor, he threw me out of his office, as if he was a fashion designer who did not like my portfolio. Even with proof in his hands, he still didn't believe me. Maybe he thought that I had stolen the MRI film from somebody?

In order to get approval to go to the E.R., I had to get a referral from a doctor in the army. I refused to go see the orthopedic doctor again, so instead I went to the base's head doctor. I had arrived there just as he was leaving for lunch. Instead of deciding to take five minutes to look at me and write a referral to the E.R., he went to go eat while I sat outside his door in pain for the next hour. I shouldn't have been surprised that *hurry up and wait* applies here.

"Jasseeeka Feeshman." My name is finally called in the E.R.

I limp into the room.

"You know there is a song about you?" the doctor asks.

"I've heard," I say, hoping that he won't sing it.

"So, you are having some knee problems?"

"Yes." I can already tell that this doctor is a better diagnostician than the one in the army.

I explain that the pain has been getting worse for the past few months and detail the incompetence of the army doctor on base. He does not seem surprised and gives me two weeks of sick leave, a prescription for inflammation, and a referral for crutches. Unfortunately, I don't get approval for surgery. For approval, I have to go to the central medical base to be seen by a specialist.

With all of its tanks, APV's, F-16s, and helicopters, the IDF cannot even provide me with a simple pair of crutches. I have to rent them from *Yad Sarah*, an organization that aids the disabled, poor, elderly, housebound, and now, one lone soldier.

While the crutches prevent me from having to put weight on my knee, they don't help me become more mobile. I can't figure out how to use them. They fall out of my arms. I slip. My armpits get chaffed. And I get tired after walking with them for less than thirty seconds. I thought that getting two weeks of sick leave was going to be great. I'd have time to rest in bed. My knee wouldn't hurt as much. And I could just have some down time. But by the end of the two weeks, I'm suffering as much mentally as physically.

I'm bored out of my mind. I didn't think that I could be any more bored than I was in the army, but I am. At least there I had people to talk to. Here I feel like I am in solitary confinement.

I can barely leave my house. The crutches limit me to a fifty-meter radius. I'm alone all day with nothing to do but watch reruns of trashy American TV. My friends are busy with their lives. It's hard buying and making food on my own. I can't carry a glass of water into my room because of my crutches. Without money for an air conditioner on my lone-soldier's salary, I sweat profusely in my bed. I feel trapped between the four walls of my bedroom. I've lost hope that I'll ever get better. I feel more useless than the UN peacekeeping forces in southern Lebanon.

I'd rather be on night guard duty.

*   *   *

"Yep, I see a small tear," the orthopedic surgeon says while holding my film up to the light. "I usually see this type of tear in knees of eighty year olds and don't recommend surgery for them. But since you are young and active, you should have surgery, especially considering the amount of pain and immobility you are experiencing."

This is the first competent doctor I have seen in Israel. It is probably because he is a civilian doctor. Serving as a doctor in the army is only part of his reserve duty.

"You definitely think I should have surgery?" I ask.

"Yes, the tear will only get worse. It is like when you have a small tear in your jeans. It will keep getting bigger if you don't patch it up. You will come to my office at the hospital for another checkup and there we will schedule a surgery date." He has a quiet voice and a serious demeanor.

Hearing someone from the army finally recognize my pain is as big of a deal as if the Palestinian Authority was to actually recognize Israel's right to exist.

Jagged Little Pill

I just threw up at the Tel Aviv central bus station. The pain killers, which were supposed to ease my knee pain while walking and riding the buses, didn't sit well with my stomach. No one noticed me in my army uniform puking next to the drunks who were pissing all over the place. The foreign workers and North African refugees just kept walking past me as I heaved, and the homeless people barely even tried to avoid my puke.

I couldn't sleep the night before when the army called me unexpectedly and told me that I had to come to the medical base. I was so nervous that they were going to delay my surgery again.

Two months after my doctor's visit, I'm now heading back to the central medical army base. I'm still limping. I'm sweating. I've been here three times already and my surgery still hasn't been scheduled. I feel like I'm being tossed back and forth between bureaucrats, as if I am just another file that ends up on someone else's desk.

Just as I start to feel faint, my bus arrives. Holding onto the poles and the back of seats, I finally find a seat. I sink into it.

"Jeeessikah? Is that you?"

I try to open my eyes.

I see a girl wearing a long, flowing skirt and a baggy shirt. I focus on her face. She was in boot camp with me. Why isn't she in her uniform?

"Oh, you're still in the army?" She seems shocked.

It hasn't even been a year since boot camp ended. Both she and I have at least another year of service left.

"Of course. You're not?"

"No. The army isn't for me. I'm pretending to be religious so I don't have to serve. I go to yeshiva a few hours a day and then I spend the rest of the day at the beach."

It seems as if everybody knows how to work the system except for me.

She gets off at the next stop.

I close my eyes. I think back to last week during my pre-surgery checkup in the civilian hospital. While waiting for my turn to see the doctor, I looked around the room. Across from me, there was an elderly woman clutching her purse like it held a million dollars. A man in a wheelchair, who was probably a Holocaust survivor, had been parked next to a chair where his Filipino foreign worker sat.

"What happened to you?" The twentyish-year-old guy sitting next to me with orange-ish hair and a matching scruffy beard asked.

The two of us started comparing our "war wounds."

"Oh, so you *really* do have a torn meniscus?" he asked me suspiciously.

"Yeah, I do. I've been trying to get approval for surgery for the past few months."

"Oh . . ." he said, contemplating if he should say more. "Well, I actually have approval for surgery, but I am trying to get it cancelled. I don't actually have a bum knee. I just knew what to say so they would think I do. You see, a lot of my friends were killed in an army operation. I only have a few months left of service, but I can't go back in the field after seeing my friends dying. I just want to finish my service on sick leave."

"Why haven't they given you an MRI to confirm it?" I asked.

"It's just cheaper to do exploratory surgery."

I wanted to keep talking with him, but my name was called.

I walked into the room and was greeted by a new doctor who made Dr. House seem like Mr. Rogers.

"On the exam table," he ordered me with the arrogance of a surgeon and the rudeness of an Israeli.

Without saying anything he began moving my knee in ways that not even acrobats in Cirque du Soleil can.

I cry out in pain, but he doesn't seem to hear me.

"You don't need surgery. I'll inform the army." And then he motions to the door.

I couldn't believe my ears. I couldn't speak. I couldn't move, but this time it was not only because of my knee that I was left paralyzed. This army is so backwards. There was a soldier sitting outside who is supposed to get surgery who is pretending to have the exact same condition that I actually have, but they won't approve surgery for me even though I actually have proof of a tear. I felt like my life was turning into a Greek tragedy. The irony in my life makes that of Oedipus' life seem mundane.

"I need the surgery!" I yelled at him.

"No, you don't. All you need is physical therapy."

For the past two months I have been going to physical therapy. All I got out of that was electric shocks to my knee like I was some kind of serial killer.

He opened the door and pushed me out, without even a sticker or a lollipop.

"I want my dad," I cried to myself.

I open my eyes. Trees and buildings are rushing past us. The bus comes to a stop. We've reached the army base. I slowly get up, hoping not to puke. I'm still sweating. I probably look like I'm hung over. My stomach hurts so much that I can't stand up straight. I limp off the bus.

After everything I have been through, I'm as bitter as a cup of Starbucks. All I want is to have the surgery that I so desperately need so I can go back to serving in the IDF Spokesperson Unit. Maybe when I get back to the unit, I'll actually be able to have a more meaningful service.

I slowly make my way to the base. Soldiers walk past me. I'm envious of them for being able to walk . . . no, I'm mad at them for being able to walk.

Limping down the long path to the army base, I'm out of breath and dehydrated. When I finally make it onto the army base, I slouch down in a chair. I put my head in my hands to keep the room from spinning.

When my name is called, I hobble into a female officer's office. My army shirt is untucked and partially unbuttoned, my hair is a mess, and I am wearing flip flops. I no longer care about meeting dress code.

As I sit down, the officer looks at me, but doesn't really see me. Without feeling, she says, "Your surgery is not approved. You will report back to your unit tomorrow for duty."

I'm a piece of paper to her.

I no longer care about the consequences of the army. I don't care about this woman. Who the hell is she to tell me that I'm not going to have surgery? My eyes narrow. I'm happy that I am not holding a weapon. I don't say anything. She may not be the one making my decisions about my surgery, but she is the only person I have to yell at. It is too hard to fight a system; it is much easier to fight a person.

The storm hits.

"I refuse to return to base until I have surgery. Release me from the army. I'll go back to the States and pay for my own surgery out of my own pocket. Then I'll return. I'm a volunteer soldier." I'm so mad that I'm shaking. "I'm not trying to get out of my service or my duty. I even asked my officers for permission to work from my home. I'm sick of being in pain every day. I'm sick of dealing with this army bureaucracy." Words just keep flying out of my mouth. "The army is supposed to give its soldiers medical care. You take better care of your M-16's than your soldiers. You better figure out how to approve my surgery before I give myself the surgery with a kitchen knife!"

I'm not sure who is more surprised by my rant—her or me. It was the type of rant that would make Glenn Beck's seem sane.

She stares at me blankly. She doesn't say anything for a few seconds. She looks down at the file in her hands.

I get up to leave, but before I do, I say, "I'll be at home. Call me once the surgery is approved."

Chicken Soup for the Nose

"Have you had any surgeries?" asks a religious nurse and a nurse in training.

"Yes, on my *oaf*," I say, wearing a hospital gown that looks like it has been around since the creation of the State.

They both give me a strange look.

I point to my nose.

"Oh . . . *off*." They laugh. "Not *oaf*."

Oops, *oaf* is chicken. This type of misunderstanding is bad before surgery. I need to make sure that I remember how to say left versus right in Hebrew so I don't tell the surgeon the wrong leg. My nerves are getting to me.

It turned out that my rant worked. I'll need to remember this in the future.

When I received approval for the surgery, my mom decided to fly in to take care of me. It suddenly feels strange to me that my mom is here for me. I feel like I have been trying to escape her history all my life. Back at the sorority in Indiana, I was embarrassed by my mom. All of my sorority sisters' mothers had come to help them move in. Their moms were sociable, fashionable, and outgoing. They were typical Jewish mothers. My mom was nothing like them. I had told my mom that I didn't need her help. My mom wore Birkenstocks and Patagonia. When their moms gossiped, my mom was quiet; when they were out looking for fur coats, my mom was volunteering at the zoo, and while they were out shopping for Fendi purses, she was praying in synagogue or volunteering as the Hadassah chapter president.

I wonder if moving to Israel was also part of me trying to redefine her history. But it seems as if no matter how much I push her away, she is always the first one there to help me when I need her. I wonder if this will always be true. If she will always be there for me. But before I can further contemplate, I am wheeled into surgery.

*   *   *

It didn't take me long for me to recover from surgery. In fact, I was able to *walk* out of the hospital holding my mom's hand. Walking out of there, I had a renewed sense of hope. I felt like after getting my way in the Israeli army, I could accomplish anything—maybe I could even become useful in the IDF Spokesperson Unit. After all, I had now acquired Israeli super powers.

7

A New Leader

Arafat, the man who popularized suicide bombs, is on his death bed and I'm right in the middle of the controversy.

During my four months of sick leave, the Rapid Response Department had been dismantled, like some temporary settlement in the West Bank. Shmuel had left for the Galapagos Islands, now enjoying his retirement and his new tooth. The other two girls had been transferred to other departments, and a whole new branch was created in the IDF Spokesperson Unit. The new departments are usually as ineffective as the last. But this branch feels different. We are actually making an impact here.

"Jessica! You sit with Bar and start contingency planning for Arafat's death," Yoni, my new head officer in the Strategic Initiatives and Research Unit, delegates. "How will his death impact the security situation? What are all of the threats and opportunities? Will this bring about a new peace deal or more terrorism? How will the global community view this? The two of you will have a great international perspective." He never commands us. He has too much respect for us to command us. Despite his short stature, he knows how to control a room. While Yoni is a *sgan aluf*, lieutenant colonel, he is not obsessed with his rank. He jokes around with us, informs us of the workings of the upper echelon instead of just barking orders, and is the first officer that treats me as more than just an eighteen-year-old soldier. He actually recognizes that my degree and experience can benefit the army. He sees my potential. I feel as if I'm actually making an impact in the IDF, that my contribution will be a part of Jewish history.

Bar and I head into the other room to brainstorm the different outcomes of Arafat's death—from Arafat coming back to life to the Palestinians being ready for a peace deal (with the first one seeming much more likely), and the IDF's response to each.

Bar, a new immigrant from France, is the first soldier I have met who is older than I am. With his quiet and calm demeanor, I'm surprised Israel let him into the country, much less the IDF.

We sit down side by side on two chairs with one laptop. The room is small, with the only window covered by bars. The florescent light is almost greener in tint than our uniforms. It is already dark outside.

"Where should we start?" Bar asks.

Bar arrived to the branch a few weeks after me. Until he joined, I had been the only soldier with three other officers in the Strategic Initiatives and Research Unit. When I first met Bar, he was sitting at Yoni's desk. Excited to have another soldier in the department, I bombarded him with so many questions that he must have thought that I was part of the army's security clearance team. Despite the intense introduction, Bar and I have become quite close.

"It looks like we'll be spending the weekend in the office. There has been another report that Arafat died, but it seems like this time it's real," Yoni says half-jokingly as he walks into the room. His bald head reflects the green lights from above.

"He is like Kenny from South Park," I joke, now that his death has been reported four times.

Yoni laughs, exposing a jagged tooth, and asks "How are things coming?" Yoni looks at the computer to see our progress. "Are you two done with the contingency planning? The chief of staff wants to see it so we can get all the ground forces and the media relations prepared for Arafat's funeral. They are saying that there will be a funeral in Egypt and then he'll be buried in Ramallah. You know, depending on how we have prepared the army for this, Arafat's death could be either a media disaster or a success."

There is hope in the air that this could be a turning point for Palestinian-Israeli relations and I'm excited to have some impact. I'm sitting on my hands, trying to act cool and composed. I can't believe that I'm part of this major Israeli event. Going to synagogue or being in a Jewish sorority never made my Jewish identity feel this strong.

On Thursday morning, Arafat dies. On Friday there is a funeral in Egypt and then he is buried in the West Bank city of Ramallah. The entire army is put on high alert. My new unit is camped out in front of the TV, switching between CNN, BBC, and FOX to watch the coverage, and to see if all of our planning prevents mass chaos or greater tragedy. With Palestinians mourning, wailing, and shooting guns, the scene in Ramallah looks like a violent version of Woodstock. But all of the planning is a success. There is no actual violence. The media, despite its typical tendency to do so, does not blame Israel for Arafat's death. And I can't wait to see what else we will be able to accomplish in the department.

Pro-Choice

Our small branch of five people is sitting at a table for twenty. As a new branch we don't have offices, so we sit in the unit's conference room. The room is meant to be used for media briefings, but since that rarely happens, it is used for the unit's ranking ceremonies, release celebrations, and something called *ha'ramat cosit*, which means to toast a drink (usually for the holidays). To my American ears, this had initially sounded strangely close to *ha'ramat cusit*, literally translated to lifting up a hot girl—so I was quite confused and a little concerned regarding the sexual harassment policy of the army.

Only a few weeks ago, in this very room, Yoni gave me my corporal insignia. This entailed him pinning a piece of cloth with two stripes onto my sleeves. The ceremony felt less formal than my AEΦ pinning. In the evening, after the pinning ceremony, most soldiers take their ranks back home and have their mothers sew it onto their sleeves. But people like me, lone soldiers, who do not have their mothers in Israel to sew on their ranks, end up looking like a mix between G.I. Joe and Raggedy Anne, with messy cross stitches embroidering crooked ranks. The stiches I made reminded me of the ones I had in my knee, which was a bit disconcerting, but so far I hadn't had any pain or problems.

Today we are again sitting at one end of the long table. I am sitting next to Bar. We have grown even closer since the night a few weeks ago when he had nighttime guard duty and was supposed to simultaneously finish a presentation for the head of the IDF Spokesperson Unit. I had volunteered to go in and help him. Knowing that we had each other's backs made us feel like we weren't completely lone soldiers.

At the head of the table is Yoni and across from me, wearing a knitted kippah, is Yehuda, the other officer in our branch. We are all waiting for Yoni to make his announcement. He enjoys theatrics and keeping us guessing.

"We have a new addition to the branch," Yoni says with great pride.

In walks a girl straight out of a Moroccan Abercrombie and Fitch catalogue.

"This is Tali. She will be my secretary."

Tali smiles shyly. I expected someone this beautiful to be more outgoing.

Bar and I welcome her in our differently accented Hebrew.

Yehuda pauses and thinks before he says anything, as if the weight of the entire world is on his next sentence, or God might strike him down if he says the wrong thing. "Shalom Tali," he finally says.

Yoni is beaming with pride at the growth of the new branch. "Now everyone should make Tali feel welcome," Yoni declares. He turns to Tali, "If you need anything, come to me right away."

After a month, Yoni found offices for our branch. Unfortunately the offices are not in the "S" House, where most of the Spokesperson Unit sits and army rules only partially apply. The new offices are inside The Campus base, which has real guards at the gates, who check our IDs before entering and military police who make sure our uniforms meet requirements.

More unfortunately, Yoni decided that this move would be a good *gibbush* experience for the now four soldiers in the branch—by painting the offices. A *gibbush* in the army is usually a physically strenuous activity that forces soldiers to bond. Most of the time the bonding is formed over complaining about and cursing out the commander behind his back. So far we have been working in silence and the only bonding has been over the toxic paint fumes.

We are all in our work uniforms, which, as *jobnicks*, we haven't worn since boot camp. Bar and Chagai, the new male soldier who recently joined the branch, have plastic grocery bags around their boots that are closed at the ankles with rubber bands so that they won't be stopped by the military police for spots on their shoes. We hypnotically paint the walls with industrial-sized brooms. We look like soldiers who have escaped a mental ward.

Just as I begin to think that this *gibbush* doesn't seem to be working out so well, Tali puts down her broom and takes of off her button-down army-issued shirt. Exposed and stripped down to a grey tank top, she breaks the silence with barely a whisper, "My dad died when I was four months old. I never met him."

Surprised by this confession, we all stop sweeping the walls with paint and turn to her.

"My parents met when they were soldiers. Our age. They fell in love and got married. It was a fairytale romance. When I was only a few months old, my dad was on his way home from the base one night and an Arab terrorist saw that he was driving an army vehicle and intentionally crashed into him. He died at the scene."

None of us knows what to say. The only thing filling the room is the paint fumes.

"I'm proud to be in the army, but it is strange. That's why I'm so quiet," explains Tali.

I walk over and hug Tali.

"My mom converted to Judaism," Bar says quietly.

With my arms still around Tali, my head turns towards him. Why is it that saying your mom converted to Judaism is like coming out of the closet? When I was younger I would announce with pride to everyone that my mom was a Jew by choice. My mom had consciously chosen to be a part of the Jewish faith, where everybody else had just been randomly born into it. Is that why he moved to Israel? Is that why I did?

After hesitating, I say, "So did mine." It was the first time I had admitted this to anyone in Israel.

I let go of Tali. Bar's and my eyes catch for an instant. The white paint in his hair mixes in with the grays. I look at his uniform and think that I never would have known. He does a good job of hiding it.

Come and Knock on Our Door

After a few weeks in the new office, things finally fell into place. We worked long, hard hours on different types of operations. Bar, Tali, and I worked together seamlessly. Bar was the research specialist. I was the strategic specialist, and Tali was our native Hebrew speaker who double-checked all of our documents. We became the IDF's version of *Three's Company*. I never thought that my best friends would be a French man and an Israeli girl five years younger than me. We knew everything about each other's lives, our history, our likes, our dislikes, our families, and even the most private and embarrassing stories. During lunch, we would make a finely-diced tomato and cucumber Israeli salad[14] with handmade tahini. On the weekends, Tali would invite us over for Shabbat dinner and then we would go out to the bars together.

I began working in Hebrew, writing documents in Hebrew, and conducting meetings in Hebrew. I still needed somebody to review and edit everything, but as time went on, the mistakes became fewer and fewer. It was as if I had found my place in the Israeli army. I even mastered typing in Hebrew without looking at the keyboard instead of having to peck at each letter.

With an open-door policy in the branch, I worked closely with all of my officers. Yoni was always challenging me with interesting projects. Yehuda would call me into his office to ask my opinion about different missions and how to conduct them. I was treated like an officer among them, and respected for my motivation.

I saw the impact that the department was making when I went home and watched Israeli and international news. I saw how operations were covered, based on recommendations we had made. I heard the chief of staff saying quotes that I had written for him.

Yoni took me under his wing. He would call me into his office and ask me how I was doing, if I was enjoying my work, and he'd make sure that things were not too difficult for me as a lone soldier. I would chat with him as if he were a friend. He seemed sincerely concerned

14. For an Israeli salad receipe, please see the appendix.

about me and my welfare. I was finally living the life that I had dreamt about when I decided to make *aliyah*. I couldn't imagine it getting any better.

It is early Sunday morning and we are sitting in front of Yoni's desk for our daily meeting, in which we will be updated on new projects. Looking forward to the meeting, we look like kindergarteners at snack time.

"I'm glad everybody could make it." Yoni is sitting behind his desk with his foot rest hidden underneath so that his feet won't dangle from his chair. "I have an announcement to make,"

He waits to build up anticipation. "Jessica will be receiving the award for excellent soldier." He looks at me, beaming with pride.

I can't believe it.

"And I am recommending her for Officer's Training Course," he adds. "But either way, from now on, Jessica will be considered a captain in this branch and the entire unit. She will attend officer meetings, she will no longer have to do kitchen or guard duty, and she will receive an army phone."

Surprised by the announcement and slightly embarrassed, I look down trying to hide my smile.

Everything I have been through has been worth it just to get to this point. Nothing is more Jewish than being an officer in the IDF.

"*Mazal tov*," Bar says to me while giving me a hug. He knows how much this means to me.

"Guess what!" I scream into the phone while lying on my bed at the end of the day.

"What?" my parents ask simultaneously, each on a different phone at home. They just woke up. They are used to hearing my disappointment and complaints about the army.

I tell them the good news.

"That is great," they say.

"So that means you will be serving another . . . how many years?" my mom asks hesitantly.

"Three," I burst out in excitement.

"Oh, okay. I'm really happy for you," my mom says.

"We both are," says my dad. "We love you and are so proud of everything you are doing."

I'm so thrilled that I don't pick up on how much they miss me.

"Thanks! I love you guys too," I hang up the phone, impatient to get up tomorrow and go to the base.

Engaged

We are all gathered in Yoni's office again, but this time it feels different. He is not joking around. The air is tense, but I am still on a high from getting a recommendation to become an officer.

Earlier this week, guard and kitchen duties were handed out and now that I am an officer, I didn't get any. This morning, I went to the officers' meeting to be debriefed.

"We just got handed a big project from the IDF spokesperson," Yoni announces. "This project is going to be the only one we work on from now until the operation ends in another five months."

No one speaks. No one moves. We are all waiting to hear what the new assignment is.

"From this day forward we are going to be planning Israel's disengagement operation from the Gaza Strip. While this is a politically controversial operation, it is one that the army has been tasked with implementing. It is our branch's duty to decide everything from the name of the operation to which type of uniforms soldiers should wear. We will plan contingencies for every single situation so that the army can be prepared for anything. It is our duty to make sure that the IDF is ready to carry out this operation, does it in the best possible manner, and gets positive media coverage. This is an historic operation and you get to be a part of it."

Wide-eyed, Bar and I look at each other, intimidated and excited to have the opportunity to take part in this daunting event. We were going to be a part of, not an observer to, Israel's history.

Disengaged

"Everyone is released. Get back to work!" commanded Yoni after another daily meeting. "Jessica you stay here and shut the door."

I solemnly sit down and wait. I already know it is bad news.

"I heard back from the spokesperson. Despite my recommendation, you did not get accepted into Officer's Training Course. It was purely politics," Yoni tells me.

Unable to respond, I just stare at him.

Trying to reassure me, Yoni reminds me that even though I won't have the rank, I will still be considered a captain for all other purposes. I've gone through so many bureaucratic ups and downs since I've been here, I'm not surprised. Despite being disappointed, I head back to my desk to begin working on our new operation. It is almost enough for me to feel useful. I don't need to be an officer.

After that, the entire department begins working twelve- to fourteen-hour days. As we are dedicating ourselves to the mission, Yoni's personality suddenly changes, as if he was transforming from Dr. Jekyll to Mr. Hyde before our eyes. We are all taken by surprise. No one understands why. We speculate that it might be because the new spokeswoman doesn't believe in our department.

One morning, I walk into the offices at 7:00 A.M. and Yoni is standing in front of my office door with his arms crossed, ranks shining on his shoulder, eyes squinted, and red in the face. Without raising his voice, he says to me, "You're late."

Not sure if he is joking, I take my phone out of my pocket to look at the time. "I'm a minute late. What's the big deal? Did a war break out?"

He reaches inside the room and shoves the floor squeegee in front of me.

I look at it and laugh. "You're joking, right?" I haven't had to clean in months.

"The bathroom needs to be cleaned. If you don't do it, then I'll make the entire branch do it. It is up to you. Do you want the entire branch mad at you?"

After the squeegee incident, Yoni starts demeaning everyone in the department. He begins every day with cleaning rituals, screaming ceremonies, and degrading orders. He isn't doing anything that is specifically illegal, but he also isn't doing anything that is worthy of a medal of valor. He is manipulative and cruel.

He begins using against us all of the personal intelligence he had gathered about us when he was nice to us. We all feel betrayed and completely alone. He has isolated us from the rest of the unit, both physically and mentally. He keeps a close watch on us, not letting us communicate with anyone outside our branch. He holds early meetings and late meetings so that we have as little contact with the outside world as possible. He makes us feel like we have no one to turn to for help.

And even if we could turn to someone for help, what could we say? That he makes us clean? That we work hard, long hours? That we are far away from our friends? There is nothing that we can specifically point to that he has done wrong. These are all things that are typical of the army. But he seems to be doing it with a different intention.

One morning, while I am sitting at my desk looking for something in my purse, Yoni walks into my office with two other soldiers and blurts out, "Jessica! Stop looking for your vibrator!"

I freeze. I stare at him like a deer caught in head-lights. I know that I didn't misunderstand him; my Hebrew is too good for that now. What should I say? He crossed the line. This was completely inappropriate. I almost want to tell him that his wife asked to borrow it, but considering the fact that he has a gun and the authority to throw me in jail, I decide to not insult his masculinity.

I can't understand what happened. One day he was a benevolent yet sarcastic garden gnome, and then the next he was living proof of the Napoleon complex.

The harassment and abuse continue to get worse. He yells at us more and more, treating us like we are insignificant. Calling us names. Insulting our work. Giving us dirty looks. He pulls us into his office to try to gather information on other soldiers in the branch. He tries pitting us against one another by punishing the entire group if one person screws up. He asks us to do demeaning work. Clean up after him. Get him coffee. He even tries to manipulate us into refusing orders so he can punish us more.

Facing this daily psychological warfare, our *Three's Company* bunch falls apart. Tali asks to be transferred. Bar pulls into himself and begins befriending the two doves outside his window. Until that is not enough and he turns to religion. He begins wearing a *kippah*. He stops going out with me on Friday nights and won't answer my phone calls on Shabbat. He thinks that religion will help him cope with the stresses of being abused in an army that we had so desperately wanted to be a part of.

"What the hell are you thinking?" I asked him when I first saw his *kippah*. I was concerned that he was going through an army conversion. I felt betrayed, like he was leaving me alone and wounded on the battlefield.

"I just need something," Bar had said to me quietly, not wanting to fight.

"But the religious don't even accept us as Jews," I say quietly, not wanting to upset him too much, but still feeling hurt.

I, on the other hand, reacted by fighting with Yoni every day, until I got sick with mono.

But through all of the abuse, both Bar and I stay dedicated to our work. It was the one thing keeping us going. While our branch seems to be falling apart, the rest of the country is on the verge of a civil war. Even though Israel is not the country of brotherly love, it is the country where everyone considers one another brothers. Jewish residents in Gaza are threatening to lift up arms against the army to protect their homes—something unthinkable in Israel. The threat of soldiers refusing to participate in Disengagement is looming. Half of the country is wearing bright orange to show their support for the settlers and their disapproval of Disengagement. Jewish settlers are wearing orange stars that resemble the yellow stars from the Holocaust to express their pain from being expelled from their homes.

It feels as if the entire country is about to implode and we are trying to prevent it, all the while simultaneously suffering under the reign of a tyrant who isn't even tall enough to ride the roller coasters at Disneyland.

"The research says that the public does not approve of soldiers disobeying orders, but they do understand and even agree with soldiers not wanting to participate in Disengagement," Bar says, reviewing the statistics with me at 7:00 A.M.

Bar speaks fluent French, Hebrew, and English. We could speak English, but it doesn't feel right speaking English when we are talking about such an historic Israeli event.

"Is there any information on soldiers' opinions and what they think about refusing orders?" I ask, trying to figure out how we are going to tackle this issue. We can't have soldiers refusing orders or justifying it; this would cause the entire army to collapse.

Strangely, I feel like my Hebrew is best with Bar. I don't stumble over any words or sentences. I wonder if it is because I don't feel like I need to prove anything with him.

"It says that soldiers disapprove of refusing orders, but it might be hard to actually rely on those polls since soldiers may be scared to say the opposite." Bar has stopped wearing his *kippah* by now. Just like a zit, it disappeared one day. He realized that prayer was not going to stop the harrassment from Yoni, and now our friendship is getting back to normal.

"If the public thinks that it's okay for soldiers to refuse orders, then the public will disapprove of punishing soldiers who disobey orders. We have to change that," I said. "The first step is to prevent soldiers from disobeying by letting them know there will be consequences. The threat of punishment has to be real. We should make an example of any act of disobedience, and the punishment should be publicized. We shouldn't hide it, pretend it isn't happening, or try to bury it. I'll work on the report and develop specific tactics. It will take a few hours. You'll get the data and figures ready to present?"

By late afternoon our report is ready. For the first time in a few months, I finish all of my work before 19:00. I call Yehuda, my commanding officer, who left for home hours ago, to let him know I'm leaving early.

"Hi Yehuda. How are you?"

"*Baruch Hashem*, bless the Lord" he says. Religious people use this as an answer for every question, from "How is the weather?" to "How is your dying grandmother?" Even though I'm now almost fluent in Hebrew, I still don't know if this answer means that things are good or bad.

"I finished the report and the recommendations on refusing orders. Tomorrow I'll work on the recommendations regarding dismantling of the houses, synagogues, and army bases in the Gaza Strip. I wanted to leave early today. It's almost 18:00," I say, feeling demeaned just having to ask, but more so after I have already put in over eleven hours of work today.

"Wait for another forty-five minutes and then you can go," Yehuda says calmly.

"I'm done with my work today. You're telling me that you want me to spend forty-five minutes staring at my computer? Doing nothing?" I'm close to yelling. I almost wouldn't mind if there was something specific that needed to be complete urgently. This reminds me of the beginning of my service.

"Yes. What if something comes up?" he says, calmly.

"I'll come back. I only live five minutes away from the base," I reply. I'm in shock. Yehuda is the most reasonable officer. Ever since Yoni turned into a rabid munchkin, I have turned to Yehuda for support. He is nice, kind, and caring. He has been my only redeeming officer in the army so far. And now he is turning on me. I yell in the phone, "I am not going to sit here and stare at my computer screen for no reason."

"Yes, you are."

Instead of replying, I hang up. I can't figure out why Yehuda is treating me this way. I turn my phone off. I don't want anyone to be able to reach me.

I walk out of the base.

I disobey orders.

I am fed up with the army. I've given up. I no longer care about my fate here. I no longer respect the ranks of the IDF. I have given everything to the army and all I get in return is humiliation and degradation. I don't need this army to prove my Jewishness anymore. I just want my service to end. I only have four months left.

I aimlessly walk around Tel Aviv. I'm not ready to go home. I don't even know where I want to go. I just don't want to be here anymore. I see billboards and graffiti protesting Disengagement with pictures of little children who are going to lose their homes. I see stickers plastered on walls, bus stops, and cars that are pro-Disengagement. I walk through a huge rally in Rabin Square, where the mayor of Sderot is prophesizing more Kassam rockets hitting his city and even Tel Aviv following Disengagement. Pictures of houses, buildings, and kindergartens that have been hit by Kassams illuminate the large screen. The picture changes to the face of a woman who was killed by a rocket fired from the Gaza Strip. She stares back at me from the screen.

While walking through the crowd, I see the faces of the people, of the families, who will be losing their homes and livelihoods in less than a month. A little girl, who is holding her mother's hand, is crying. I have no emotional reaction to any of it. I don't even know how I personally feel about Disengagement. I have been too close to the process, too involved in the details to actually develop an opinion about the whole picture. Too wrapped up in my personal pain.

By the time I get to my apartment building three hours later, it is dark outside. I turn my phone on and I have ten voicemails from Bar, Tali, and Yehuda all making sure that I'm okay. As I open the door, I see a note wedged underneath. It is from Yehuda. On one side are his daughter's scribbles. On the other side is a note from him: "I was in the area and I stopped by to see how you are doing. Be in touch with me. And don't say that my daughter isn't talented!"

I hold the note to my chest. I try to picture this happening in any other army in the world. I can't. This compassionate gesture is exactly what I needed to remind me why I'm proud to serve in the Israeli army.

Disengagement

Thirty of us soldiers are sitting on the hard, cold tile floor of the makeshift *chamal*. *Chamal* is usually the abbreviation for War Room, but since Disengagement is not a war, it now stands for Situation Room.

As a representative for our department during Disengagement in the field, I am now stationed in Oshkol, right on the border of Gaza, for Disengagement, while the rest of the department is at The Campus. The entire area is swarming with reporters from all over the world. We are in Kassam rocket range, but I figure I have a better chance of surviving a rocket attack here than Yoni's rage if I were back at The Campus.

However, Yoni intentionally separated me from Bar, the only person I can rely on. I don't know how I'll be able to get through the next week or two without him.

Normally the Situation Room is loud with phones ringing, people running in and out, and multiple TVs blaring, but at this moment everyone is still. No one says anything. No one is sending emails, faxes, or answering phones. It's as if even the phones know not to ring.

Time seems to stand still.

We are all staring up at the large-screen TV, waiting with the rest of the country for Prime Minister Ariel Sharon to make his speech on the eve of Disengagement.

He finally comes on air.

"It is out of strength and not weakness that we are taking this step. I understand the feelings, the pain, and the cries of those who object. However, we are one nation even when fighting and arguing." Sharon's words are broadcast across the country and simultaneously across the world.

Despite it being stifling hot in here, I have goose bumps all over my body.

Then, the second that Sharon finishes his speech, the Situation Room comes back to life. Everything that we have been planning for the past six months is about to start.

At midnight, the attention of the entire world turns to Kissufim Crossing, the main gate between Gaza and Israel, for the opening ceremonies as if it were the Olympics. The location is symbolic as it has been the target of numerous terrorist attacks throughout the years. Top IDF brass are standing at the gate. All the international media cameras are pointed at it. The gate of the crossing is lowered for the final time to signify Israel disengaging from the Gaza Strip . . . and then it pops back up. It is lowered again and then it pops back up again. It takes another three times of putting the gate down for it to stick. It sort of ruined the symbolism that we intended. With the IDF looking like it can barely even handle a garage door opener, it doesn't seem like we are off to a good start.

Having been assigned the night shift, I spend the entire night scanning the TV and Internet to monitor the media coverage in case we need to make any adjustments to our messaging or operations. But since there are no operations planned for the night, nothing is happening. I wonder if Yoni purposely wanted me to feel useless.

The next morning at sunrise, Disengagement begins. Israelis are being uprooted from their homes. Residents are forcefully removed. Others passively follow the soldiers, who are evicting them, as if they are being lead to the gas chamber. Every scene is more heartbreaking than the next. Soldiers cry on the shoulders of the settlers. Settlers cry on the shoulders of eighteen-year-old soldiers. Soldiers weep in each other's arms.

As I'm watching CNN, I'm surprised that these scenes are actually broadcast. They are showing the settlers' pain, the compassion of the Israeli soldiers, and not treating Israelis as vicious Arab-hating Jews. For the first time, the international media is showing the human side of Israelis and IDF soldiers versus their typical biased narratives.

All of our hard work is paying off.

As I'm watching the scenes unfold, a reserve soldier not much older than me comes in. He treats me as if I'm nothing. He has come to take over. He doesn't know that I have spent the past months planning for Disengagement. All he sees is a lowly soldier. He has seen the way Yoni treats me and pushes me aside like I'm nothing.

"Jessica! What are you doing here! Move! Give the reserve soldier your seat! Get out of here! Did you even do anything during your night shift?"

I freeze. I'd know that voice from anywhere. It's Yoni's voice. I feel like prey that has just realized she has been spotted by a predator. I don't have anywhere to run. Where did he come from? He isn't supposed to be here.

I leave the Situation Room for the first time in over twelve hours. I feel as disillusioned as the settlers who moved to Gaza to reclaim the land of Israel. I wonder if they still think that their sacrifices for the country were worth it. I wonder if they feel as betrayed by their leaders as I do.

As I walk outside into the daylight, my eyes slowly adjust to the sunlight. I pull out my phone.

"Baaaaarrrrr," I cry into the phone. "He is horrible. I need you. I can't do this without you."

"Jessica, I can't understand you when you cry. Calm down and speak clearly."

I sniffle.

"Yehuda is wearing his work uniform," Bar says on the other end. "You know how he looks so dignified with his air force uniform on? Well, his work uniform is tight and high-waisted. He looks like Mr. Bean."

I snort all the snot up my nose while laughing in between sobs. What would I do without Bar?

I sleep all day. When I wake up, instead of heading back to my station in the Situation Room, I pack up the same backpack that I used during boot camp, but by now I'm used to its weight on my shoulders. After getting off the phone with Bar, I call a friend, a doctor in the army. I ask him to give me sick leave. I have learned how to work the system like an Israeli.

I know that I can't face another day with Yoni.

I walk over to the Situation Room to fax my sick leave to the logistics department. Once I verify they have received it, I head out of the Situation Room, forgetting about everything that is going on in Gaza. It is time to take care of myself. To look out for my own health. My own well-being. I've given enough to the army.

I walk out of the Situation Room's doors and turn into the hallway. The sun shines through the big windows. The warmth reminds me how close I am to escaping.

"Where do you think you are going?" I hear from behind me.

I freeze. He is still here? I feel like the girl in a horror scene who thinks the bad guy is dead, but then he comes back to life to kill her.

"I . . . uh . . . I have *gimelim*. I'm going home."

People inside the Situation Room are staring.

"You have sick leave! When did you get sick leave? How did you get sick leave? Why do you have sick leave? You know not every sick leave is at home!"

Who does he think he is with all these questions? Oprah?

A male officer is not allowed to ask a female officer why she has sick leave. And it is an outright lie that *gimelim* are not at home. I can't stand the sight of him anymore. I don't have the strength to answer him. It takes all my power to turn around. I run down the stairs and head for the bus station.

With each step my backpack feels heavier. Silent tears start rolling down my face. My lungs constrict. I know I can never go back there. I know that if I do go back that I won't survive.

Luckily, the bus comes quickly. I get on and find a seat.

I call the new logistics officer. Nimrod is no longer there. "If I stay under the command of Yoni for one more day, I might do something drastic." *Drastic* is the safety word in this sadistic game and I chose it carefully.

On the bus radio, I hear the announcer describing the events of Disengagement unfolding like it is a football game. Up until now, the settlers have gone peacefully for the most part, but in the settlement of Shirat Ha'Yam the settlers are taking a stand, a violent and religiously-inspired stand. They have barricaded themselves on a rooftop. They are refusing to leave. They are throwing paint, acid, and other flammable liquids on the Israeli security forces. Israelis are turning on one another. It is a war of brothers.

"And it looks like the IDF spokeswoman has just been hit in the head by a can that somebody threw off the roof. It looks like a can of *loof*," the announcer on the radio screams as if someone has just made a touchdown. He does not clarify who threw the can—a settler protesting Disengagement or a soldier protesting being fed *loof*.

"Okay, Jessica. Take the weekend to relax. Sleep. Rest. Next week you can meet with the head of logistics. From this point forward, you don't answer to Yoni anymore."

For the first time in months I breathe without having to hold back tears.

8

Released into Civilization

I am twenty-five years old and this is the first time that I've had to look for a real job. I've run out of Jewish programs to participate in.

"Nice to meet you," said Carmella Uziel, the head of the public relations department at Mitoog, one of the top marketing firms in Israel. She smiles. It seems forced. It looks like the smile of someone who lost facial muscles in a horrible accident and went through physical therapy to smile again.

I shake her hand with confidence. I'm ready to begin my civilian life in Israel now that I'm armed with my military experiences.

"It is a pleasure to meet you. Please allow me to give you a copy of my résumé," I say, using professional Hebrew.

Carmella puts on her glasses with her long bony fingers and scans my résumé.

"I served—" I begin to tell her about my army experience, but she stops me by using the Israeli signal for hold on, but I'm not used to this gesture. It doesn't bother me that she cuts me off like that. I got used to dealing with brashness and pushiness in the army.

"Our main client is a government department that attracts international investors to Israel. Do you think you can support them?" Carmella asks me with doubt on her face.

"I handled the planning of Disengagement; I should be able to handle this," I say, trying to joke around while working in some of my experience.

With dark circles under her eyes, Carmella glares at me through her glasses. Her nose is pointy and her hair is fried. I guess she doesn't like humor.

By the standards of my other interviews, this one is actually going well. In previous interviews, most of the time the interviewer asked in roundabout ways if I was planning on getting pregnant soon. It made me feel like I was at Planned Parenthood. I was surprised that they didn't ask me how many sexual partners I'd had and what form of protection I use.

"I can see you have experience in media relations and quite a bit of work in strategy," Carmella says, "but I want to see if you can write a press release. Read this and write a press release about it for me."

This is the most reasonable and appropriate request that I've had from an interviewer so far. At another PR company, they asked me to give them a writing sample so they could do a hand writing analysis of my personality. It seems as ridiculous as a life insurance company reading my palm to determine my rates.

"Is it okay if I send it to you this evening?" I ask.

"That is fine. But do it all by yourself. Do *not* get help from anyone else." Carmella hands me her business card, but not before she crosses out her cell phone number. "Send it to this email address."

She then sends me out of the office.

"Thank you," I say as I walk out.

The bus stop is right around the corner from the offices. As I'm waiting, a military police soldier starts walking towards me. My heart skips a beat and I hold my breath. I look down to check my uniform and realize that I'm in civilian clothes. I relax. I must have the *jobnik* form of PTSD.

I look up and smirk, happy that the military police soldier can't write me a ticket.

My bus pulls up. As I board the bus, I try to fish my army ID out of my back pocket, only to realize that I don't have pockets in these pants. Again I am reminded that I'm a civilian. It has already been a few months since my release, but I'm still adjusting.

"How much is it?" I ask the driver. I'm no longer scared to use my Hebrew with strangers. I thought that once I was released from the army and no longer had my army uniform to show that I belong, that I would go back to feeling like an outsider, but I don't. I feel like I fit in.

I hand him the money and he hands me a ticket.

I look at all the open seats and decide where I want to sit.

I spent my last days in the army like most Jews throughout history—wandering. I worked on a number of different projects in a number of different departments. Yoni was forced out of the IDF Spokesperson Unit and the entire army, for that matter. I was honorably released.

The commute back to my apartment is short. Only fifteen minutes. At Rabin Square, I get off the bus. Today the square is empty. There are no rallies. The displaced Gaza settlers have already been forgotten about.

*　　　*　　　*

"How was your interview? Tell me all about it! Do you think you got the job?" Orli greets me as soon as I open the door to the apartment.

When I was released from the army, Alon, my weird roommate, who would sit on the couch without moving for so long that there were times I thought he had died, decided to move out. I was not particularly sad that Alon left.

In his place, Orli moved in.

"I see you borrowed my shirt for the interview. It looks good on you. I borrowed your shoes for work," she says. Both of our closets have doubled in size since she moved in. It is nice coming back to an apartment that feels like home versus something that feels like some type of boarding house. The apartment feels like a sorority, except that we actually like each other. I look at a picture of Orli and me from three years ago that is on a shelf. I can't believe how far I have come, how close we have become.

I tell her about the interview.

"I'm sure you will get the job. You have so much to offer. You have great Hebrew. English is your native language. You have a lot of experience. They would be fools not to take you!" Orli is always encouraging me. Without her support, I don't think I would have had the courage to move to Israel in the first place.

"Thanks. What salary do you think I should request?" In the army I made less than a thousand dollars a month. I'd be thrilled to make minimum wage.

"I'll call Carmit. She works in PR. I'll ask her what she makes." In the US it is rude to ask people about their financial situation, but in Israel it is completely acceptable to ask people their salary, rent, level of debt, and how much their shoes cost.

Orli hangs up the phone. "Don't expect more than eight thousand shekels a month[15]—before taxes. And don't expect overtime pay, but do expect to work overtime."

"So, like the army?" I remark sarcastically. "But this time without an officer who torments me."

"When are you supposed to hear back if they offer you the job? Would you accept?" Orli asks.

"Well, Mitoog is one of—" I begin.

"The best PR agencies in Israel," Orli finishes my sentence, as usual.

---

15. Approximately $2000 USD.

The Early Bird

I go through my closet like I'm skimming a book.

It feels strange having to pick out clothes for work. I'm used to putting on my uniform every day. I've forgotten how much time it takes to express my identity through clothing.

I can't find anything good to wear. Nothing fits. Nothing looks good. I don't have anything appropriate for work. I don't have anything that looks like it has been bought recently. I haven't gone clothes shopping since before the army.

I wish I still had my army uniform.

I finally find a plain button-down shirt and pants. Besides the color, it looks exactly like my IDF uniform.

Walking through the huge glass door of the offices, I see a pendulum the size of a wrecking ball swinging back and forth. A silver-haired janitor is on his hands and knees picking up the little pegs that the pendulum knocks over.

"Good morning," I say to him, as I walk past him to the reception desk.

"In Russia," he grumbles in Hebrew with a thick Russian accent, "I was an electrical engineer."

I don't know how to respond. I guess it makes sense that in Israel where an immigrant who is a nuclear physicist can be a maid, an engineer can be a janitor.

"Hi, this is my first day. I'm supposed to start in the PR department," I say to one of the receptionists.

"*Nu* . . ." she says as if I'm bothering her while she is busy doing nothing. Her makeup is plastered on. She is chomping her gum like a horse. And she has an unlit cigarette in her hand. She reminds me of Dan's secretary.

"Where should I go?" I ask firmly, with three years in the country, including two in the army, backing me up.

Without saying anything she makes a phone call. "You can go wait in there. Someone will come get you."

As I'm sitting in the waiting room, the secretary, who was too busy to help me a moment ago, comes in and lights up a cigarette as if it is some type of smoking room. When I start coughing, she looks at me and rolls her eyes.

A tall, thin, blond-haired girl comes into the room, pulls out a cigarette and lights it.

After they finish their cigarettes and a conversation about celebrities, the blond-haired girl stands up, looks at me, and says, "Follow me." She turns around and I see her butt crack peeking out. This place seems more like a bar than an office. I hope I made the right choice.

"The woman you are replacing is not here yet. She is driving in from Jerusalem. The boss isn't here yet, either. You can just stand next to my desk until one of them gets here."

I had gotten used to waiting in the army, so I didn't mind. This feels strangely similar to guard duty.

At 9:45 A.M., Carmella marches down the hallway as if she is the meanest model on the catwalk. I quickly straighten up to greet her as if I were at army roll call.

"Hello," I say with a big smile and my hand stuck out.

She walks right past me.

An hour later, a woman no taller than five feet waddles in. Wider than she is tall, she looks like she might give birth in the hallway.

"Hi! Sorry I'm late. I'm Galit," she chirps while turning towards her office and motioning me to follow.

She braces herself while slowly sitting down.

"I don't know how many more days I'll be in the office, so learn fast," she says while pointing to her large baby bump.

I wonder why they would wait until the last moment to hire me. And then I remember that procrastination is an art form, if not government policy, in Israel.

"When are you due?" I ask.

"Not for another few weeks, but . . ."

"That is stupid! Why did you mention it? Do I have to do all the work? Do you even think?" I hear Carmella scream.

I look at Galit. She rolls her eyes.

"That is why I don't think I'll be coming in anymore," she says, motioning her head towards Carmella's office.

I have a bad feeling in the pit of my stomach. I wonder if she got pregnant to just leave this job—like what the religious do to avoid the army.

Galit scrolls through emails, erasing most of them. "I usually start my day by looking through all the English newspapers to see if any of our clients are mentioned. I also look for any relevant Israeli investment information—M&As, new R&D sites in Israel, and anything related to VCs . . ."

"What?" I know what APVs, M-16s, and NCOs are, but I don't know any of these.

Seeing my confusion, Galit explains. "Most of your job will be writing a newsletter about Mergers and Acquisitions of Israeli companies and Research and Development deals in Israel for the Israeli Investment Encouragement Department. Just to give you a hint of who we are dealing with, it is a government organization . . . in Israel," she says without taking her eyes off the screen.

I flash back to my experience at the Israeli Interior Ministry.

"So, will I work with the media?" I had expected this job to be a bit more glamorous.

She looks at me, puts her hand out, palm down, fingers spread out and shakes it back and forth. The Israeli gesture for "ehhh, sort of."

The phone rings. Galit answers and hangs it up without saying anything.

She turns to me, "Carmella wants us in her office." She says it like we are about to face a firing squad.

When we enter, Carmella takes her glasses off and looks at Galit as if she's thinking, *If your water breaks in my office, you are cleaning it up yourself!*

"So Galit, you are going to the client's tomorrow? Jessica, I don't want you going. You stay and learn the material. That is all," Carmella says as she turns back around to her computer.

We walk out and Galit whispers, "I think she has a coat made of Dalmatians in her closet."

In Israel the Devil doesn't wear Prada

"Is it 'in' or 'on'?"

"It is 'in,'" I say mechanically, knowing that she isn't going to believe me. I knew I shouldn't have answered my phone when I saw the numbers 666 appear on the caller ID.

"I think it is 'on,'" says Lital, my client from the Israeli Investment Encouragement Department. She never listens to me. I don't even know why they bother wasting their money on our services.

"Yes, it is definitely 'on,'" she says. "Microsoft buys Israeli Gteko specializing on providing networking and supporting software to digital homes. Wait, should it be 'to' or 'for' digital homes?"

I roll my eyes.

We are working on developing the monthly newsletter. Lital and her boss treat this newsletter as if it is the most important published piece of work in the world, as if it has a greater readership than the Bible . . . or even Harry Potter.

"Lital, it is 'in.' I'm positive," I say.

"I'll get a second opinion. Let's come back to it." She says this as if it is as crucial as getting the right cancer diagnosis.

I wonder if she has OCD, like the officers who made us clean in the army.

"Okay. The item titled: Israeli Yellow Pages sold to Australian firm Babcock & Brown. You wrote for the history of the company that Yellow Pages was created in America, but it is an Israeli invention. We made up the saying 'let your fingers do the walking.'"

"No, Lital. I researched it. Yellow Pages is *not* an Israeli invention and neither is the saying." I try to remain calm. I'm sick of these ridiculous conversations. I can't believe that I made *aliyah* and served in the army to do this.

"It is an Israeli invention," she responds, determined. Israelis think that everything was invented in Israel. They don't get that just because the pillcam, the USB flash drive, and ICQ were all invented in Israel, that other technologies can actually be invented in other places around the world.

I feel like I am talking to a three-year-old.

"Would you like me to send you the source?" I ask after a deep breath. I've spent over two hours immersed in the history of the Yellow Pages.

"Yes, I'd like to read it," she says, as if I'm illiterate.

"Okay, but I have to go to a meeting now."

I hang up the phone slowly and then I bang it down three more times. I've been here two months now and I don't know how much longer I am going to be able to put up with this client. Galit is long gone. She was supposed to be here for a month to train me, but she disappeared after the first week.

I walk into the meeting room. There are fifteen people sitting around the table. No one is talking. Everyone has their notebooks out. I find an empty seat and sit down. We have these meetings every week.

Carmella walks in with her lunch and shuts the door behind her. She is wearing a greenish-orange tie-dye T-shirt that says in sparkles MY TIME HAS COME. She sits down at the front of the table and scowls at everybody before saying, "I don't have a lot of time. Let's begin." I guess she forgot that she is the one that insists on having this meeting every week.

"We need to think of different ways to promote one of our new clients. We are going to brainstorm together. Everyone has to give an idea. The new client is a radio station that is promoting peace between Israelis and Palestinians." She begins eating her lunch while everybody else's stomachs growl.

"We could have a music concert with both Israeli and Palestinian bands," says Shannon. She is one of the best PR people here. She is the first one to arrive in the mornings. She always gets her stories in the paper. And she has a good relationship with all of the journalists.

Carmella stares at her and says, "Can't you think of something a bit more original? Really, Shannon!"

"We could have a sports tournament in which Israelis and Palestinians play together. Like soccer! Sports are always a uniting endeavor," says Ehud, the in-the-closet religious guy.

"That's been done before," Carmella says, but without a stare. Her jowls are as droopy as a bulldog's from never smiling.

"Yeah, you're right," he responds while re-adjusting his knitted kippah.

Suck up! I yell in my head.

"We could stage a hot air balloon race in the skies," says Timnah.

"That is a stupid idea! I can't believe you would even mention that! Do you people even bother thinking before you talk? If you don't have a good idea, then don't say anything at all!" she screams at all of us with food flying out of her mouth. "Who's next?"

No one volunteers.

"Why isn't anyone saying anything?" Carmella yells.

To say that Carmella stifles creativity would be an understatement. Communism is more conducive of creativity than she is.

"Jessica, what is your idea?" Carmella demands.

I freeze in silence. She usually never calls on me during these meetings.

"Well, the station could do prize contests, or make bumper stickers, or interview celebrities at events, or partner with night clubs," I say, hoping to give her enough ideas so that at least one will warrant her not yelling at me.

"Jessica! This station is just starting out! How do you expect them to have the money or the connections to do any of these things?! What did I just tell all of you? Think before you talk! And be creative!"

I stare at her bony, sunken-in face while she is yelling. I wonder if the artists of *101 Dalmatians* used her as inspiration when drawing Cruella de Vil. Not only does her name sound eerily close to the villain's name, but she looks a lot like her.

More people give ideas and more people get yelled at. At the end of the hour-long meeting, Carmella turns perky for a second. It feels like when a serial killer tries to befriend his victim before killing him.

"I just saw *The Devil Wears Prada*. Has anyone else seen it?" she asks. This is the third time I've heard her mention the movie.

All of the females mumble "yes" suspiciously.

"Wasn't it a great movie? I really liked it," Carmella states.

I bet you did, I think.

"Although I couldn't believe how Miranda treated her employees. It was just awful. I couldn't imagine treating anyone that way," Carmella says in the most sincere voice and without an ounce of sarcasm.

Of course none of us mention that if Carmella had a better fashion sense, the movie could have been about her.

In the War Zone

It is too hard to get any work done. I can't concentrate. My head is somewhere else. Instead of working, I'm toggling between all the Israeli news websites trying to get the most recent updates. Eighteen days ago a soldier, Gilad Shalit, who looks like a little boy, was kidnapped at the Gaza border when terrorists infiltrated Israel. Ever since, there has been heavy combat in the Gaza Strip and depressing music on the radio stations. It makes me wish that I was back in the army. But instead I'm visiting my client in Jerusalem like every Monday.

I hear a noise behind me and quickly turn around to see if my client is watching. Luckily, no one is there.

I click refresh on *The Jerusalem Post* site.

2 Soldiers Kidnapped, 8 Soldiers Killed in Tank Attack by Hezbollah on Northern Border, F-16's take off for Lebanon

I blink hard.

The headline is still there when I open my eyes.

I can't believe that after the past two weeks of Israelis being kidnapped and killed in the West Bank, and the conflict in Gaza, this can be happening now. It doesn't seem as if the news can get any worse. It feels like we are being attacked from every border. I read the article.

How can Hezbollah do this? They aren't playing by the rules. It is like in a boxing match when a boxer kicks his opponent in the nuts when he is already down. If this had been boxing, the referee would have blown his whistle. Instead the UN will probably blame Israel for the escalation.

On the bus back home, the mood is tense. Everyone is silent. We are all straining to hear the latest news on the radio from the front of the bus.

When I get home, I sit in front of the TV. Every Israeli news station is trying to be first to coin a name for the conflict. It looks like the front runner is The Second Lebanon War, even though the IDF continues to claim that this is not a war. I bet that it was decided in my old department not to call it a war.

So that is it. We are going to war.

This isn't my first war in Israel. During my volunteer program, I experienced the Second Gulf War. The night before the war started, my group celebrated Purim, the holiday commemorating Jews being saved from Haman, yet another evil, mustached dictator in Shushan, which is now modern-day Iraq. We were given gas masks in case of chemical weapons. When I tried mine on, it felt like I was wearing a fish tank. We were then forced to carry the gas masks around for a week, even though the threat passed. The rest of the country had already put them in storage. We felt like we were carrying out-of-fashion purses. This war feels more real.

BEEP. BEEP.

I look at my phone. It's a text message.

We're heading up north. I'll talk to you later.

The text is from Liel. He is heading to the front lines. I take a deep breath in.

Liel is still in my life. I had tried to disconnect from him, but I couldn't. He keeps coming back into my life—like herpes, which luckily he doesn't have. I still see him every now and then. I think back to our first date. It was the first date I ever had with an Israeli.

While teaching English at a high school during my volunteer program, I was trying to understand what one of my students was saying in Hebrew over the other kids yelling in the background. I was concentrating so hard that I barely heard my phone ring.

"*Ahlan*, it's Liel. Remember me?"

I remember thinking that Orli must have told him about my crush, but I was too excited that he called to be mad at her. He told me that he was calling me from his army base, but would be heading home for the weekend and wanted to know if I wanted to go out on a date.

We went out for drinks at a bar on the Tel Aviv beach and then headed to his house since there weren't any buses at that time of night to my place in northern

Israel. As he opened the door, I expected to see a bachelor pad. He told me to be quiet since everyone was sleeping.

"Who is everyone?" I whispered, not knowing then that it is standard for Israeli men to live at home well into their twenties and bring their dates home.

"My parents, my younger twin brothers, my older sister, her husband, and their three-month-old baby boy." Seeing that this Israeli officer still lived at home with his family made me realize that all the other soldiers probably lived at home too. With their moms doing their laundry, they no longer seemed as tough as CNN made them out to be.

I thought about the notorious walk of shame from fraternity row during college and tried to imagine what it would be like in front of his entire family, even though I had no intention of sleeping with him that night.

The next morning, I sat down with his whole family to enjoy a full breakfast platter that his mom had made. Dating in Israel was so different than dating in America. When I would visit my American boyfriend at his parents' house during college, even after we'd been together for two years, his parents still made us sleep in different rooms. Liel's mom was almost acting as if she was happy that her son might be getting some action.

In the afternoon, Liel took me to the Carmel *Shuk*, the open air food market in south Tel Aviv. We bought fresh fruits and lemonade with mint leaves that was so sour it pinched our cheeks. Hand in hand, we strolled down *Nachalat Benyamin*, the artist market, and gazed at pictures, paintings, pottery, and jewelry. We went to the beach to watch the sunset. Then, wearing a helmet and carrying a bouquet of flowers, I jumped on the back of his motorcycle.

Driving back to his place at dusk I fell in love with Tel Aviv—with its romance, trendiness, liveliness, sexiness, sacrilege, and Jewishness. It was everything the rest of the country was not. It was me. It was my future.

I never wanted to leave. As the wind swept through my hair, I squeezed Liel tighter as if trying to hold on to that moment.

I slowly exhale. I wonder when I will hear from him again.

I text Yehuda, my old officer, who is still in the army.

If you need me to come in for miluim, *reserve duty, just let me know.*

Experiencing this war in my twenties, while in the Middle East, feels very different than when I was ten and had watched on CNN Iraqi scud missiles pound the Jewish nation during the First Gulf War. Then I had experienced the war with my family from the safety of our kitchen, protected by the vast and insignificant corn fields of the upper Midwest. Now, I'm ready to be in the middle of the action.

Isaiah 2:2

The war has been going on for more than two weeks. In the beginning, our air force took out all of the Hezbollah strongholds and it looked like we were winning. But last week our ground troops went in and now it feels like we are losing the war. Soldiers are being killed. Rockets are slamming into the north every day. And even though Hezbollah dragged us into this war, Israel is being blamed by the media and the international public.

I check my phone. I looked at it five minutes ago, but I want to make sure it is working. I haven't heard from Liel since he told me they were entering Lebanon.

I look at the TV screen in our living room, which has been constantly on; maybe he will be on the news. He was on the front page of *Yediot Acharanot*, the leading Israeli newspaper, yesterday.

I look over at Orli. How is she so calm?

"Orli, aren't you worried?" I ask her again, just like I've asked her every single night. I feel as if the country might cease to exist if we lose this war.

"No. *Yihyeh b'seder!* Everything will be okay!" she always replies confidently.

The typical Israeli answer for everything also applies to war? However, I've begun to notice that no one ever mentions *when* everything will be okay.

"Listen, Jessica, Israel has been through many wars and we've always been fine. The nation has always survived. We will survive this one too."

"Do you promise?" I ask, worrying about Liel.

"Yes."

She is the same age as me and she has already lived through the First Lebanon War, two intifadas, Scud missiles during the First Gulf War, and many other war-like operations. Her parents have lived through the Yom Kippur War, the Six Day War, and the War of Independence.

I look back at the TV. An Israeli reporter, with our northern border in the background and the sounds of war surrounding him, begins his report. "It has now been cleared that we can announce that there has been intense fighting in Bint Jbeil. Hezbollah ambushed the Israeli forces and killed eight soldiers."

A graphical re-enactment of the ambush is shown. It almost looks like a video game. I see little cartoon Hezbollah terrorists circling and killing Israeli soldiers.

But they aren't just soldiers, they are kids. They have faces. They have families. They had lives. They could be my friends. They could be the kids I volunteered with.

Then the reporter announces the names of the soldiers who were killed. On the screen are the pictures of the soldiers. I watch carefully, hoping not to see somebody I know. The pictures look like they are from a high school yearbook.

I don't recognize any of their faces. My friends are safe for now. And that means Liel is still alive. I realize that I've been holding my breath and force myself to exhale.

Then a crying woman is on camera. Her son was one of the soldiers killed in the attack. Every mother in Israel knows that tomorrow she too might be mourning the loss of her child.

This has been the worst battle so far. I look over at Orli, hoping to get some encouragement.

"This was just one battle. We have a whole entire war to win."

*   *   *

I can't get any work done. I'm again staring at my computer in my office. I'm looking through the names of the soldiers who were killed yesterday, again hoping not to see Liel's name.

I hate not knowing what is going on behind the scenes. I used to help determine what the IDF released to the media. Now I'm dependent on what the media releases.

The radio has been playing sad songs for over a month now. The entire country is in mourning. The reports from the front lines keep getting worse. There are civilian and soldier deaths every day. More rockets. The entire population in the north is holed up in bunkers. There is more and more ridicule from the international community about how the IDF is handling the war.

I should be in reserve duty, but Yehuda never got back to me. This war is turning into a PR disaster for Israel. I should not be sitting in this office, flipping through the newspapers. I should be influencing them.

I look at my cell phone to see if Liel texted from his bunker in Lebanon.

I wonder why Yehuda hasn't called me back about doing reserve duty.

RING. RING.

It is my office phone.

"Carmella wants everyone in her office now," says Carmella's secretary. I don't know why Carmella has her secretary call us when she, herself, can obviously yell loud enough for all of us to hear.

"Why?" I ask, but the secretary has already hung up.

I walk into the room. The entire department is standing in front of Carmella's desk. Carmella, of course, is sitting in her big, comfortable chair.

"As you know, Hassan Nasrallah has been threatening to send rockets into the heart of Tel Aviv." She stops to look at an email that just came in, which is obviously more important than our safety.

Hassan Nasrallah is the leader of Hezbollah. If Nasrallah says something is going to happen, then it usually does. The other day he said rockets would hit as far south as Hadera, and they did. Israelis are now looking to him to know what is going to happen during the war.

"As I was saying," Carmella begins without apologizing for making us wait. "The threat of a rocket attack on Tel Aviv is growing. So, I just wanted to let you know that the stairwell is to be used as a bomb shelter."

She makes this announcement as if this a normal working day in Israel.

"However, until you hear an air raid warning, I expect all of you to be working as normal. Just because there is a war going on doesn't mean that you don't have to work. I don't care if the media is only covering stories about the war; I want to see stories about our clients too! About the new falafel-flavored cracker or the updated new software release or a real estate investment that a client just made."

The newest girl at the agency naively speaks up. "Carmella, if I may say something, it is—"

"I don't want to hear excuses! Just get your work done!" Carmella roars.

I look around the room. No one says anything. I begin to wonder why I am still at this job. I'm not fulfilled.

I'm not challenged. I have an abusive boss. This is not the army. I don't have to wait for a release date. I need something more.

"Why are you still here? Get to work!"

On the Home Front

BOOM!

I slam the door at 9:30 P.M.

"*Orli!* I'm going to kill her! I can't stand her! That woman is ruining my life! I feel like I'm at a work camp."

Work has gotten back to normal and so has the rest of the country. With no clear victor, and after thirty-four days of fighting, the Second Lebanon War came to an end. Yehuda, my old officer, never called me to serve in reserve duty. The falafel-flavored cracker never made it into the newspaper. The UN forces deployed in southern Lebanon. But with the effectiveness of the UN forces, it would have been just as useful to put some mall rent-a-cops on the border. Hezbollah has probably already started stockpiling weapons for the next war.

"Are you just getting back from work? You have been working fourteen-hour days non-stop."

"Orli, you don't understand. I sit at my desk and daydream about Carmella dropping dead from an aneurism while she is yelling at me. I will her to be hit with that life-size pendulum at work."

"What happened today?" Orli asks, used to my rants about Carmella.

I walk into Orli's room. Wearing a dress and high heels, she is standing in front of her mirror, putting on makeup.

"Are you coming out with the girls tonight?"

"No, I'm tired. I'm going to bed early," I say as I fall down onto her bed.

"So tell me about it."

"I have a few new clients now. But at least I got rid of the client in Jerusalem. So the newest client is that radio station for peace. Why a radio station thinks that it can solve the problems of the Middle East when no one else has been able to, I don't know," I fume. "Anyhow, they are planning a big launch. I barely even have time to get up to go to the bathroom, much less eat during the entire day. Well, my senior account manager tells me to send out the invitation to the press conference after approving it and then after sending them out to CNN, BBC, and the AP, I realized that the date was wrong. Well, I got really upset. Just as I started tearing up, Carmella walks in."

"*Nu*, go on . . . Did she ask why you were upset?"

"No. Do you think she cares? She started yelling at me for crying!"

"What did she say?"

"She said 'Don't you dare start crying! Do you think your life is so hard? I pull these hours all the time! I'm not going to feel sorry for you! Now, knock it off and get back to work!"

"Did you say anything?" Orli asks.

"No, I never answer her back." I learned that it is never worthwhile getting into a competition with an Israeli woman about whose life is worse. I could have been hit by a bus, robbed, and diagnosed with cancer all in the same day and they still would have found something worse in their lives to complain about. It's like a contest to them. "She just walked out of the room."

"I think she needs a heart transplant, because hers definitely isn't working."

I laugh. Orli always knows how to cheer me up.

"Why don't you just quit?" Orli asks me.

"Because, it is the best PR agency in Israel. Once I pay my dues here, I will be able to get a good job . . ." I say out loud, but hope that the personal sacrifices I'm making now will actually pay off down the road. "Oh, and I didn't tell you what happened to me today at the bus station."

"What?" Orli is used to me always having funny stories.

"I was running late for work, so I walked across the street on a red light by the train station."

"Oh, no. Jessica, don't you know that lazy police officers hide out there to ambush jaywalkers instead of doing actual work?" she asks.

"I know now," I say. "But get this, the police officer said she would give me a warning, but then when she saw on my driver's license that I have only had my license for three years she said she had to give me a ticket."

"What? Why?" Orli asks.

"I don't know, I guess in this country first you have to prove that you don't know how to drive before you have the right to be able to walk illegally," I sarcastically say. "Well, have a good night out. I'm going to bed."

*   *   *

BEEP. BEEP.

It is two in the morning. Who could be texting me now? I roll over and grab my phone.

The text is from Liel. *Are you awake?*

I haven't heard from him since the war. This is how he lets me know he is alive—with a booty call? Wait, he isn't even bothering to booty-call me . . . he is booty-texting me! I can't believe this. After I spent the entire war worrying about him. And after the day I had at work.

I don't have the energy for this anymore. I'm sick of waiting for him to be ready for a relationship. I need to cut him out of my life. I want something real.

Working Nine to Five, What a Way to Make a Living . . .

"Jessica! Jessica! Are you listening?" Cruella yells at me, trying to snap me out of my gaze.

"Uh, huh," I say . . . *24, 25, 26.*

"Well, then why are these logos in Hebrew? Do you think that means anything to a client who can't read Hebrew? Do you even think before you do things?"

31, 32 . . . "You wanted those clients' logos. They don't exist in English. I checked." *33, 34, 35* . . . I'm counting the number of floors on the building that is being constructed across the street from our offices.

"Is that supposed to be an excuse?" Carmella bellows rhetorically.

Wait, where was I? 34 . . . 36. Damn. "No, Carmella. It is not an excuse. It is a fact," I say, no longer caring how she is going to react. *1, 2, 3, 4, 5* . . .

Carmella takes off her glasses so that the lasers in her eyes can better penetrate me. "Why do you even bother responding to me?"

12, 13, 14, 15 . . . I tune her out. I'm not going to let her get to me like Yoni did. I'm stronger now.

Days turn into weeks. Weeks into months. Months into a year and a half. I have no social life anymore. All I do is work. I need something more, so I decide to start an MBA program. At the very least, it gives me an excuse to leave work by 7:00 P.M.

As much as I hate my job, I'm actually getting scared that I'll get laid off. A few months ago, I had a dream that when I walked into my office one morning, I found my desk completely cleared off. In the dream, I walked over to Carmella's secretary and asked her, "What is going on? Where is all of my stuff?"

She responded, "Didn't you get the text message? Carmella fired you."

Ever since that dream, I started noticing that I was no longer invited to meetings with my clients. I didn't get as many emails from my manager or co-workers. I felt like I was getting pushed out.

"I think I'm going to get fired," I tell Orli and the other girls at a café.

"Don't you hate your job?" asks Limor, one of the girls in Orli's group of friends.

"Yes," I say.

"Well, then this is great," says one of the other girls.

"But, I don't want to get fired," I whine. I'm terrified of losing my job. For some reason, maybe it is because I don't have any family here, I'm afraid I'll end up homeless and on the street.

"Jessica, you should have left that job a year ago. Any other company would be lucky to have you!" Orli says.

"Listen, this is great news," Limor says. "If you time this just right, you can find another job and get fired at the same time. That way, not only will you have a new job, but you will also get compensation."

I smile and think to myself, "*I can do that.*" After surviving the army, I can survive anything. I'm a real Israeli after all.

Psychological Warfare

At work, I start acting like Peter Gibbons in *Office Space*. I show up late. I take long lunch breaks. I stop answering emails. I take an hour and half to go through the newspapers in the morning. I take naps in the bathroom. I never gutted a fish on my desk, but that's only because I'm a vegetarian.

At the same time, I start interviewing for a new job in high-tech. A high-tech job with a car in Israel is what a house with a white-picket fence in the suburbs is in America. It is the Israeli dream. The high-tech world in Israel is dynamic and creative. Having a high-tech job in Israel means that you've made it. It's where all the most successful people in Israel work. The benefits are better. The work is better. The pay is better. I'll get a car and gas paid for. It is the Israeli dream so now I'm trying to achieve it.

After a few months of trying to get laid off, Carmella upped the ante. One day I walked past her room when she was interviewing someone for my position, with her door open. She would leave mean notes on my desk— just like a bully in high school. I would just crumple them and play basketball with them. She did not realize that I had dealt with the devil in a beret while I was in the army and survived.

On Thursday afternoon, nearly two years after the Second Lebanon War started, my war with Carmella feels like it is about to come to a close.

"Hello?" I answer my cell, even though I know who is calling.

"It's Mati, how are you? I'm calling because I would like to officially offer you the job," he says.

Yes! I got it! I've made it in Israel! A high-tech job! And I'll get a car! In my new job, I'll be making more than my current managers are making, with better benefits and conditions. I do a little party in my head and stomp my feet up and down in excitement. "And I would like to officially accept," I say as professionally as possible.

"I'll send you the contract. You can start in a month, right?"

"Of course," I say.

Damn. Carmella still hasn't fired me. Now I'm going to have to quit and I'm not going to get any compensation . . . and after all of that hard work I did to get fired. I thought I had played my cards just right.

I had a feeling I was going to get this job offer. I have been trying to time it so that I'll get fired this week. For the past two weeks, I have been sending emails to Ronit, another manager of mine who works under Carmella, asking her why I wasn't being invited to meetings with my clients. After not hearing back from her, I told her it was rude that neither she nor Carmella were getting back to me after I put in over two years at this company. I told her that I wanted a promotion, and I gave her a list of new responsibilities that I could focus on. I wanted to make it clear to them that I was planning on staying, that I saw my future at Mitoog. If they wanted me to leave, they would have to fire me. But if I don't get fired today, I'm going to have to quit first thing next week.

In an attempt to get laid off I marched into Ronit's office two days ago and asked her, "Do I need to get my résumé ready?"

Ronit didn't know how to respond. She stared straight at my forehead and didn't move for an entire minute. She was hanging onto the arms of her chair for dear life, trying not to scratch her nose, since just a week beforehand, we had been to a body-language expert who told us that people subconsciously touch their nose while lying. I thought she'd had a stroke until she finally said, like a true PR person, "You should do whatever you think is best."

I got up and thought, *checkmate!* I know Ronit will call Carmella and tell her to lay me off now because they are afraid that I know something.

But Carmella still hasn't fired me and it is nearly afternoon on the last day of the week—which is the day that people always get laid off.

I stare at my computer screen thinking about what to do next.

NEW MESSAGE.

It's an invite from Carmella's secretary for a meeting with Carmella at the end of the day today. That can only mean one thing.

Yes! I'm getting laid off today!

I start packing my belongings. I clear off my desk. I distribute my work load to all the different people I worked with.

At 4:00 P.M. on the dot, I walk into Carmella's office. She closes the door behind me.

"Jessica, we both knew that this was coming. You . . . um, well . . . have been here for two years. It is just that . . . well, you can tell people that . . ."

This is the first time that I haven't heard Carmella yelling. Maybe she doesn't know how to talk in a normal tone and that's why she is so confused. Either way, I'm enjoying hearing her struggle and babble, so I let her continue.

"I don't know . . . I looked for a solution . . . but we just don't have the money . . . you will be able to find . . ."

After listening to her trying to avoid saying the words, 'You're fired,' for five minutes I finally say, "So, this is it? You're laying me off?"

She looks down, flustered. "Yes, I'm sorry. But you can use the office space. You can use the computer here to look for another job. Whatever you need. No one is going to fill your position; we just don't have the money to retain you anymore."

What the hell happened? Had she finally gotten that heart transplant? The only other time I saw her like this was when she asked me to put ear drops in her ear one day. I shiver at the memory.

"What should I do? Where should I look for a job?" I ask her, pretending that I'm shocked.

I may still look like an innocent American, but I know how to work the Israeli system. It's the best of both worlds.

"You will have three months of compensation. You will be fine. You will find a great job."

I try to look sad, but all I want to do is jump up on her desk and do a little jig.

"Okay," I say as I get up.

I walk out of the office singing "Freedom" by George Michaels in my head and decide to go buy a new summer dress, just like I did after my interview for the army, to celebrate fulfilling another of my Israeli dreams.

9

Professional Life

I'm standing in front of the company CEO, president, and all of its VPs. I'm about to present the company's new website, which is set to launch in a few weeks. I've spent the past four months creating the entire site and preparing the launch campaign. I should be nervous, but I'm not. I'm excited. I'm confident.

I love my new job.

This morning, I came in early just so that I could start work. I worked from home last night, just so that I could get more done.

The company has its problems. Mainly financial ones. The CEO is from an intelligence unit. Used to keeping information secret, he doesn't believe in marketing. So, the job can be a bit difficult, but I'm always up for a challenge. Besides, I'm used to nothing being easy in Israel.

The presentation goes well. There are a few changes, but I'll still make our launch date.

I look at my phone. No missed calls. It is 6:30 P.M. I'm going to be late. I have to get to class.

I run downstairs. My company laptop on one shoulder, my purse on the other, and my car keys in my hand. The sun hits my face. It is beautiful outside.

There it is. My car. My baby. It is mine. It is all mine. It is my chariot of freedom. It may be small and by

American standards, it is really nothing special, but to me it is shiny and new and it will take me anywhere I want to go. Unfortunately, I have to go straight to class.

I look at my gas tank. It is full. I smile. The company pays for my gas. Since all of Israel's oil neighbors hate us, the gas prices in the country are exceptionally high. It would be cheaper to run a car on Absolut vodka.

I turn the radio to Galgalatz and start singing along with Shlomo Artzi at the top of my lungs. I might be making up half of the words, but I don't care. I'm on top of the world. I feel like I have finally made it in Israel. I feel like I have paid my dues to this country and now my life will be easy. I have worked hard for years and now feel as if I have finally achieved many of my goals. I feel stable and secure here. I'm no longer worried that I will ever leave the country, like so many other American girls. The chorus of the song starts and I join Shlomo Artzi in singing about how much he loves his wife. I sing louder, almost willing myself to be that woman.

The traffic outside isn't as bad as normal. I'm used to bumper-to-bumper traffic. Instead, it is just the typical hectic driving. Cars switching lanes without blinkers. Drivers cutting me off. Motorbikes and motorcycles swerving in and out of lanes and driving on the shoulder. It doesn't bother me anymore. In fact, I drive the same way now.

Nefesh B'Nefesh, the organization that helped me make *aliyah*, might consider living in Israel three years a measurement of success in the country, but many new immigrants consider their *aliyah* a success once they have a car. Maybe it has something to do with the 150% tax on cars in Israel.

After parking on campus, I run into the school. I'm late, but not panicked; everybody is late in Israel. Our finance professor during our first semester told us that we could never be late, and then he was a half an hour late to the next class.

After stopping to get a cup of *nes* coffee and a bureka[16], I walk over to our usual classroom. When I enter, I see that it is completely empty.

Damn! I hope they didn't change the date of the class again. I shouldn't be surprised. Everyone in our MBA program has complained about the administration problems, from scheduling a class on Memorial Day to changing a test time an hour before the test. In answer to our complaints we got the same response that Israel gets from the UN when it makes a complaint against Hamas—we're ignored.

Where is class? I text one of the other students.

After getting a text with the room number, I make my way across campus. I am now fifteen minutes late. When I get there, I see a group of students from my MBA program sitting outside the classroom.

"What are you doing out here? Why aren't you in class?" I ask the forty-year old businessman in Hebrew.

When I signed up for the MBA, I was hoping to meet some eligible Israeli bachelors to jump start my love life in this country, but I quickly gave up on that hope when I realized everyone was already married and fifteen years older than me. However, it would be nice to have a relationship. I feel stable enough in this country that I'm ready for something serious. I'm even beginning to look forward to starting my own Israeli family.

"The professor said we have to wait and then all come in together at half past so we don't disturb him."

"I was only thirty seconds late and he wouldn't let me in," says another guy.

---

16. A popular Israeli fast food, a bureka is a baked filled pastry made of a thin flaky dough (phyllo). A bureka can be filled with spinach, potato, cheese, or meat.

"That's bullshit. I'm going in. We are paying him to teach us," I proclaim like a veteran Israeli. Hopefully that line of reasoning will work better on him than it does with police officers.

"He'll kick you out."

"Watch," I say confidently.

"Really, Jessica, it might be better just to wait," says an American who is just in Israel for the program and hasn't spent any time really living in the country. He is used to following the rules. He is used to raising his hand in class, instead of just blurting out comments, like a real Israeli.

I throw open the doors and start making my way to my chair like I belong there.

"As you will see, if you apply the —" the professor at the front of the large lecture hall abruptly stops his explanation to the seated students. "You have to wait outside until half past. You are late. I don't like interruptions."

"Yeah, I tried to get here on time. But I had a work meeting," I calmly reply as I continue walking to a seat.

"Well, those are my orders."

Orders? "I was released from the army over three years ago. I don't take orders anymore."

"You can't sit down in the middle of the class. I have rules," the professor demands.

"And if I do?" I ask. What the hell is he going to do? Court martial me?

"I'll leave," he proclaims.

Damn. I walk out. Guess I still have room for improvement on being an Israeli.

Negative Space

"So, how long did it take you to learn Hebrew?" the girl asks me from across the table.

"Well, I'm still learning. Every day I learn at least another word. But I finally started feeling confident in Hebrew towards the end of my army service," I say.

"Oh," she says, disappointed.

"But you can learn Hebrew without the army. You just have to be stubborn about it. Force yourself to speak only in Hebrew. Read as much as you can," I say, trying to cheer her up. "You know, when I first came here, I could barely even formulate a sentence. I made so many embarrassing mistakes."

Nefesh B'Nefesh asked me to meet with a new immigrant so that she could get advice from me on how to succeed in Israel.

"What about work? How did you find your job? Do you like your job?"

"After the army, I worked at a company called Mitoog," I start.

"Really? That is like the top PR agency in the country! How did you get a job there?" she asks.

"Well, the army again. I mean, my experience in the army helped, but someone high up in my unit who used to work there gave me a recommendation. It was pure chance, but that is how Israel works. It's so small," I say, suddenly realizing how much the army has affected my life. "Now I'm the marketing communications manager at a high-tech company." I smile, thinking about it.

"That is my dream job. But, I'm too old for the army. Do you have any other suggestions?" she asks, concerned.

"Oh, there are many immigrants that don't do the army," I say. *And those are the ones that don't learn Hebrew, don't find a good job, and then end up going home,* I think to myself. "You don't have to do the army to succeed here. Just make sure to meet people. It will be hard, but stay determined. It will pay off," I say, trying to encourage her.

"How long until you felt settled here? Like you succeeded?" she asks.

"Like five years," I think. Wow, that was only like half a year ago.

"Do you have lots of Israeli friends?"

"Yeah, I do. Many from the army. Then there is Orli, my roommate, and all of her friends," I tell the story about how I met Orli.

She looks sort of jealous.

"You'll make friends. It takes time. You should come out with us!" I offer. "I'll call you next time we go out."

"Do you have a boyfriend?" she asks.

I wince, but hope she doesn't notice.

I think about my friend who was on my volunteer program and made *aliyah* like me. She just got married. It must be so nice having someone to really depend on in this country, having a family, having a place to go to for the holidays.

"Uh, no," I say, my voice shaking. I clear my throat to hide my hesitation. "I don't have time for a boyfriend. I've dated, but I just sort of decided a long time ago that I want to be completely settled here before I get into a serious relationship. There are too many American Jewish girls who fall in love with Israeli guys and then leave after breaking up. I'm determined to stay here, so I'm being cautious. I didn't come here for a guy and I'm definitely not going to leave here because of one."

I may be able to convince everyone around me that my life is complete, but I still haven't been able to convince myself.

Unholy Sex in the Holy Land

Dating in Israel hadn't been as easy as I expected. The probability of finding a nice Jewish guy in Israel, the Jewish homeland, should have increased since I was surrounded by eligible Jewish men. The country is a Jewish mother's dream come true for her daughter. However, I have now been in Israel for more than half a decade and have yet to find anyone that I'd like to be in a serious relationship with.

The First Officer

The first Israeli man who I fell in love with was the young Israeli officer who trained our group of American sixteen-year-olds for a week during *Gadna*, army training, while we were on a trip to Israel. The first time I saw him, he looked like a dark-skinned Jewish Rambo with his hair slicked back. The entire group of girls was standing around giggling in our too-big army uniforms, but when he walked up, we all froze. We stared at him without breathing. We wanted to be with him. The guys in the group puffed out their chests, stood up taller, and raised their heads. They wanted to be him.

He was everything that American Jewish guys aren't. He was tough and commanding. The first night of *Gadna* in my shared room, I drifted off to sleep thinking about him, but was then awakened when one of my roommate shrieked, "A cockroach just crawled over me!"

Having joined in with our roommate's shriek, we barely heard the knock on our door. We all turned to the door simultaneously but didn't answer.

Another knock. More silence.

"Why you yell in there?" a deep voice asked from the other side.

In my pajamas, zit cream, and retainer, I turned on the lights and opened the door to the officer who looked like a Greek god.

"What is da problem, girls?" he asked.

We began drooling at his magnificence—me a bit more thanks to my retainer. My roommate managed to explain that a cockroach crawled over her and that we were now afraid to sleep. He looked at us, probably trying not to laugh, and said as convincingly as the Terminator, "I be back."

When he shut the door, we grabbed each other's hands and jumped up and down. We had never been so happy to have seen a cockroach. I quickly washed my face and took out my retainer.

The officer of our dreams was back at our door in less than five minutes with a device that was supposed to keep away cockroaches. He stepped into our bedroom and plugged in the gadget. He said good night and walked out. In bed again, we had completely forgotten the cockroach, but still couldn't fall asleep. We were too excited that such a hot IDF soldier had been in our bedroom.

That was not the last time an IDF soldier would be in my bedroom, but more unfortunately, it was probably the best.

Adam

Adam got my number from a mutual friend after we met at a party. He invited me out for a coffee. While sharing a drink at a café, we began debating the modesty laws in Judaism. He told me that he thought that women who wear provocative clothes were asking to be raped. I, wearing a short jean skirt and a tank top, became concerned for my safety. When I told him that I thought that many of the religious were hypocrites, he revealed to me that he was religious and kept Shabbat.

Despite his commitment to the Sabbath and women's modesty laws, he did not refrain from touching or sleeping with women, as later that evening he asked to receive a massage from me and tried to kiss me.

When I got home from that date, I called up my friend and told him to never give my phone number to anyone, ever.

Dr. Big

Dr. Big, the second officer I dated, was a doctor in an elite unite in the army. He always tried to impress me with stories of his army service that seemed as far-fetched as crop circles, but were much more exciting. Dr. Big and I played an over-dramatic cat and mouse game for a few years, until I uncovered his pathological lies. After suspecting that he was lying about his whereabouts, I found out that Dr. Big claimed that he was on base when he was really off for the weekend. All I had to do to confirm it was simply to call up Israel's 411 for the number of his war room to get the information. Given how much the IDF prides itself on being one of the most secure and impenetrable armies in the world, it shouldn't have been so easy. We never talked after that.

Later, thanks to Facebook, I found out that Dr. Big never was cured of his pathological lying. His profile picture was a graphic that read, "I just wanted to ask for forgiveness" and his relationship status had changed from being engaged to single. Even though he was the one who survived many dangerous operations, I was the one who dodged the real bullet.

Kyle

While I was in the army, I dated Kyle, an American guy who had also moved to Israel and joined an elite unit in the Golani Brigade in the IDF.

Since we were both in the army, I wasn't looking for anything serious with Kyle and I thought he wasn't either, until one night when he showed up drunk professing his love for me. He told me that during his navigation training missions he would get lost because he couldn't stop thinking of me. Yes, ladies, that is what passes for romance in Israel.

Dror

Dror was someone I met randomly on the street. One of the perks about Israel is that you can meet Jewish guys everywhere and not just at some painful Jewish event. We went out on one date to a bar and I instantly regretted it. The conversation was as bland as the beer that I ordered. I drank as quickly as possible so that I could end the date. And then on our way out, the conversation got even more odd.

As if the country isn't chauvinistic enough, there is actually a smell of testosterone in the air—and I'm not using that as a metaphor. Carob trees are planted on nearly every boulevard in Israel. When the tree blooms in September and October it gives off the smell of . . . well, there is no politically correct way of putting it . . . semen.

As if the smell of jizz on a first date isn't awkward enough, the guy started discussing the smell by saying, "I hate this time of year. The smell is awful." And then added, with a crooked smile, "But I bet you women love it!"

I froze with my mouth hanging open from shock, which probably was not the best reaction, considering the subject matter.

Ido

A friend of mine kept trying to set me up with one of his friends who was in *Yamam*, the elite Israeli police department. He repeatedly told me all of the reasons that we would be a good match. After refusing for nearly a year, I finally caved. In the middle of the date, the guy claimed that he had been called into an emergency mission and I never heard from him again.

He either died on the mission or he just wasn't that into me.

JDate

I went on a few dates from JDate in Israel. I never thought that a Jewish dating site would be necessary in Israel until I actually started dating here. Unfortunately, I did not have much luck with the online dating scene either. Most of the guys I ended up dating were shorter than me because I didn't know how to convert feet and inches into the metric system.

Tal

During a Rosh Hashanah that I spent with Orli, we went to a club which was supposed to be the biggest party of the night. It was in some type of warehouse. One guy came up to me and started talking to me. He ended up being the party producer. He was tall, dark, and handsome. I ended up giving him my number. He embodied Israeli persistence. The very next day he begged for me to come out, even though I had to get back to Jerusalem for *ulpan*. The day after, he drove to Jerusalem to take me out for some coffee. Even though the two cities are only an hour apart, for a Tel Aviv resident to drive out to Jerusalem is like a New Yorker flying out to California for a date. Our next date was during Sukkot, and I spent the holiday at his house with his entire family. Luckily, thanks to Liel, I had grown used to meeting guys' families by the second date.

Things didn't work out between us, but the story didn't end there, because two years after that, when Orli and I would spend every weekend at Zamir, the dance club where I hurt my knee, it turned out that Tal owned that place also. This is one of the most unfortunate parts about dating in Israel—you are more likely to run into an ex at a club than meet someone new.

Tzachi

I, of course, could not miss out on the most important part of the IDF experience: having a fling with someone in my unit. As with most army flings, mine started with Tzachi when he was on duty over the weekend. Since the army is an expert at wasting people's time, he was just sitting around doing nothing, waiting in case something happened. Since he was not doing anything, he invited me over to the base to watch a movie.

We ended up taking ten army cots and stacking them on one another and putting a movie in the projector, which is supposed to be used for viewing army operations, but we used to create our own personal movie theatre experience.

After that, Tzachi and I ended up spending nearly every weekend together, but when we saw each other on duty, we would pretend as if we barely knew each other. We would pass each other in the hallway and barely make eye contact. We would be sitting alone together in a room and not say anything to each other. After all, a unit called the spokesperson unit has its fair share of gossipers.

Yoel

Over six feet tall, dark hair, and blue-eyed, Yoel was considered hot by most women, but I had never been particularly attracted to him. I had met him years ago, and then while coming back from Independence Day celebrations at 3:00 A.M., I ran into him and he suddenly looked much cuter. So when he asked me for my number, I gave it to him.

We went out the next week. I couldn't tell if we were just going out as friends or if it was a date. But when he walked me home and tried to stick his tongue down my throat, I knew that he definitely thought it was a date.

We dated a few times, but there just wasn't a click. Unfortunately, I could not get rid of him. Since he was living in Haifa and working in Tel Aviv, he had basically moved into my apartment after two dates—as if he thought my place was the newest settlement in Israel. If I hadn't been involved in planning Disengagement, then I would have had to call the border police to evacuate him.

After so many bad dates, I had nearly given up on finding a Jewish guy in Israel, but there was something that told me to keep holding onto hope. I thought that finding love would be like all my other experiences in

Israel; maybe the person with whom I would fall in love would be worth all the previous struggles.

Love Life

The *aliyah* posters and fliers never told us young, idealistic Zionists about the lonely Friday nights, about desperately trying to find somewhere to spend the holidays, the longing to feel like someone needs and wants you with them during the holidays in this small and overcrowded country.

Rosh Hashanah is approaching. I'm dreading it. The holidays always remind me that I am alone here.

I go to Orli's family for every holiday, but I want to celebrate with a family of my own. I want to feel like a true part of a family here in Israel, not just a guest at someone's table. It is the one thing that I still need to achieve in this country.

The rest of the country can't wait. Everybody is in a good mood. People wish each other *chag sameach*, happy holiday, in the streets. There are pomegranates and apples and honey everywhere. There is even apple-smelling toilet paper, which I find particularly odd. I don't even like the perfume samples in magazines. I do not want my toilet paper smelling like apples any more than I want my tampons smelling like bananas.

Sometimes it is easier just to pretend that it is only a normal day.

Sitting in my office, a few days before Rosh Hashanah, I'm reading through my emails. No one has gotten back to me about anything that I requested. Nobody, except for me, is doing any work. Most people are already at home with their families. For the next two weeks, everyone is in holiday mode. But I dive into work to try to forget that it is Rosh Hashanah.

I look outside. It is already dark out.

I look back to my computer when I hear it chime.

NEW MESSAGE.

I open it.

It's an email from Jeremy, who is a friend and colleague of mine from the states. That's strange: I usually send him emails. I usually need his help. I wonder what he needs.

From: Jeremy
To: Jessica
Subject: Favor
Time: 9:31 p.m.

Hi Jessica,

How are you?

A friend of mine is coming to Israel for a few weeks during Rosh Hashanah and will be moving there shortly. I wanted to know if I can give him your number?

Thanks and shana tova,

Jeremy

- -

I hit reply.

From: Jessica
To: Jeremy
Subject: RE: Favor
Time: 9:33 p.m.

Hi Jeremy,

All is good here. Sure. That is fine. You can give your friend my number.

When do you think you are going to visit again?

Jessica

- -

After being in Israel for nearly six years now, I'm used to people wanting to give my name to others who want to move to Israel. I have seen so many wide-eyed Americans move to Israel and then leave after it is too hard that this country feels like a revolving door. But I'm always happy to offer them advice on how to make it in Israel.

*   *   *

Orli's house is chaotic as usual. Her mom is cleaning the apartment and cooking her special, Afghani rice[17], for Rosh Hashanah dinner. Leah, Orli's sister, is re-checking everything her mom is doing to make sure it meets the strictest Jewish law. She was released from the army around four years ago and ever since has become more and more religious. She only wears long *frummy*[18] skirts. She picks through each grain of her rice to make sure there are no bugs in it. She doesn't touch boys. She studies in an all-girls yeshiva. Solomon, the middle brother, is now in the army and working towards his graduate degree at the same time. Doron, the younger brother, just had his bar mitzvah and is starting to become a rambunctious teenager. And to think that when I first met him, he was still playing with toys.

RING. RING.

It is probably someone calling to wish me a happy Rosh Hashanah. The more calls and text messages I get on this day, the better and less alone I feel.

I've never seen this number before.

"Hello?"

"Hi, it's Meydan. Jeremy gave me your number," the guy says in perfect Hebrew.

---

17. For an Afghani rice recipe, please see the appendix.

18. *Frum* is a Yiddish word that means devout. Someone who dresses *frum* wears very modest, often baggy clothing.

"Oh, hi. How are you?" I ask, surprised that his Hebrew is so good. I figure that his parents are probably Israeli. They probably spoke Hebrew at home. That isn't fair, I think. I had to work so hard to understand this language.

"Good, good. I'm going out with some friends after our Rosh Hashanah dinner. Do you want to come?" Meydan asks me, sounding confident that I will say yes.

He already has friends here? I wonder where he is spending the holiday dinner. He seems to know a lot of people here already.

"Um, yeah sure. You want to pick me up?"

*   *   *

Outside of my apartment, Meydan is standing on the sidewalk, in the glow of a street light, wearing a big smile and a just-tight-enough Hebrew Coca-Cola T-shirt. He has a buzz cut, glasses, broad shoulders, and strong biceps. There is something about the way he confidently stands or how he greets me with a hug that makes me feel like we are meant to be together.

I've never felt like this before. Especially not in Israel. Especially not after training myself to be cool-headed to protect myself from a broken heart. I've always been afraid that a broken heart would ruin my success in Israel. And if I fail at being Israeli then my Jewish identity would be at stake.

"Are you ready?" he asks, smiling at me.

My eyes light up, a smile spreads across my face, and my heart becomes lighter. At that moment, I decide to let myself fall for him. There is something about him that I see instantly. His openness. His fun-loving attitude. His Zionism. His strength mixed with sensitivity.

On the way to the *kibbutz* to meet his friends, our conversation flows; we laugh, and joke around together. We spend the entire night with his friends sitting in the fresh air, drinking beer, snacking on nuts, and talking. At the end of the night, he takes me home. When I get out of the car, he doesn't try to kiss me. We both smile at each other. I hope that I'll see him again before he leaves.

The next night Meydan comes over to my place. We talk the entire night.

"So, you are planning on moving here in a few months?" I ask excitedly. Outside it is completely dark, but my room is filled with light.

"Yeah, January first. I can't wait."

"Do you know where you are planning on living?" I wonder. *Say Tel Aviv, say Tel Aviv!* I think to myself.

"No, I'm not sure yet. Probably Tel Aviv though," he replies.

Yes!

Outside it is steamy. The room is boiling hot. I wonder if it is from the chemistry between us. The air conditioner is working full force. I had finally saved up enough money to install the one that was sitting under the kitchen table for the past few years.

"Well, if you need any help looking for a place let me know . . . Wait, how do you know Hebrew so well?" I ask.

"I was born here."

"Oh, so you moved to the states with your family when you were really young and you just spoke Hebrew at home?"

"No, I grew up here," he replies.

"Well, I don't get it. Where are your parents now?" I wonder, not understanding what is going on.

"They live in Petach Tikvah," he says.

"So you were in the army here?" I ask, still confused.

"Yeah. I just spent the past few years studying and working abroad. Now I'm moving back home, to Israel."

He is perfect. He is both Israeli and American. He is macho, but also polite. He is Jewish, but also liberal. He is smart, but also fun.

Why does he need me? He knows more people here than I do. He has friends. Family. He knows the language.

All of the sudden I get it. I feel like I am on the final episode of *The Bachelor* and have just been let in on the secret. This is a setup!

We spend the rest of the night talking on my bed, but again he is a gentleman and does not even try to kiss me. We talk until the light of day sneaks up on us to remind us that we are tired.

When it's time to go, I walk him to my door.

"I'll see you when I get back," he says and kisses me on the cheek.

"Sounds good," I say and shut the door as he walks away.

I get back into bed and fall asleep with a smile on my face.

10

A Hard Candy Shell

KNOCK. KNOCK.

"Orli? Are you expecting someone?"

"No."

"Who is it?" I ask through the door.

"Your boyfriend," the voice says. I love how that sounds. Three months after I met him, Meydan moved back to Israel and as soon as he did, we started dating.

I swing the door open. "What are you doing here?" I ask with excitement.

"I missed you," he says. He grabs me in his arms and gives me a kiss. Israeli men are so affectionate.

We saw each other yesterday.

"Have you eaten yet? Because I brought food to make dinner," Meydan says, as he smiles at me. He is always in such a good mood. He takes out all the vegetables to make a salad and puts some fresh bread in the toaster oven. He does everything with both enthusiasm and care.

I love the fact that Israeli men make dinner, fix a car, and serve in the army.

"I hope you don't have plans this weekend, because we are going up north with some friends of mine."

Israeli men are so spontaneous.

*   *   *

"*Shalom. Shalom,*" I'm greeted by the smiling and inquiring faces of Meydan's mom *and* grandmother who are checking to see if I'm good enough for their favorite son/grandson. We have only been dating three weeks and I'm already meeting his entire family. While in the US, meeting friends and family is a stepping stone, in Israel meeting parents is somewhere between the second and fourth date. This way, the mother can give her approval or disapproval before the man invests too much time and money into a relationship. "I'm Meydan's mother, Mira. This is Mor, Meydan's grandmother. Moti, Meydan's dad isn't here right now. But he will be soon. You can meet him then."

His last name, Macabbi, starts with an M too. Did they do that all on purpose? Is having a name that starts with an M a pre-requisite to being a part of this family? I wonder if there are any other requirements.

"How are you? Come on in. Sit down. Meydan is in his room on a phone meeting. Here, I made dinner. Are you hungry? What do you want? I have soup. I have potatoes. I have fish. I have chicken. I have kugel. What can I get you? What do you need?"

I'm offered more dishes than are listed on the Cheesecake Factory menu.

"Oh, I'm fine. Thank you."

"No, no. Sit down. Here, have some soup to keep you warm. It will be cold up north." She sits me down at the table and puts some soup in front of me. "Do you have a coat? Let me go and find a coat for you."

"Oh, thank you. I have a coat." It is nice having someone take care of me. I haven't had this since I lived at home.

She doesn't listen. She is digging through some clothes stacked up in the living room. I look around the apartment. It looks like it should be featured on A&E's *Hoarders*.

Against my will, I start eating the soup. It is delicious. Nobody has made me soup in years. Mira comes back with enough fleece coats and blankets to outfit an entire army. "Here, take them all, just in case," she says as she shoves them at me. She sits down at the table. What am I going to talk to her about? I'm so bad at this. I'm even worse at making conversation in Hebrew. What should I say? I want to make a good impression.

"Ignore the mess. I've been so busy. I took my father to the doctor. And my mother too. I'm so busy. And then I had to make dinner. And I work at night. I'm so tired. And lately I've been having these bowel problems. I don't know what to do about them. My stomach keeps flipping."

I barely even know this woman's first name and now I know more about her gastrointestinal system than her doctor.

"Where are you from in the United States? I love traveling. I would go and visit Meydan when he lived in New York and Florida. But we also went all over Europe. Have you been anywhere in Europe? We go to Europe all the time. I used to take care of this woman's parents and now we go and visit her in Switzerland every year."

I guess I shouldn't have been worried about finding something to talk about. Having a conversation with her is like listening to the radio.

"You should come with us. Mikah, Meydan's younger sister, and I are going to England. Why don't you come with us?" she asks, completely serious, even though she has just met me. I have never met anyone who has welcomed me into her family so quickly and who is so giving.

Meydan walks into the room and smiles at me. We look at each other and both light up. He claps his hands. "I'm done with work. Are you ready to go?"

We gather up all of our stuff, say goodbye, and head out the door together.

"So, how was meeting my mom and grandmother? They didn't overwhelm you, did they?" he asks me as he takes me in his arms. He always wants to make sure that I feel comfortable.

"No, they were great." I love feeling his arms around me. I try to breathe him in as he gives me a kiss on the forehead.

"Oh, and I brought a bunch of vegetarian food for you," he says, always attentive to my needs.

Bedside Manner

After that weekend in the north, things with Meydan quickly become serious. We spend every weekend together. We spend all of our free time together—going out to dinner, on long walks, bicycle rides, sitting on the beach, hanging out with our friends. He sleeps over at my place and I sleep over at his. When spending the nights at his house, we sleep right next to his parents' bedroom and I can hear his dad snoring as loud as a tractor, which is probably the only time that he makes more noise than his wife. I meet his entire family, his grandfather, his siblings, his nieces and nephew, his aunts, uncles, and cousins at different family events.

When I forget my keys in the door one day because I was thinking of Meydan, I realize that I have been walking around with a smile on my face ever since I met him. Every day I feel myself letting go of my fears and feeling more secure.

This is the first time in more than six years in the country that I actually begin to feel like I have a home here. Whenever I need help or advice, I know I can call Meydan and he will be there to help me. In fact, I know his entire family will be there to help me. I'll always have a place to go for the holidays. I won't have to ask my parents to fly to Israel at the last minute for a surgery. I no longer have to take a taxi to and from the airport. I'll always have someone to greet me when I land.

When I'm with him, I feel like I'm floating. I'm no longer afraid of falling in love. Everything feels like it's falling into place.

Even though we have spent almost every minute together, we still haven't slept together. So after a few months, I decided that it was time to take things to the next level and sent Meydan to get tested. At the same time I went for a checkup.

"Orli? Can you recommend a good women's doctor (as they are called in Hebrew)?" The last time I visited the OB/GYN was in the army. He told me to drop trow without even giving me a gown, and left me waiting for him with my legs up in the air. Since then, I've obviously been putting off another checkup.

"Yeah, I just went to one. He was so nice. He even complimented my appearance down there during my checkup," she said with a completely straight face.

"Your doctor commented on your—? That is sexual harassment! You weren't offended?" I ask, bewildered.

"No, why would I be offended? He gave me a compliment. So, do you want his number?"

"Fine."

*   *   *

"How can I help you today?"

"I want to get an annual check and be tested for all STDs."

"All? Even AIDS?" the doctor asks me.

"Yes, of course. Just to be sure," I reply.

"Why? Have you slept with someone outside Israel? Someone who isn't Jewish?"

"What? Why? What does that have to do with anything?"

This doctor has been to medical school. Does he actually believe that being "the chosen people" means that we're exempt from getting AIDS? This is as bad as when I realized that half of this country believes in Genesis but not evolution.

"Okay, you're fine. We are done here," the doctor says to me as he snaps his gloves off.

I can't decide if I should be relieved or insulted that he didn't give me the same compliment that he gave Orli.

The morning after we both got our negative results back, Meydan wakes up early and makes me breakfast as I get ready for work. As I walk to the kitchen to give him a kiss, I see something out of the corner of my eye in the living room. I look over.

It is Meydan. He is standing there, wearing a *kippah*, a *tallis*, and *tefillin*[19] . . . praying.

I freeze. I tiptoe back into his bedroom. I lock myself in there, but all I want to do is run and never look back.

We have been dating a few months and this is the first time I've seen him wear *tefillin*. What does this mean? Is he religious? Is he secular? He drives on Shabbat. He spends money on Shabbat. Based on what we did last night, he obviously is not *shomer negiah*, a religious person who doesn't touch the opposite sex. I know that he keeps kosher to some degree. What type of Jew does this make him? Is he Orthodox? His ex-girlfriend is a cantor[20], so he must be liberal, right?

---

19. Small leather cases containing texts from the Hebrew scriptures traditionally worn on the forehead and the left arm by Jewish men during morning prayer. In Orthodox and ultra-Orthodox communities, only men wear them, but in Conservative and Reform communities, both men and women can wear them.

20. A synagogue official who leads the congregation in musical prayer. A cantor is male in Orthodox and ultra-Orthodox communities, but in Conservative and Reform movements, a cantor can be either male or female.

Pacing back and forth, I wonder if he wants to be married under the Orthodox rabbinate.

My dad used to go to synagogue every morning and wrap *tefillin*, but that was in a Conservative synagogue in America. That was different. Israeli Jews aren't the same as Jews in America. When American Jews are religious they are also liberal. When Israeli Jews are religious they are Orthodox. Many Israeli Jews believe that Orthodoxy is the only real form of Judaism and give the Orthodox power over the entire country's Jewish identity.

Meydan tries to open the door, but I locked it. "Jess? Is everything okay?"

I grab my purse and open the door, "Yeah, I'm fine. I'm late for work. I have to go."

He looks at me, confused.

I run out without my breakfast, jump into my car, and drive as fast as I can away from there.

I turn on the radio. A song that was popular a few years ago is playing: "*Hamashiach Lo Yavo V'gam Lo Y'talphen*, The Messiah Isn't Going to Come and He Isn't Going to Call on the Phone Either." The first time I heard this song was on a bus from Jerusalem to Tel Aviv. An ultra-Orthodox man on the bus made the driver turn off the song.

I reach for the radio and turn up the volume.

I'm stuck in traffic in Bnei Brak, the ultra-Orthodox city right next to Tel Aviv. I look around me. I drive through this city every day to get to Meydan's, but I'm seeing the ridiculousness, the hypocrisy of this neighborhood for the first time. I look at all the men around me. They look like a swarm of penguins. Men wearing faded wool black suits, stained yellowish button-down shirts, and black hats. Why the hell are they wearing these stupid outfits?! It is 100°F outside! They are no longer in Poland! And the only ghetto they're in is this self-imposed hellhole called Bnei Brak. Do they actually think that wearing that outfit makes them more religious? I highly doubt that Moses was wandering the Sinai desert in a black hat with fur trim. And if we really are God's chosen people, there is no way that God would want us to look as ugly as these penguins with their ridiculous side-curls, and fish-tank glasses, and their wives in their potato-sack outfits and mops for wigs.

And where the hell are all of them going anyhow? It is not like anyone of them actually works or serves in the army! All they do is go to yeshiva and live off the taxes of the rest of the country. Why is it that the same penguins in New York can make a fortune selling diamonds and cameras and still have time to pray, but these ones in Israel only have time to pray? Are the days shorter here? They claim they can't work because they are too busy doing God's work, but I don't understand why, if God is omnipresent and omniscient, He would need people to do His work.

I want to roll down my window and yell at them to go join the army. To go get a job. To treat their women with equality. But instead, I look in front of me and force myself to breathe slowly.

A truck cuts in front of me. I hate driving in Israel.

I stare at the back of the truck, willing it to notice my anger. Then I see the bumper sticker on the back. It says MODEST GIRLS PREVENT RAPE.

It takes all of my self-control to not get out of the car and physically assault the driver of the truck. I want to tell him that smart non-misogynistic perverts prevent beatings.

Who the hell actually believes that? Who the hell actually puts a sticker like that on their truck? Who the hell actually mass produces a sticker like that?

I get to work half an hour late. I'm still fuming. I'm still scared about what Meydan's praying means for our relationship, for our future. I shut my door and force myself to calm down.

I sit down and start scanning the newspapers, like I do every morning.

I flip through *The Jerusalem Post*, *Haaretz*, and then *The New York Times*. An article in *The New York Times* jumps out at me.

How Do You Prove You're a Jew?
BY GERSHOM GORENBERG

The article detailed the experience of a young woman who went to the Israeli rabbinate to register to get married and she was shocked when they told her that she would have to prove that she was Jewish. Her difficult path to prove her Jewish identity included having to take a picture of her dead grandparents' tombstone to prove her Jewishness. I can't imagine the humiliation that she must have gone through.

And then I start wondering if my parents' forged *ketuba* may not be enough to prove that I'm Jewish. What should I do? How should I handle this? Should I tell Meydan?

I'll call Orli, hoping that she will have an answer. She is always so good at these things.

Orli is a typical Israeli when it comes to religion. She kisses the *mezuzah* every time she walks out a door, but when we go out she kisses random guys in the club. She refuses to cook on Shabbat, because using fire is forbidden, but she still smokes cigarettes on the same day.

I turn my radio up on my computer so that no one can hear me.

I find her name in my phone and push SEND. It feels like she is taking forever to pick up.

"Orli, I have to talk to you!" I yell, but in a whisper. I tell Orli how I caught Meydan praying this morning wearing tefillin. I finish the story by saying, "You don't understand, I actually locked myself in the room and then ran out of his house! I would have rather caught him with another woman."

Orli and I both laugh at the absurdity of it all.

"Jessica, don't worry about it. Praying, to him, is probably like yoga is to you. It is a form of meditation. Everybody has their own connection to religion. Like you, you don't believe in God, but you are more religious than I am."

"Yeah, I guess that is true. What do you think Meydan was praying to God about? Was he thanking him for the sinful pre-marital relations that we had just had the night before?"

Orli laughs, but she knows my sarcasm is masking my biggest fear. "I wouldn't worry about it. If he loves you, then marriage won't be an issue."

"I guess that's true. I'll tell him about it when the time is right and I'm sure everything will be okay." I know I'm trying to convince myself. "Thanks for the help. I'll see you at home."

After I hang up with Orli, I make an even bigger decision than my *aliyah* decision. I decide to stay with Meydan. I hope Orli is right and that love will win. If I want him to accept me for who I am, then I have to accept him for who he is. Besides, this is Israel. If it is a problem, anyone here can be bought off—especially the religious.

Mazal Tov

"If I forget thee, O Jerusalem, let my right hand wither, let my tongue cleave to my palate if I do not remember you, if I do not set Jerusalem above my highest joy," the groom repeats after the ultra-Orthodox rabbi who has a long beard and is wearing the traditional penguin nineteenth-century ghetto garb.

The groom lifts up his leg and stomps on the wine glass.

It's Carmit and Dror 's wedding. Carmit is the first one of us getting married from Orli's group of friends.

CRUNCH! The glass shatters. Everyone cheers.

I look over at Meydan. He is smiling and clapping his hands.

He looks back at me. I wonder if he can see in my face the pain I'm trying to hide.

He leans over and gives me a kiss. "I love you," he tells me.

"Me too," I say. And I really do. I decide to push all my fears away.

I look back up at Carmit. She looks so beautiful, so happy. Everyone is at the wedding. All the girls and their boyfriends.

Meydan squeezes my hand. I look over at him again. He looks so handsome. I wonder when that will be us under the *chuppah*[21].

The bride and the groom kiss. She is wearing a white version of J-Lo's green Versace dress, which is a lot prettier and more modest than some of the see-through dresses, short skirts, and poofy cupcake dresses that I have seen through the store windows on Dizengoff Street, the main shopping street in Tel Aviv. I wonder how is it that in a country where marriages are still controlled by the religious ultra-Orthodox, the wedding dresses are so revealing. The groom is wearing a laid-back suit, without a tie. The bride and the groom almost look like they are attending different functions and they both look like they are in a completely different century than their rabbi.

"How do they know their rabbi?" I lean over and ask Orli.

"They don't. They got a list of rabbinate-approved rabbis and picked one who happened to be available," she replies.

I balk. I can't imagine playing roulette to pick the rabbi who would officiate at my wedding. My rabbi is

---

21. A canopy under which a Jewish couple stand during their wedding ceremony.

our good family friend. I wouldn't want a stranger at the most important day of my life.

"Why didn't they ask their rabbi to do it?" I ask.

"They don't have a rabbi. It is not like they actually go to synagogue."

Then why are they getting married in the rabbinate? I wonder to myself.

This is the first Israeli wedding that I have attended. It is quite different than American weddings. The first thing I noticed when we walked in was the dress code. Most of the men are wearing jeans and the women are wearing their highest heels and fanciest dresses—not even bothering to hide the fact that they are trying to upstage the bride.

Everyone starts rushing up to the *chuppah* to congratulate the bride and the groom and then the ceremony turns into a rave.

The religious part of the ceremony is over, but that is not the most sacred part of the wedding. The most sacred part is the fireproof, bulletproof, locked, and guarded security safe, in which people deposit their checks.

I found out that weddings in Israel are less of a ritual to declare your love for a person and more of a business opportunity. In Israel there are no wedding registries. People prefer cold, hard cash. When I asked Orli how much to give the bride and groom, she referred me to a website which allowed me to put in different variables, from how many guests are invited, how close I am to the bride and groom, what my income is, what month the ceremony takes place in, and on what day of the week, to figure out the exact amount I should be giving.

When we walked in and I put the check into the lock box, Meydan leaned over and whispered in my ear, "Do you think that they will consummate their marriage tonight or count their checks?" and then chuckled from deep in his stomach.

Oh, how I love his laugh. It is contagious.

I look over at him and smile when I think about our future.

Predictions

All the girls are sitting around in white bathrobes. None of us are sober. We all just had massages. We are all celebrating Lital's bachelorette party. She is the second one of the group getting married. It feels weird that Orli isn't here. She is in the hospital. Her appendix just burst. I feel out of place with her friends without her.

"So, who wants to go next?"

"Jessica! Go! It's your turn," the girl next to me says as she pushes me forward.

I sit down in front of the numerologist. I tell her my name and my birth date.

She writes it down and begins translating the letters in my name into numbers. She looks up at me.

"Your destiny number is 4. This means you are sensible, hard-working and you live with integrity. Your feet are on the ground 24 hours a day."

She looks back down and does some more calculations.

"Your personality number is also a 4. Your friends see you as loyal and honest. You are also extremely patriotic. You love this country. You are very Zionistic."

Gee, I wonder if she figured that out from my accent. This is such bullshit. I can't believe people actually believe this stuff.

"Your emotional plane is 2 and it looks like you will be married within a year."

My head snaps up. What? Really? I smile and think about Meydan. I wonder if he has texted me.

"Okay, who's next?"

*   *   *

"How are you feeling?" I ask Orli.

"Ugghhhhh," she groans.

"We missed you last night," I say. I turn to Tova, Orli's mom, and ask, "How long have you been here?"

"I slept here."

"Do you want me to get you anything? Have you eaten?" I ask, but she waves her hand and makes a tsking noise, that means, "don't be silly, don't worry about me."

She looks me up and down and says, "You have lost 5.3 pounds since I saw you last." Whenever she sees me, she lets me know my weight. I'll never need a scale as long as she is in my life.

"Well, I'm sorry that the first time you are meeting Meydan is in the hospital, but I'm glad you are finally meeting him," I say, hoping that she will like him. Meydan extends his hand and says hello to Orli's mom.

Earlier that morning Meydan came over to surprise me with breakfast in bed. I had given him a key a few weeks ago.

"Well, we will let Orli rest. We just wanted to see if you needed anything," I say. I wonder if the doctors said when she would be released. I'm so lonely in the house without her.

After saying goodbye, Meydan and I go for a long bicycle ride in the park. While we are riding, Meydan gets a phone call.

"You'll never guess who that was."

"Who?" I ask.

"It's Jeremy!"

"Really, what is he doing here? Why didn't he tell us earlier?" I think about how much I owe Jeremy for setting us up together.

"He came in last minute for work. He wants to have dinner. I told him we can meet him on the Tel Aviv *tayelet*, boardwalk, in fifteen minutes."

When we reach Jeremy's hotel, we are thirsty and hungry. The three of us go sit down at a restaurant overlooking the beach.

"So, you guys look great!" Jeremy says. He seems proud that he has done such a good job playing Cupid.

"Yeah, we are," Meydan says as he pulls me in with one arm.

"Jessica, I've never seen you happier," Jeremy says.

"Yeah, I'm really happy," I say as I look over at Meydan and realize that this is really the first time I've been so happy in Israel.

Bonne Année

"Baaaaarrrrrr," I cry into the phone.

"What happened?"

I sniffle. "He broke up with me . . . and on Rosh Hashanah. This was going to be the first Rosh Hashanah that I didn't have to worry about where I was going to celebrate. I finally felt like I had a family. I thought that Meydan and I were going to be together forever. How am I going to get through this holiday on my own?" I weep and blubber into the phone. It has been exactly a year since Meydan and I met each other under the street light and it has been nine months since we started dating.

"Jessica, I can't understand you when you cry. Calm down and speak clearly," Bar says.

"And I bet it is even harder to hear me since you left me! I can't believe you moved back to France and left me here all by myself!"

"I'm sorry. Why did he break up with you?"

"I don't know. He just did. He has been stressed with work. We were going through a tough time. What am I going to do? I thought he was the *one*. I need you." I feel so weak and alone without Bar.

Ever since Jeremy left a few weeks ago, Meydan has been distant and irritable. It has taken a toll on our relationship, but I thought we would get past it. I never imagined that we were heading towards a breakup.

"Do you want to come to Paris for Rosh Hashanah?" he asks.

It would be nice to see him. I miss him so much.

"Umm, okay," I agree without fully thinking it through. I don't care how much the ticket is. I have to get out of here. I can't spend another holiday here alone. I doubt it is going to be easy for me to try to get over a breakup in the most romantic city in the world, but at least I'll be with Bar.

"Really?" Bar asks, surprised that I agreed so quickly.

I start making arrangements to fly.

"Hi, Nachama. It's Jessica," I say, trying not to let my banker hear my tears.

"Hi darling, how are you?"

I burst into tears. "My boyfriend just broke up with me," I whimper into the phone.

"Oh, honey. I'm sorry. Do you have anywhere to go for Rosh Hashanah? Do you want to come over to dinner with my family?" Nachama asks.

"No, I'm fine. Thank you so much," I smile, thinking how much I love this country. Only in Israel would my banker invite me to a holiday dinner with her family. "I actually need to buy some Euros. I'm going to Paris for the holidays."

*   *   *

"Oh, good. I'm glad you called. I'm just at the grocery store. I'm trying to figure out what to make for you for Rosh Hashanah lunch. I was thinking that I could make—" Mira, Meydan's mom, says without pausing for a breath.

I can't believe him! It is the day before Rosh Hashanah. Meydan and I broke up three days ago. I can't believe he still hasn't told his mom that we broke up. Does he think that people won't notice that I'm not sitting at the table? I was just going to politely say *chag sameach*, happy holiday, but it looks like I'm going to have to tell her that Meydan and I broke up.

His younger sister called me earlier today while I was at work to wish me *chag sameach*, and to make sure I was still coming to lunch on Saturday. When I told her that Meydan and I had broken up, she started crying and told me that if I ever needed anything, their door was always open. I thought I had cried all my tears, but she made me weep all over again. I had to hide in the bathroom because I was crying so hard.

Now in Orli's room for emotional support, I'm listening to Mira on the phone, listing the different foods that she can make for me.

"Mira, wait. I have to tell you something. I'm sorry that it has to be me to tell you this, but I'm not going to be coming to the holiday meal. I'm flying to Paris tonight. Meydan and I aren't together anymore." I'm holding Orli's hand. We rehearsed exactly what I was going to say to Mira. I squeeze Orli's hand even harder so that I won't start crying.

"Oh, no. I see. Okay. Tell me, who broke up with whom?"

"I think you should ask your son," I say.

"I see. Well, don't you worry. He is just stressed. I know my son. He gets this way. I will talk to him. If you don't hear from him by the time you get back, you call me at work. I'll work this all out for you," she declares with the utmost confidence. "And don't forget to get international medical insurance!"

*   *   *

The taxi window keeps fogging up. I have to wipe it every few seconds so that I can see outside into the dark. I have no idea where I am. I'm looking for Bar. He is supposed to be waiting outside his apartment for me.

Five hours ago, while the entire country was surrounded by laughter, love, food, and family, I was on my way to the airport . . . alone.

"*C'est votre destination,*" the taxi driver says.

I look up and see Bar. I jump out of the car and run into his arms.

"I'm glad you are here. Now, the rule is that there is no crying from here on out. We are going to have fun!"

On Rosh Hashanah, I visit Notre Dame—a church, of all places. It is like my Jewish identity is already slipping away.

I walk around the city, visiting the Louvre, the Eiffel Tower, and other tourist sites. All I can think about is how cold it is here and how warm it is in Israel right now. I eat buttery croissants every morning. I take selfies in front of all the landmarks, planning to put them up on Facebook to show Meydan how much fun I am having without him. The whole visit is a blur. All my energy is focused on trying to forget Meydan.

On my last night, Bar and I go out to a special dinner.

"No more crying, Jessica. Do you hear me? It is going to be hard to go back and face reality, but you have to be strong."

"I will. Why don't you come back with me?" I ask.

"I've had enough of the country," he says, looking down at his food. I understand why he left. Israel is a hard country to live in. Everything there is a struggle and a challenge.

Bar's support recharges and strengthens me.

The flight back is almost as depressing as the arrival. Hoards of families are waiting at the arrivals for their loved ones. Not one of them is here to greet me.

I want to cry, but I promised Bar that I wouldn't.

Back at my apartment, I take a shower. I have to get ready to go back to work and school. I can't show up with my eyes bloodshot. I can't cry another day at work. I have to be strong. *I have to be tough*, I think to myself in the shower. I try to be Israeli and convince myself, *Yihyeh b'seder!* Everything will be okay!

The steaming hot water is pounding down on my back.

"Jessica! Your phone is ringing!" Orli yells at me.

"Who is it?" I ask.

"It is Meydan!" she yells back.

I haven't even been home for an hour and he is already calling. This is a good sign.

"Tell him I'm busy," I say. He can wait. He ruined my Rosh Hashanah.

*   *   *

"So, here is the thing. I missed you. I can't stop thinking about you," Meydan says as he stares into my eyes and holds my hands.

I feel the sand underneath my feet. I hear the waves crashing in front of us. It is dark outside. People are chattering, laughing, and smoking hookah all around us.

"I love you," he says and steals a passionate kiss.

"I love you too," I say. "Don't ever do that to me again!"

"I won't," he promises.

He kisses me again, but I don't kiss him back. I'm scared. What if he does this to me again? What if his love isn't strong enough? I don't know if I can handle this emotional roller coaster.

He pulls me into his arms.

I kiss him back. I'm ready for a relationship. Even though I'm scared, I'm going to have to face my fears.

Family Matters

"You put da powderrr in bowl wid waderrr and flowerrr. Stir . . . harrrd," Mira, Meydan's mom, makes a stirring motion with her hand to show what she means. I have never heard her speak English before, but she is trying to show my mom how she made the bread that she is serving for lunch.

My mom is smiling sweetly and quietly, trying to understand Mira's broken English, but I know she has no intention of ever making the bread. Meydan is playing with his nieces and nephew. Looking at him, I feel almost as if we never broke up. I smile, thinking about what a good father he will make.

Nearly thirty of us are sitting in the Macabbi's cluttered dining room, which has become a backdrop for the smiling faces, open arms, and laughing children who all hold a place in my heart and my life. Moti, Meydan's dad, insisted that they use the nice plates for this meal with my parents. As punishment for this request, he is now in the kitchen, cleaning those dishes.

My parents always visit me in Israel during Sukkot. But this is the first time my parents have come to Israel and I haven't had to take them to a restaurant during the holidays. This is the first time they are experiencing a real Israeli Sukkot, with lots of love, noise, and food.

Sitting at the table are four different generations. There is a mixture of languages and cultures. It reminds me how much I enjoyed the Jewish holidays with my family growing up. When I was a child we would make and decorate a *sukkah* together; when I got older I would help my mom make potato latkes for Hanukkah, and during Passover we would always have a large meal with lots of food and guests.

"Who from the Passover story is not mentioned in the Haggadah[22]?" my father asked our twenty-odd guests of family and friends at our seder table when I was in high school. That year, he had decided to play a trivia game as part of the retelling of the Passover story.

I was used to my dad trying to make Judaism interesting and fun, but sitting next to me was Chris, my high-school boyfriend, who clearly felt out of place. Even though my parents weren't happy that he wasn't Jewish, they still invited him so he could learn about the Jewish tradition. He was just like all the other boys at my high school—he drove a pick-up truck while blaring country music, he wore a large belt buckle that was big enough

---

22. The Passover prayer book

to be a trash can, and often wore a wife-beater tank top, which he had fortunately left at home that night.

My dad received blank stares to his question. Breaking the silence, thinking that he was either courageous, funny, or a combination of both, Chris proclaimed "Jesus!"

Everyone stared at him. The room was completely still, except for me kicking him under the table.

My dad finally broke the silence, "That is . . . accurate, but it's not the answer we're looking for."

That was the first year that we put oranges[23] on our seder table. I wonder if Meydan's family would be willing to do that too.

I look over at Meydan, who is wearing his *kippah*, and smile. Everyone seems to be getting along and like each other despite the language barriers.

"What do I do? There are no serving spoons," my mom leans over and whispers to my dad during the meal.

"Just take a piece with your fork," my dad says.

"Oh." My mom grimaces. "That is not sanitary." She manipulates her fork to try to not touch it to any other pieces of chicken. Meydan's family is simply grabbing food with their hands. The cultural differences do make for a funny backdrop.

I walk into the kitchen and ask Mira what I can take out to the table.

"No, you just go sit down. I'll be out in a minute."

I sit down in between my parents and Meydan. I feel at home.

---

23. Years ago, Dr. Susannah Heschel came across a student-written haggadah in which a fictional girl asks a fictional Orthodox rabbi what a lesbian's place is in Judaism. He answers that a lesbian belongs in Judaism the way bread belongs on a seder plate. Since bread is clearly forbidden, Dr. Heschel chose an orange to represent the "fruitfulness" of women's contributions. Many Reform and Conservative Jews put an orange on their seder plates to represent women's equality in Judaism.

Mira walks out with a huge chocolate cake that she made. On the cake is written, "Mazal Tov Jessica."

"*Yom huledet sameach!*" Everyone starts singing happy birthday to me in Hebrew.

I look around and am so grateful that on this holiday, which celebrates the abundance of life, I am surrounded by so many people whom I love. My life is exactly where I want it to be.

"You know, at this age, I was pregnant with my oldest daughter, Maya," says Libbi, Meydan's older brother's wife.

"Thanks!" I say sarcastically.

"You don't look a day past twenty-three," her husband, Mati, says.

"That is what I like to hear!" I thank him.

"Wait, wait! I'll take a picture," yells Mikah, Meydan's younger sister. "Ready, 3, 2, 1."

We all smile.

"Oh, it turned out great! Come see!" she says.

I look at the picture. I can see the rest of my life in that picture. I see my future. I see our future. I see our wedding. I see the birth of our children. I see anniversaries and holidays to come. I see my home.

I think back to when Meydan and I first started dating and he told me that he couldn't wait to have kids. Then it scared me. Now, I can't wait to start a family with him.

For the first time, I *know* that I will be in Israel forever and will fulfill the dream I've been struggling to achieve. I'm no longer worrying about failing. My Jewish identity is finally mine.

II

The Next Step

"I have hamburgers, skewers, and steak ready. Who wants what?" Meydan yells to the large crowd of his family and friends in the yard of our new apartment in a *kibbutz*. In true socialist fashion, the yard is shared with everyone else living in the building, which was converted from the old communal dining hall.

Today is a day of celebration. Meydan and I are having a *hanukat bayit*, a house-warming party. We just moved into an apartment on the same *kibbutz* where we had our first date. It feels symbolic, circular. Last weekend, we painted the apartment and moved in all the furniture, but tonight will be the first night that we sleep here.

A real estate agent would describe the apartment as cozy, but it's actually just small and cramped. The entire apartment is smaller than my childhood bedroom. It consists of one large room which serves as the kitchen, the living room, and Meydan's home office. There is a small bedroom which is barely big enough to fit Meydan's childhood bed and then an old Israeli-style bathroom that is basically a toilet, with a showerhead over it.

I still have my apartment in Tel Aviv . . . just in case. I know that as long as I have it as a safety net, it will protect me from becoming another statistic on the list of girls who made *aliyah* and then left after a breakup. I worked hard at establishing my life here before I got involved in a serious relationship and I don't want to lose it. There is something inside me that won't completely let go, relax, and take the leap of faith into this relationship.

"Jess, *mammi*, hun, your veggie skewers are ready. I'm saving them for you over here on the side," Meydan yells over to me.

"Thanks *motek*, sweetie," I yell back. Hopefully, I will be able to get to them while they are still warm, I think. I'm busy making a large Israeli salad of diced cucumbers, tomatoes, and onion.

The guests suddenly begin to scatter. Everyone runs for cover, but no one leaves. It is the first rain of the season. It is a blessing. The manly Israeli men keep barbequing, while the rest of us crowd under the awning to continue eating and talking.

I look over at Meydan and smile. He looks so content with everyone around him.

By sundown, everyone has gone home and Meydan and I are cleaning up. As I'm washing dishes, he comes up from behind and gives me a hug.

"Why don't you go shower. You have work and school tomorrow. I'll finish up here," he says.

As the hot water is pounding down on my back, I think about how different my life is today than it was a year ago. Before I felt like an American living in Israel, but now I feel like an Israeli with an American accent. I have friends who are like family here. I have a boyfriend. I have a home for the holidays. I do Israeli things on the weekend, like barbeques and family lunches. I no longer feel like I'm alone here.

I turn off the shower and at the door is Meydan, ready to wrap me up in the towel that he thoughtfully warmed up on the radiator. He holds me in his arms.

I feel as if I can finally put down my guard that I have spent the past seven years building up.

You want to watch a movie together?" he asks.

"Sure," I reply.

I feel as if getting through the breakup actually made our relationship stronger, as if we will be able to survive anything that life might throw at us in the future.

We both put on our pajamas. Meydan makes us some hot herbal tea. We curl up on the couch together. This is the first night that we have spent in an apartment all by ourselves.

I look around at the bare walls and wonder how we will fill them.

Meydan starts kissing me. I guess we aren't going to be watching a movie after all. I try to forget that he found this couch on the side of the street.

I think to myself, *maybe I should get rid of my apartment.*

Oedipus Effect

"I'll take the trash out. I'll be right back," Meydan says as I clean up after dinner.

During the week, I work hard at school and at the office, but during the weekends, Meydan and I play hard. I smile, thinking about our romantic weekends at bed-and-breakfasts. Our drives to the Golan Heights to see the flooding streams after heavy rainfalls. Our hikes and four-by-four driving along Jeep paths with friends. Our picnics in the fields and making tea and coffee on portable gas burners in the forest. Our walks through the alleyways of Jerusalem. Our visits with friends for dinner or dessert. Our walks hand-in-hand on the beach.

Ten minutes later, as I'm finishing the dishes, Meydan opens the door.

"Look what I found!" he exclaims. Knowing that he inherited a bit of his mother's hoarding habit, I turn around worried that it is probably another piece of junk that he thinks is a treasure.

But instead, a spunky, copper-colored, medium-sized dog darts over to me as if he is a self-guided missile. With what seems to be a smile on his face, the dog starts licking mine. For the second time in my life, I fall in love at first sight.

The dog keeps running around in circles. Sniffing everything. Looking for food. But he always comes back to give one of us a kiss. He can't sit still for a second. He looks healthy, but without a collar it is obvious he has been abandoned, just like the many other dogs that people dump at *kibbutzim*.

Exchanging only a quick glance between the two of us, Meydan and I know that we are going to keep him. As I take our new dog to the shower to rinse him off, Meydan hunts through the cupboards to find food for the hungry dog.

After I dry him off, the dog returns to his spunky self and darts back and forth in the room until he finally settles down and curls up on our small beige bath rug.

Meydan hands him a can of tuna fish, which the dog eats in record time.

"Let's name him *Jinjy*, redhead," Meydan declares triumphantly, as if he had a stroke of utter genius.

"Well, it seems to fit his personality," I reply with a smile. I'm reminded how his family has a weird thing about naming everyone with a name that starts with an M and it makes me happy that he doesn't want to continue this tradition with our dog. The tradition made me feel as if I would have to change my identity to become a part of his family.

When we get into bed, Jinjy follows us into the bedroom. He slowly climbs into bed and curls up between us, as if that is where he belongs. It feels like we are becoming our own family.

I take a deep breath. Everything seems to be in place in my life. Having grown up with dogs, I've been waiting for the time when I could adopt a dog in Israel to really make me feel at home. I have always dreamed of living on a *kibbutz*. I speak Hebrew fluently. I have a high-tech job. I'm nearing the end of my MBA. I have a wonderful boyfriend, whose family loves me and has taken me in. I cuddle up under the warmth of the covers and for the first time feel completely content with where I am in my life. I no longer need to work towards something. I'm no longer concerned about struggling in this country. I am exactly where I need to be.

All I need is my happily-ever-after and I'll be in the company of Snow White, Cinderella, and Sleeping Beauty. I hear the pitter-patter of little *sabra* feet in our future—but that may be the leaky faucet in the kitchen. I close my eyes and see my life roll out in front of me like a red carpet being unrolled at the Emmys.

My parents' forged *ketuba* flashes in my mind.

My eyes snap open. My breathing is shallow. I look over at Meydan and Jinjy. They are both sleeping soundly. My mind starts racing. My jaw tightens and I feel a migraine coming on. I am living the *aliyah* dream that I have worked so hard to achieve. What am I afraid of? Why is there an awful feeling in the pit of my stomach? Am I so consumed by worry that I'll eventually bring about my own worst fear?

I look back over at Meydan. He is still fast asleep. I wonder if he will be my Clyde? My Romeo? Will he be my Superman or my Robin Hood? Will he defy the stars? Will he be above the law? Will he rebel with me against the authorities? Will he still love me after I tell him about the forged *ketuba*? Will he care more about marrying me than being married by the rabbinate?

If he broke up with me just because he was stressed, what will he do when I tell him that I can't get married in the rabbinate? I already told him that my mom converted, but I get the feeling that he doesn't know what that actually means for marriage.

I think back to Lital's bachelorette party when one of her friends told me that she had to get married in Cyprus because her husband is a kohen[24] and she was a divorcée. They had found a way around the rabbinate. I hope we will too.

"Ugh, Jessica . . . did you eat too much dairy tonight?" Meydan blames Jinjy's fart on me after he wakes up from his sleep.

"No, that was Jinjy. I guess that tuna didn't agree with him."

Meydan instantly falls back to sleep.

Yihyeh b'seder, everything will be fine, I reassure myself. Self-fulfilling prophecies are for Greek tragedies.

Rock the Vote

"So, who are you voting for? Are you voting for Bibi?" Meydan's aunt uses Benjamin Netanyahu's nickname as she yells to me over the commotion of twenty family members talking, eating, and laughing during one of the weekend lunches.

Unlike in the U.S., there are no topics that are inappropriate to talk about during an Israeli meal. With the elections quickly approaching, everybody is talking politics.

"Umm," I mumble, "I'm voting for this new party that promotes the environment and religious freedom."

After living here for seven years, this is going to be the first time that I vote in Israel. I can't believe I'm still experiencing firsts here. I'll feel like a full citizen. Cast my vote. Be a part of this democracy that I have defended and help shape the future of this country.

---

24. *Kohen* means "priest" in Hebrew. Anyone with the last name Cohen, Kahn, or Katz is considered to be a descendant of a priest from First Temple times. The ultra-Orthodox believe them to be of a higher caste.

"No, no. Vote for Livni. We want Livni to win," Mira, Meydan's mom, says.

"I'm voting for them because they want to make marriage more pluralistic. They want to take the power away from the ultra-Orthodox rabbinate," I say, but they have already started talking about who is going to take which leftovers home.

"Jessica, you can vote for whoever you want," Libbi, Meydan's sister-in-law, says to me. We have grown close over the past months.

*   *   *

On Election Day, I go to my designated voting location—a high school in Tel Aviv. It is bustling with people. I wander around the hallways until I find my assigned room. I wonder what it would have felt like to go to high school in Israel. I'm jealous that my future children will get to experience high school here.

I walk into the room and see four kids sitting at a table.

"Is this where voting is?" I ask, thinking that I must be in the wrong room.

"Yes, what is your name?" one of them asks.

"Jessica Fishman."

"Jessie, Jessie, Jessie, Jessi-caaaaah ooh ah ooh ah! Now she is far away . . ."

I roll my eyes. After seven years, people are still singing that song to me. Don't they get it? I'm not her. I'm here to stay, unlike the girl in the song who runs away after a heartbreak. People will probably sing this song at my funeral. "Is this the right place?"

"Yep. Can I see your ID?"

I hand them my Israeli ID card. One of the kids gives me an envelope.

"What am I supposed to do with this?" I ask out loud.

"You put the slip of paper in it. That is how you vote."

I stare at the envelope in utter confusion and then look back at up them.

They point to a cardboard divider.

I walk behind the divider and see a bunch of pieces of cut-out paper with letters on them representing the different parties. I am supposed to pick a letter, put it in an envelope and bring the envelope back out and put it in a box. I feel like I am voting for prom king and queen—not the prime minister of one of the most recognized countries in the world. It is such an anti-climactic experience. It is so simple that even Floridians would not be confused.

After I vote, I hand them my envelope and with it my hopes that maybe things will change. Maybe my vote will make a difference. Maybe the conversion thing won't be an issue. Maybe I'll be able to get married in Israel without any problems after this election.

A few days after voting, a coalition is formed. The political system in Israel functions like a game of musical chairs. Every few years the leaders of the different parties swap positions. The new prime minister, Bibi, has already been prime minister before and he failed miserably the first time. The foreign minister is an outspoken racist. And of course there are right-wing religious parties in the coalition.

It doesn't seem like this is the type of change we need.

Car Crash

This year, the spring holidays in Israel fly by more quickly than ever. I celebrate all of them with Meydan's family. Celebrating Passover, the holiday that celebrates Jews being set free, feels so different when it is with people who I know will become my family.

On Independence Day, we celebrate by having a barbeque—just like every other Israeli. The small size of the country becomes abundantly clear on Independence Day, when every single Israeli is trying to find a spot to barbeque that some even set up on the grass median on highways.

During our barbeque, Meydan's best friend announces that he and his girlfriend got engaged. His fiancée sticks her left hand in my face to show off her ring. As I tell her how beautiful it is, my throat closes up. I can't believe that for the past few weeks, I have been celebrating the freedom of the Jewish people and of the land of Israel, when I'm still not free as Jew in my homeland. Trying to pretend that the tears I'm shedding are for their joyous occasion, I congratulate them, with an overly enthusiastic, "*Mazal tov*, congratulations!"

Now that all of the holidays with the family are over, tonight, Meydan and I are planning on spending some time alone. We're on our way to see a show together. In the passenger seat, I look around the car and think back to how I felt when I first got it. I remember how getting a car in Israel felt like a symbol that I'd survived here and that this country was really my home. The car had given me the freedom to go wherever I wanted. I was no longer stuck to the confines of walking distance or public transportation. The car had already been through an accident and had a throw-up stain in the back seat from the dog. I looked over at Meydan, who always drove my car whenever we were together.

"So, I was thinking that once the contract is up on the apartment in the *kibbutz*, we should move into another apartment together," Meydan tells me.

"Well, you know how I feel. I don't want to give up my apartment until we are engaged," I say.

Whether it is the intimacy of being close to one another in the car or the detachment of being able to look out the windshield and not having to look the other person in the eyes while talking or the combination of both, we often have serious conversations while driving.

"I know. But listen, my grandfather bought me an apartment years ago in Petach Tikva. We could live there and not have to pay rent. Plus we would be right across the street from my parents and grandparents," he says, incorrectly thinking that somehow this last point might convince me.

Even though I love his family, I think we should live more than walking distance away from them. And besides, Petach Tikva! Ick! Even though it means Gateway of Hope, it symbolizes the exact opposite to me. I have no desire to live in bleak, dreary, over-crowded, shoddy, and religious Petach Tikva. There is a Facebook group of Israelis that calls for the city's destruction. Recently, the religious families of the city protested against having their children study with Ethiopian children. If I had wanted to live in a racist city, I would have married Chris, my high-school boyfriend, moved to the US South, and hung up his Confederate flag. I want to live in vibrant Tel Aviv, where I can smell the sea air, where there are young, liberal people.

"Well, I don't know how I feel about that. I mean, are we planning on getting married first?" I ask. He knows that I'm afraid to leave my apartment, my only home in Israel, before our future is set.

Meydan doesn't answer. Instead his whole body tightens up. He stares straight ahead and grips the steering wheel. "Well, there are a few things we need to work out," he says, uncomfortably adjusting his body-weight in the car seat.

When he says this, I'm transported back to the first night that I met Meydan's cousin and her boyfriend. After a lovely dinner at a café in Tel Aviv we said goodbye to them and Meydan turned to me and said, "You know, he isn't *really* Jewish."

I let go of his hand and froze. Not wanting to hear the answer, I forced myself to ask him, "What do you mean?"

He nonchalantly replied, "His mom converted, so he isn't technically Jewish."

I had snapped back at him, "What do you mean? Of course he is! He was in the army. He speaks Hebrew. He has lived in Israel his entire life. He grew up Jewish.

He knows nothing else than being Jewish. His identity is Jewish. And if his mom converted, then they both are Jewish. Don't you, someone who prays every morning, know anything about *halacha*? You are never supposed to remind a convert that they weren't born Jewish!"

"Yeah, I guess you are right," Meydan had quietly conceded, maybe trying to avoid a fight.

I didn't have anything else to say. I was too busy choking back my tears. I could not believe his ignorance, the blatant discrimination. How could one Jew whose grandfather had survived the Holocaust say such a thing about another Jew? Didn't he know that Jewish converts were gassed, burned, and tortured right along with other Jews? All of these questions had stormed through my head as I wondered to myself, what will he think when I tell him the truth about me? Will he reject me?

As we drive around a curve, I'm jolted back to the present, into my car, which used to feel like my freedom mobile, but is now suffocating me.

"If you want to marry me, then you have to go through a rabbinate conversion," Meydan stipulated.

Every little girl dreams of a romantic marriage proposal from the fairytales. No one ever dreams of getting a marriage ultimatum. Hamas has made better proposals to Israel than Meydan is making to me.

I stare out of the window feeling rejected by both the man and the country I love.

I don't understand what is happening. No one ever pays attention to any laws in Israel. When it became illegal to smoke in public places, police officers wouldn't even bother coming to bars to hand out tickets. Nobody parks legally. People don't even bother slowing down to the speed limit when they see a police officer. I can't understand why all of a sudden people actually care about this law.

We keep driving forward through the night in silence. The seatbelt around my waist tightens as if trying to protect me from a crash. My heavy, uneven breathing is the only noise either one of us hears. Each of us continues to look forward through the windshield, not daring to look at the other person. The red lights of the cars in front of us become blurry and the bright white lights of the cars coming toward us seem to get brighter like stars scattered across the night sky. I hold my breath, hoping for one of those cars to crash into us and change this ill-fated path we are driving down.

However, the cars keep zooming past us. I look outside the passenger-side window. A car full of people laughing and enjoying their time together pulls up next to us. I long to be with them, but I am sucked back into the car, into this new reality. I do not know how to respond to him, I cannot find my voice. I feel my hands shaking and quiet tears begin streaming down my face.

When I finally look at Meydan, I see his face, with his eyes fixed forward, showing no empathy and a stubborn, clenched jaw. It does not matter to him that I walked to synagogue in the freezing Minnesota winter every Shabbat, that I went to Jewish summer camp, that we lit the candles as a family every Shabbat, that I fasted every Yom Kippur, that we said the blessings before every meal, that I said the *shema* as a child before I went to bed every night, that my family kept kosher, that my dad was president of the synagogue, that I went to Jewish day school, that my mother was the chapter president of Hadassah and gave up her family and her past to keep a Jewish household, that my family had participated in Jewish Agency missions to Hungary and Romania, that I made *aliyah* to Israel, that I struggled to survive here, that I learned Hebrew, that I volunteered for the IDF. No, what matters to him is the opinion of some primitive male rabbis who are busy trying to get as much *gelt* as possible from the state by exploiting God's name. I can't help thinking about my sorority sisters, the girls who preferred Prada over Israel, and how they would be considered more Jewish than I am in this country.

Meydan refuses to look over at me to see my tears that he caused.

I want to jump out of the car, but the seatbelt holds me in place. With each tear, I feel my jaw getting tighter and breathing getting shallower. With all of the things I'd been through here, I think that this might be the thing that breaks me.

It makes me think that my friends and family spent a lot of wasted time distressed about terror attacks, because all the major traumas in my life in Israel have not come from terrorists, but from Israelis themselves.

I wrap my arms around myself, trying to hug myself, trying to calm myself down. I don't think I have any energy left to survive this country. I thought that I was tough enough for anything, but I realize that I might not be.

Meydan parks the car and we get out without looking at each other. When we shut the doors, it almost feels as if the conversation is left inside the car, like a rancid fart that has been contained. He takes my hand and we walk into the show. I try to forget what we talked about, but it feels as if my life in Israel will forever be changed by this night.

*   *   *

The next morning, I wake up in the same bed as Meydan, but in a completely different world.

There is a piercing pain inside my left ear. My body must be trying to physically reject what it heard the night before. I look over at Meydan sleeping peacefully. I get out of bed. I don't even want to be in the same room as him. I pack my things. I grab Jinjy and head to my home in Tel Aviv. I'm so happy that I never gave up my apartment.

I'm in the same car as last night, but this time I'm in the driver's seat. I drive down the same road as last night, but in the light it looks completely different. Everyone is going about their Shabbat as if nothing happened. Their world is completely the same. It's only mine that has turned upside down.

I call Bar in Paris.

"Baaaaarrrrrr," I cry into the phone. "You won't believe what Meydan said to me last night."

"Jessica, I can't understand you when you cry. Calm down and speak clearly."

"Baaaaarrrrrr, it's the worst. I can't even say it," I'm weeping so hard that I can't even see in front of me. Thankfully, I'm at a red light now.

"Oh, Jessica, don't even say it. I don't want to hear." Bar knows that Meydan asked me to convert without me having to say it. He knows it's my worst fear, because it's his worst fear also.

"What am I going to do?" I ask.

Neither of us have an answer.

*   *   *

At my apartment, I sit down with Orli on her balcony. I'm stroking Jinjy to calm myself down.

"Jessica, don't take it personally. It's not about you," Orli says.

"How can I not take it personally? He's asking *me* to convert! Why can't he just realize that the rabbinate shouldn't have a stronghold on religion? I don't understand why he wants their approval? He isn't religious!" I weep.

"Listen, I know you don't want to hear this, but I'm not religious, and I still want to get married in the rabbinate. It's important to me," she says. "Listen, you can get married in Cyprus, just like Lital's friend, the divorced one who married a *kohen*."

"Why should I have more rights in a country where I'm not a citizen than in a country in which I live, served in the army, and call home?" I ask, but still thinking that I'll mention it to Meydan.

"Hey! What's up?" Hadas, one of Orli's girlfriends with whom we used to go dancing on Friday nights, walks in. "What is wrong? Why are you crying? Why are you holding your face like that? Did you get hit?" she asks as soon as she sees me. Her boyfriend walks in right behind her.

"Oh, it's nothing. I think I have an ear infection," I respond.

"I know what will make you feel better," she says, smiling and pulling out a joint.

"You should ask their opinion about this," Orli suggests.

I tell them about Meydan's ultimatum. Orli looks over at Hadas' boyfriend and says, "Don't you want to get married in the rabbinate?"

"I don't think I really care. But if there was anybody causing that much pain to the woman I love, I'd say fuck them and throw a Molotov cocktail on their front step," he says as he stands up and makes a throwing motion with his arm.

I look over at him and smile. I wish Meydan would say that. I wish Meydan would have that desire, that strength to rebel against the authorities, and stand up for me.

*   *   *

When I get back to our apartment on the kibbutz, Meydan and I barely say hello to each other. The pain from my ear has increased and radiated out to the entire left side of my face. I can't touch it without being in pain. I can't chew. I can't smile. I can't kiss. Not that I'm interested in doing any of those right now.

Meydan, fixated only on my physical pain, insists that I go to the doctor the next day.

The doctor tells me that it isn't an ear infection. "Your jaw is inflamed from clenching. Has anything stressful happened that would cause you to clench your

jaw?" the doctor asks in a heavy Russian accent. And I
burst into tears.

Gotta Have Faith

I stare at my computer screen at work. I can't get any
work done. I open Google and type in "Conversion and
rabbinate"

I'm holding my jaw. It still hurts, even though I'm
taking anti-inflammatory pills. I wonder what would
happen to me if I actually went through a conversion. I
would probably get lockjaw.

I read article after article about the monopoly the
rabbinate has over religion and their crooked, corrupt,
and criminal actions. I read an article about how
women were refused a *get*, a divorce certificate, because
in the Orthodox system, husbands have total control
over divorces. I read articles about how the rabbinate
blackmails organizations and accepts bribes. It seems
the only difference between the rabbinate and the
Vatican is that Dan Brown has yet to write a book about
the corruption of the former.

I read horror story after horror story about how
the rabbinate humiliates American immigrants by
doubting their Jewish identity and demanding unat-
tainable proof. About how the rabbinate has begun
retroactively revoking women's conversions, making
their marriage and all of their legal rights null and void.
About entire families whose lives have been destroyed
because of political rifts between the rabbis in the
rabbinate. About women being thrown out of conversion programs for being seen wearing pants on the
street.

Friends have suggested that I go through the
Orthodox conversion and just pretend. But if I refuse
to fake orgasms, then there is no way that I'm going
to fake being ultra-Orthodox. Orthodox Judaism is
against everything that I stand for as a feminist and as
a free-thinking, intellectual human being. They make

women sit in the back of buses. They don't even count women as human beings for prayer purposes.

All of a sudden, I have an idea. This is Israel; everyone can be bought, especially the religious.

I type into Google search: *Bribe the rabbinate*
No search results.

I type into Google search: *Deceiving the rabbinate*
No search results.

I type into Google search: *Lying to the rabbinate*
No search results.

I guess I found the one thing that Google doesn't have the answer for.

As I'm deep in thought trying to find a solution, my phone rings. Maybe it's Meydan, apologizing, realizing that he made a big mistake.

"Shalom, Jessica."

"Shalom"

"This is Rivka, I'm calling about the graphic project that you asked us to work on."

"Yes, thank you. Will it be done by the deadline?" I ask, looking at my watch.

"*B'ezrat Hashem*, with God's help," Rivka, one of the multiple religious women working at the company, responds.

I've been in Israel nearly a decade and I still don't know if this means things are good or bad. "Well, is it going to be done by the end of the day, per my request?" I ask, getting annoyed.

"*B'ezrat Hashem*," Rivka responds again. Probably looking at her watch, because at 4:00 P.M. on the dot she will leave and go back home to make dinner for her eight kids and her husband who refuses to work because he is too busy praying all day.

"Rivka, I don't want God's help! I want *your* help! I'm paying *you* to get it done, *not* God! I want *you* to work on this, *not* God! God hasn't done anything for me lately! It isn't like we're talking about the messiah!" I erupt, misplacing my anger. "So, is it going to get done?"

"*B'ezra* . . ." she stops before going any further, "I'll make sure of it."

I try to imagine what would happen if the IRS responded to tax refund questions or if FedEx answered package arrival questions by saying, "with God's help."

I go back to looking for a solution, knowing that as long as I'm dealing with the primitive rabbinate, I'll need something a lot stronger than God's help.

Facebook:
Not Just for Jewish Geography or Stalking Your Ex

The same people who don't even know I'm alive are ruining my life. They're taking over my life. Every conversation I have is about them. Every thought I have is about them.

After meeting with Tali, from the army, for a cup of coffee last Shabbat, I've become more outraged with Israeli society.

When I was telling her what I've been going through and my outrage with the rabbinate, she stopped me and said, "This is a Jewish country. I think that the rabbinate should have *more* control."

"Are you serious?" I asked.

"Yes," and then she tried to connect religion with the security of the state. She sounded like the Taliban to me.

"You know Tali, if the rabbinate had more power, then we wouldn't be able to sit here right now drinking coffee on Shabbat. You wouldn't have been able to drive here. And you would certainly not be able to wear that shirt with your boobs hanging out," I said.

She didn't even try to button up her shirt after I said that, in fact she arched her back a bit more.

The only reason I could think of for these obvious inconsistencies in Israelis' logic is that they have been brainwashed by the rabbinate. The fact that they are sanctioned by the government gives them the type of legitimacy that the ultra-Orthodox are not afforded from Jews in the United States.

I start posting a new Facebook status every day to express my outrage with the rabbinate and how they're corrupting Judaism.

Jessica Fishman: "Absolute faith corrupts as absolutely as absolute power but absolute power is corrupt only in the hands of the absolutely faithful." —Anonymous
10 Likes

Jessica Fishman: "I distrust those people who know so well what God wants them to do because I notice it always coincides with their own desires." —Susan B. Anthony
5 Likes, 3 Comments

Jessica Fishman: "With or without religion, you would have good people doing good things and evil people doing evil things. But for good people to do evil things, that takes religion." —Steven Weinberg
12 Likes, 5 Comments

Jessica Fishman: "Men never do evil so completely and cheerfully as when they do it from religious conviction." —Blaise Pascal
7 Likes, 1 Comment

Jessica Fishman: "The word god is for me nothing more than the expression and product of human weaknesses, the Bible a collection of honorable, but still primitive legends which are nevertheless pretty childish. No interpretation no matter how subtle can (for me) change this." —Albert Einstein
3 Likes, 6 Comments

Jessica Fishman: "Few people are capable of expressing with equanimity opinions which differ from the prejudices of their social environment. Most people are even incapable of forming such opinions." —Albert Einstein
2 Likes, 4 Comments

The last one is for Meydan, hoping that he'll realize that he's stuck in his thinking because he grew up in a country where there is limited religious freedom.

I hope he'll see that the reason he's stuck thinking that there's only one true form of Judaism is simply because the state sanctions and supports only one form. Just as I had wanted to understand what it was like to live here as an Israeli, I find myself wishing that Meydan will also come to a broader understanding. I wish that he would understand that there is a more progressive form of Judaism and that he doesn't have to be held captive by his surroundings, his family, or by his family's history. I wish that he didn't have to cling onto this faith to make sense of the world, to make sense of the atrocities during the Holocaust, or to make sense of the threats against Israel. I wish that he could find the strength to break free from this oppression and his self-imposed pressures to be the ideal Jewish son and grandson, and be strong enough to be my partner.

Double Standards

"I prefer not to say my name," I say, afraid that the rabbinate might have wire-tapping capabilities or a black book of names of people who aren't allowed to get married in Israel.

I'm searching all by myself for a solution. Meydan isn't helping me. We've grown apart. I cry every day and a few weeks ago I began sleeping on the couch with Jinjy. Our apartment has grown quiet. We barely speak to each other anymore. But I'm still desperate to make this work. My future is at stake. I'm certain that if we overcome this, everything will work out.

"That is fine," said the rabbi of ITIM, an independent non-profit that provides information and advocacy for the Jewish lifecycle.

While hopelessly looking for a solution, I remembered the article that I'd read the day I caught Meydan putting on tefillin—the article about the American woman who had to prove to the rabbinate that she was a Jew by providing a photo of her grandmother's headstone. The article had mentioned ITIM as the organization that helped her.

"Just so you know, we're completely confidential and are even going through a process of increasing our security system," he said, ineffectively trying to comfort me.

I told him my story. I told him of Meydan's demands.

This rabbi offered three different solutions: converting, having a civil marriage abroad, or having a religious, non-Orthodox marriage abroad. None of these were helpful. I knew of these options. I was fine with having a religious marriage abroad, but Meydan refused.

"I have a forged *ketuba*. I want to know what else I need to prove to the rabbinate that I'm Jewish," I said.

I don't even know why I'm searching so hard for a solution to getting married with the rabbinate's blessing. I no longer want to be married by a rabbi in the rabbinate. Not after what I've learned. I don't like that the rabbinate's wedding ceremony is not a mutual agreement. In their ceremony, the man is actually buying the woman and I'm certainly not for sale. Deep down, there had been a part of me that used to want the rabbinate's acceptance, but now, I just want Meydan to accept me.

"I don't really think that fooling the rabbinate is the route to go," he says hesitantly, but continues. "There is a double standard for Israelis and immigrants. Israelis need two male—not female—witnesses, to say that the woman is Jewish and a single virgin."

Wait! Women can't be witnesses either? Is their eyesight worse than men's? And a virgin? What era are we in? Is this Taliban-ruled Afghanistan? Or is this supposed to be the only democratic country in the Middle East?

He continues. "Immigrants need a letter from a rabbinate-approved rabbi abroad who knows you and your family. If you can't get that, then they might ask for the *ketubah* of your great-grandmother and great-great-grandmother," he replies.

"Fine, thank you," I say, now armed with all the information I need to fool the rabbinate. If they want a picture of gravestones like in that article, then I'll use Photoshop.

Not Jewish Until Proven Guilty

"Jessica, it was horrible," my dad says over the phone.

My parents had agreed to my request to find a rabbinate-approved rabbi from Chabad and convince him to give me a letter testifying to my Jewish identity. It turns out that the Chabad Houses are the rabbinate's international network of rabbis around the world—sort of like McDonald's franchises, but without the bacon.

"We felt like we were raped by this rabbi. I'm so sorry that we couldn't help you." He begins sobbing.

"What happened?" I ask, trying to hide the quiver in my voice. I don't know if I'm sadder that my parents have now been hurt by this or that this might be the end of the road for me having a Jewish wedding in Israel.

"This rabbi started asking mom and I questions. When mom told the rabbi that she had converted, he refused to even speak to her," my dad sobbed. I could barely understand him through his and my tears.

My mom, who has always been proud of being a Jew by choice, had told this rabbi the truth, fully believing that all of the Jewish people are accepting and caring. She had been taught that *halacha*, Jewish law, forbids a Jew from reminding a convert that they converted. She has now been Jewish for more than half her life.

"Then he said to her that you were not born with a Jewish soul because a Jewish soul is formed in the womb of a Jewish mother, and that Mom is not a Jewish mother." My dad continues crying.

This rabbi had penetrated and violated my mom's body with his words. He defined and symbolically controlled her body without her permission. I want to kick something. I'm furious. I can't believe that my parents are suffering so much at the hands of this man, who has the audacity to call himself a rabbi.

After I hang up with my dad, I call up this so-called rabbi.

"You just spoke to my parents. I want to let you know that you are a horrible person, rabbi, and Jew. You do more damage to Judaism than good."

He attacks me back like the rabid rabbi that he is. The conversation continues for over an hour. I argue *halacha* with him. He tells me that Reform rabbis aren't even rabbis and that they all eat bacon. I tell him that is like saying all ultra-Orthodox spit on little girls for dressing immodestly. He tries to offer me conversion classes. I tell him I'm already a Jew and don't need a conversion, and that all I want from him is a letter proving my Jewishness. He refuses. I offer him a bribe.

I hang up the phone wanting to send him a year's supply of bacon.

When I tell Meydan what happened, he is unsympathetic.

"You wanted to lie to the rabbinate? That sounds like bad karma," he says.

Despite the fact that the whole rabbinate thing is important to Meydan, he isn't doing anything to resolve the situation. He is strangely absent from all of my efforts—sort of like Bush was after Hurricane Katrina.

I explode. "What the hell does karma have to do with it? First of all, wrong fucking religion! And second of all, the rabbinate is so corrupt that just dealing with them brings bad karma. Besides, why don't you do something to help me? This is your goddamn request! Why have I been doing all of the work?"

After that Meydan agrees to talk to the ITIM rabbi and to try to look for a solution together.

Maybe things will work out after all.

12

Freedom From Religion

Sitting on opposite ends of the couch, the same couch on which we cuddled the first night we moved into this apartment, Meydan and I are watching the news.

The biggest story of the past few weeks is the reoccurring riots in Jerusalem—the religious, but not the spiritual, capital of the world. The penguins have been rioting every Shabbat against a parking lot that is open next to the Old City. The Riot of the Penguins, as I like to call it, consists of them throwing rocks at fellow Jewish police officers on Shabbat—a day when they are not supposed to be lifting or carrying anything—in order to protest other Jews desecrating Shabbat.

As I watch the news report, I think back to a hike with friends in the Golan Heights a few summers ago. It was sweltering outside. When we reached the natural pool, we were dripping with sweat. We stripped down to our bathing suits and jumped into the refreshing water with the rest of the Israelis. After cooling off, we got out and sat on the rocks and began eating our packed lunches.

As we ate, a religious woman with her two young kids turned to me and politely asked me, "Do you mind putting your shirt on? My husband just left because we are religious and he feels uncomfortable being around women who aren't modest."

I reluctantly but politely agreed.

Her husband came back. And then a second later, she whipped out her breast and began feeding her baby.

I looked at her in shock. I don't have anything against breastfeeding in public, but don't ask me to cover up my stomach when a second later you go and show your nipple to the entire world like you're at Woodstock.

Everything they do is as hypocritical as the Shabbat elevators[25]. I wish I hadn't put my shirt back on.

My phone rings in the middle of the news report and brings me back to the present. It's my parents. I walk into the other room and shut the door.

Ever since Meydan made his conversion demand, I talk with my parents every day, especially my mom. I need their support as much as they need mine. In all the years I have been here, I have never missed them as much as I do now. It is strange to me that Meydan, who seems to be so close to his family, has yet to tell them about what we are going through. I've begun to notice that even though there is always laughing and noise at his family meals, they never talk about anything real. Instead the entire conversation involves everyone asking one another if they need or want something, like food, clothes, laundry, or money. No one ever really talks about their feelings.

I hang up with my parents. I wish they were here.

I sit back down on my side of the couch. Meydan hasn't moved. He's still staring at the TV, which is now broadcasting an undercover exposé about a religious widow who has to undergo a humiliating ceremony

---

25. Shabbat elevators are elevators which are pre-set to work in an automatic operating mode in order to circumvent the Jewish law requiring observers abstain from operating electricity on the Sabbath.

called *haliza*, where in order to remarry she has to take off the shoe of her dead husband's brother.

The woman is the only woman in the room that is full of what I assume are smelly, bearded penguins, examining her as if she is a specimen in a laboratory. In the voiceover, she tells of how her religious brother-in-law has been extorting her ever since her husband died in the Yom Kippur War.

I look over at Meydan.

"What do you think of this?" I ask him, in all seriousness.

"They are crazy. They are idiots. They are fanatics," he says.

A feel a glimmer of hope. My eyes widen.

"*Really?* Then why do you want their approval? Why do you want to be married by the same people who believe in this crap?" I ask, honestly curious.

"Because, we live in Israel. We don't live in the United States where there is Conservative and Reform Judaism. We live in Israel. Here there is the Orthodox. Here there is the rabbinate," he states.

Really? You want the approval of the rabbinate? Why? They are so screwed up. The chief rabbi made an announcement during the swine flu outbreak that the media and public should stop referring to it as swine flu since pigs are not kosher. Then they went on to promote a flight full of praying and swaying rabbis to fly over the country to give the Israeli nation their blessing, as if that would work better than vaccines. Isn't it bad enough that the health minister is from one of the religious parties, and instead of allocating part of the budget to medicine and medical equipment, he decided to add more synagogues in hospitals so people can pray away their illnesses? Based on this, Scientologists Tom Cruise and John Travolta have just as many qualifications to be Israel's health minister.

"Well, I want to take our kids to a Conservative synagogue here. I don't want them raised in an Orthodox synagogue where the women are separated from the men like when the South was segregated." Trying to take a stand for my vision, I sit up a little taller.

"Are you an idiot? There are no Conservative or Reform synagogues in Israel."

My hand instinctively moves to my ear and gently rubs it, remembering the pain I had the night he gave me the ultimatum.

"Of course there are. I've been to them. There just are not as many Conservative and Reform synagogues in Israel because the Orthodox synagogues are the only ones that get government funding." I, the immigrant, understand more about the religious and political affairs of the country that he was born in. What should I expect from a guy who served in an army unit called *moran*[26]?

"Well, I don't want to go to a Conservative synagogue. Every time I see a woman wearing a *kippah* it makes me want to throw up," Meydan says, not having enough knowledge to win the argument on an intellectual level.

And why do Israelis think they are always right, even when they aren't? They're like teenagers.

"I grew up wearing a *kippah* in synagogue! Besides, it doesn't say anywhere that women can't wear them, it just says men have to," I yell back as he gets up off the couch and heads toward the bedroom. I don't bother mentioning that he isn't wearing a *kippah*.

For someone who claims Judaism is so important, he really doesn't know anything about the religion.

Turning around, Meydan says more calmly, "Listen, Jessica, the thing is that I'm just worried about our kids. I don't want them to have to go through the same thing you are going through.

---

26. *Moran* is an elite unit in the IDF that works with precise guided munitions, but to a native English-speaker it sounds like *moron*.

I look down at my hands, now in my lap, and think to myself, *the only reason I'm going through this is because of you. Because you can't see that if we marry outside the rabbinate, we would be living above the law. You see it as living below the law.*

He goes on, "There must be some easier type of conversion since you are Jewish, since you grew up Jewish, since you served in the army and all. It is not like you are going to be converting from scratch."

Did he just compare converting to making a batch of cookies?

He doesn't get it! I scream in my head. Then I scream out loud, "The rabbinate doesn't care about the army! They are the same ones that don't serve in the army. They don't think it's their duty to serve in the army. They think that praying in a yeshiva is a more effective defense strategy. They're the same people that don't even believe that the State of Israel exists because God didn't bring about its existence, but are somehow able to get over that belief and still take all of the funds of this 'non-existent' state for welfare and as a salary for working in the non-existent state's government."

He doesn't know what he's talking about. He doesn't know the rules, the laws, the politics, and the complexities of what he's asking. And he isn't doing any research to try to understand. I've called my rabbi, rabbi friends, and rabbis of friends. He says he doesn't even have a rabbi to call. I had to explain half of these laws to him. If I hadn't explained this double standard of the "who is a Jew" question, then he wouldn't even have known it existed.

Meydan walks into the bathroom to brush his teeth. Sitting on the couch, feeling completely alone, I try to figure out who he represents in this journey of mine. Is he the scarecrow without a brain to think for himself, brainwashed by the rabbinate and its control in the government? Is he the lion without enough courage to take a stand? Or is he the tin man without a heart to love me and support me, unable to forget about this whole rabbinate marriage-conversion thing?

I think back to over a year ago, when I finally worked up the courage to tell him what my mom's conversion actually meant for marriage.

Even though he had already known that my mom converted, I somehow knew that he didn't know its impact. We had been sitting in the car outside his parents' place after lunch when I, the immigrant, had taught him, the *sabra*, about the history of our country. I, the secular, had explained, to him, the "religious," about Judaism. I told him about Ben-Gurion's concession to the religious over sixty years ago. I explained to him that it meant that I couldn't marry in Israel, because the rabbinate today has complete control over marriages, conversions, and burials.

When he heard this, I saw his whole body tighten and then he asked me, "What will this mean for our children?"

Like a movie was being projected on his forehead, I could see all of his thoughts flashing through his head—his grandfather behind the fences of Auschwitz, himself wrapping tefillin in the morning, lighting Shabbat candles with his grandmother, fasting on Yom Kippur, and his mother's Jewish cooking on holidays. I saw all of his Jewish guilt from being a descendent of a Holocaust survivor cross his face. It was as if his Jewish identity was owned by his past as much as mine was.

I had told him then that they would be just like me, "Jewish in terms of the State of Israel, but not in terms of the rabbinate."

He hadn't responded. Instead he had given me a kiss, got out of the car, and shut the door.

I had sat alone in the car, with the truth out in the open.

I had tried to push the subject out of my mind after that conversation, but it stayed with me every day of our relationship. I guess somewhere, somehow, I always knew that he wouldn't be strong enough to deal with it.

I should have just told him that I preferred getting married abroad and saved myself from these fights. I should just have used the forged *ketuba* and never told him about the purgatory that the state created for me. But, deep down, I needed his full acceptance.

The subject was not mentioned again until that fateful night when I willed the car to crash.

Standing up from the couch, I yell back at him, "There is no easier way!" I feel like I'm sinking and no one is throwing me a life jacket. "Don't you get it? The rabbinate doesn't care! They just want money and control!" I don't understand how Bibi privatized everything from El Al to the Israel Electric Company, but marriage he left under the control of the Jewish Taliban.

He looks back at me with blank eyes and a mouth full of toothpaste. Meydan is as ignorant of the world around him as I had been naïve when I first came here and actually believed that the Zionism I was taught in Jewish day school was the same that existed in Israel. I grew up in a country where religion was individual, but he grew up in Israel, where the Orthodox own everyone's Jewishness. This country is not the Land of Oz for Jews. This is not a land where all Jews are family. This is not a land where Jews are not discriminated against. This is not a Jewish democracy like the founders of Israel had imagined.

If Ben-Gurion and Herzl knew what this country has become they would be turning in their graves.

He comes out of the bathroom with fresh breath and a damp face. I put my hands on his biceps and look into eyes. "Meydan, this is my identity. It's not a haircut. Being Jewish, being a Zionist is the core of my identity, and you asking me to convert is stripping that away," I say calmly, trying to get him to see my pain. I feel like my sense of self is being chipped away, my idealism destroyed, my identity stolen.

I let go of his arms and look over at Meydan's tefillin sitting on the shelf.

This Judaism, this Israeli Judaism, is not the type of Judaism I grew up with. I grew up with a Judaism that cared more about loving thy neighbor and treating life and people with respect. I grew up with a Judaism where community, justice, education, and social activism were at its core.

This Israeli Judaism is where people care more about avoiding lighting the Sabbath candles even a second too late, or picking the microscopic bugs out of rice. This is a Judaism where people throw rocks to prevent people from breaking the Sabbath, or spit at women who aren't modest enough. This is a Judaism where people refuse to make a phone call on the Sabbath to the police to save a child from being beaten, but will still use a Shabbat elevator or watch TV on Shabbat with an automatic timer. This is Judaism where the women wear expensive wigs to cover their heads after being married, but if they find out that the hair had been donated by Hindus during idol worship, they prefer to burn the wigs instead of donating them to cancer patients. This is a Judaism where they are so concerned with following the letter of the law to the strictest degree possible that they forget the spirit of it. These penguins, the rabbinate, the ultra-Orthodox, have hijacked Judaism from us, from Israel, from the world.

Meydan doesn't respond. Instead he sits back on the couch to watch more TV. I walk into the bedroom. Without changing, I crawl into bed and quietly cry under the covers. I'm scared that if we can't work this out, the life I've built will fall apart. I'm scared that Meydan will never accept me. The *ketuba* that I've been safeguarding for years to protect my Jewish identity can't protect me from my need to be loved for who I am. I feel my future crumbling away. With the noise of the TV in the background, I feel my dreams of raising an Israeli family fade into darkness as I fall into a dreamless sleep.

Kosher is as Kosher Does

"I don't understand. Shouldn't there be an easier way for her to convert? She is already Jewish. This is just a technicality, logistics," Meydan is finally on the phone with the rabbi from ITIM. We both stayed home this morning in order to make this phone call together.

Earlier that week, we had talked about the options of getting married abroad. He had finally agreed to consider it. I even made him sign an informal contract on a scrap piece of paper that he wouldn't rule out the option . . . and good thing I did, because he totally forgot that he promised. I don't understand why he keeps focusing on the conversion option with this rabbi. The whole point of the conversation was to look at other options. Options that we could both live with.

"I do have connections and could probably find an easier conversion process, but it sounds like your fiancée doesn't want to convert. I've talked to her in depth and it sounds like it is too painful of an idea, too detrimental to her self-identity. There are plenty of other options for you to marry her," the rabbi says on our speakerphone.

"Well, Judaism is really important to me. I keep kosher. I wrap tefillin every morning," Meydan states as if he is the authority on religion.

Agggghhhhh! I scream in my head as my hands pull at my hair. You think you are so special because you wrap tefillin in the morning? Well, you aren't! You are a fake! You are a fraud! You are a cliché! Plenty of Israeli men wrap tefillin in the morning . . . right after their one-night stands or right before they go to eat their bacon cheeseburger . . . Oh, my God . . . Meydan is a cliché. He doesn't even know who he is. He'll never stand up for me. He's a coward. I'd hoped for a Martin Luther King, Jr., but instead I'm stuck with an even lamer version of Kirk Cameron.

"That is something that we Orthodox do," the rabbi replies, agreeing with Meydan's comment about wrapping tefillin.

Is taking your *kippah* off as soon as you're done praying something that the Orthodox do? Is driving, cooking, and spending money on Shabbat something the Orthodox do? Is *fucking me* out of wedlock something that the Orthodox do? I want to scream out loud, but instead it all just echoes in my head.

"Okay, well, we'll look into these options," Meydan says, fully knowing that the only option he considers "kosher" enough is me converting, since he isn't strong enough to take a stand. "Thank you for your help."

He hangs up the phone and looks at me crying on the couch. "We have to go. We're late to see the apartment."

In a few months we're supposed to be moving into the apartment that his grandfather gave him.

In silence, we sit in my car. Everything outside is a blur. I can't see anything through my tears.

For the past few months the only time we talk to each other is to argue about marriage and religion. I cry every day. He has yet to shed a tear. I realized a long time ago that the affection of Israeli men should not be confused with emotions. There must be a training course in the army that teaches them how not to be emotional.

When we get to the apartment, I realize that it is literally across the street from his parents . . . and grandparents. My life is going to become the Israeli version of *Everybody Loves Raymond*, which is a hundred times worse than the American version, since Israelis are pushy, bossy, and have no sense of boundaries or privacy. It is bad enough living ten minutes from them—his dad stops over every day unannounced, his mom brings food and laundry, and they are always asking him to come over to do jobs around the house. The country, being the size of New Jersey, is small enough as it is. It is not like we can move that far away from his family, but that doesn't mean we have to live next door to them.

I get out of the car. I look at the street sign. The street of our new home is named *Asari Tzion*, Prisoners of Zion. I think to myself that there must be a God, because there is no way that this type of irony can be random.

"Isn't it great? I can't wait to fix it up!" Meydan says with enthusiasm after we walk in. We are standing in the middle of the dark, dusty, and grimy apartment. I feel as if the walls are closing in on me.

"Let's go see the bedrooms." Meydan leads me down the hall.

Israeli apartments are so small. There isn't even room to breathe. There is no oxygen in here.

"And this is the bathroom," Meydan says.

I start sweating.

"And this can be the laundry room," Meydan adds, winking at me.

I'm having a hot flash.

"One of these rooms can be my office."

There's no air moving inside. There's no light. It's dark in the middle of the day.

"This is the bomb shelter. We can use this for storage or something. And look at this big window in the living room, isn't it great?"

I feel like Carrie in *Sex and the City* when she had an allergic reaction to the cheap wedding gown. I feel like I'm having an allergic reaction to this low-class, bigoted neighborhood. Just the thought of the religious demonstrating against Ethiopian children being in schools together with the Ashkenazi children is making me sick. I don't want to raise children in a racist neighborhood like this. I don't want to raise children with a twisted sense of religion.

Or maybe I'm becoming allergic to a future with Meydan.

*   *   *

Before I know it, we've packed up everything from our kibbutz apartment into separate boxes—the things headed for my apartment and the things that will be stored at the new one until we finish with renovations. While we are still together, our future paths are looking very different. It is hard saying goodbye to the life we had here, the open door policy for dogs and friends, and even the cramped lifestyle we have shared over the past year.

Seeing the emptiness of our apartment makes me doubt that we're strong enough to overcome the reign of the rabbinate.

*   *   *

We live the next two months in transit. We spend nights at my shared apartment in Tel Aviv with Orli. Meydan travels around during the day, sometimes at the new apartment with the builders, sometimes at coffee shops, and sometimes at his parents' house. Jinjy, our dog, gets schlepped around depending on our schedules. Meydan mostly lives out of the new car he just bought, never fully moving in to any place.

As our living situation becomes more and more separate, so do our lives. Like an old sweater, our relationship is slowly unraveling. We're coming to an end. He had told me then, in his own words, that fateful night in the car that I was not Jewish enough for him, but I would not hear it. I could not hear it. He had become my future in this country. He had become Israel to me. If he can't accept my Jewishness, then the country won't either. If he can't accept me, then I won't be able to live here anymore. So, while he's busy putting all of his energy into fixing up the apartment, I keep fighting for this relationship and for what I've always hoped would be our future. I feel like I'm trying to revive a person, even though I know he's already dead.

"Mira, I need your help," I say. This is my last attempt.

I'm in Meydan's mom's crowded and messy kitchen. She is in her pajamas making a feast for a regular Tuesday night dinner.

"Sure, anything," she says.

"Well, uh . . . I don't know how to say this . . ." I begin crying. Meydan still hasn't told anyone in his close-knit family about what is going on between us. I think it is because he is ashamed, but I don't know if it is of me or of himself.

She stops and looks at me. "Did Meydan hurt you?"

"No, not exactly."

I tell her the whole story.

"Well, of course I accept you and we accept you, but what about the children?" she says, as though I'd be passing along some terrible genetic disease to them. "You know, Moti, my husband, used to be like Meydan. He used to wrap tefillin, but after we got married, he stopped," she rambles, her eyes wandering until they fixate on the corner of the counter. "Look at this! The counter is broken. You see? I have to do everything around here by myself. I super-glued this piece back on yesterday and now it is falling off again."

I've got to keep her on track, I think to myself.

"Mira, what should I do? I can't convert. I just can't do it," I cry.

Mikah, Meydan's younger sister who is twenty-five years old and still living at home, walks into the kitchen.

"Look at you, Jessica. The onions must be getting to your eyes. I'll open up a window," Mira says trying to hide the fact that I'm crying from Mikah.

She doesn't know that both Mikah and Libbi, Meydan's sister-in-law, already know the whole story. I told them the story months ago. For how close their family is, they are full of secrets. I know Mikah will keep my secret, since I'm keeping her secret about dating a German Muslim.

Mikah walks out.

"Well, Jessica, if you want him, then you need to do what he wants," she says, as if she is reading a script from *Leave it to Beaver*.

The entire kitchen turns black and white.

Scarlet Letter

After months of arguing, Meydan and I broke up. We were driving in my car and he pulled over to pick up a religious hitchhiker. I was furious, I didn't want a man who didn't consider me Jewish in my car.

"What are you doing?" I had asked Meydan.

"Offering him a ride," he replied.

Is he doing this dafka, *purposely?* I thought to myself. I made a disgusted face, thinking back to when I was sixteen years old and visiting Jerusalem on my teen tour. I had gone into Meah She'arim, an extremely religious neighborhood to buy *challah* bread for Shabbat and when I asked a religious man for directions, he refused to even look at me.

Meydan looked at me. "You shouldn't hate them. We are all brothers."

I know that the religious penguins typically inbreed, but I certainly don't consider them my family. They make me feel like a disowned child. Telling me to love them like brothers is like telling Rodney King to go up and hug the police officers who beat him.

"Where are you going *achi*, brother?" Meydan asked.

It turned out that he was going in another direction, but offered us a prayer book.

The religious man looked at me as if he knew my secret. I felt as if I was wearing a big scarlet C on my chest. *Maybe I shouldn't have had a nose job*, I think to myself, *then no one would have questioned my Jewishness.*

"Why would you do that to me?" I asked.

He looked at me, bewildered.

Why would he do any of this to me? I asked myself.

Everything we did came back to the same subject. We couldn't even talk without fighting.

After that, we both let go of each other. The rabbinate won. Our love had not been strong enough . . . or maybe he had not been strong enough.

It was all over in an instant. The fighting ended. My aliyah dreams disappeared. My future vanished.

*   *   *

Now I sit at my desk at work, trying to distract myself with a marketing project. Every document that I work on, every email that I write, every presentation that I create, keeps me in this country and proves that I have some purpose here. As I'm working on one of the projects, my manager walks over and asks me to come to his office.

"Jessica, you know we have been having a lot of financial problems . . ." he says.

I close my eyes to hide my tears.

"I'm sorry. I did everything I could to keep you on," he says. "Your work has been extremely valuable to the company. I hope you will continue to work for us on a freelance basis . . . if we have the money."

I open my eyes, but I can't look at him in the face. I stare out the window behind his desk. "Okay," I manage to say.

"You will have to return your car to the company," he says. All those years in the army and working under Cruella now seem meaningless. Everything I had worked for during the past eight years is suddenly gone.

As I walk out of the offices, the sun shines down on me as if it is actually a cheerful day. I try to reorientate myself, but the light blinds me. After all those years, I am back at square one. I don't know how to pick myself up again. Or how to start over again. Where am I going to find the energy? Or the strength? I no longer have the will inside of me to start over again.

After taking the train home, I crawl into my bed. I pull the covers up above my head and draw the blinds shut so that not even a ray of sunlight can come in. I never want to leave this spot again. I stay there for a week. The only time I get up is to take Jinjy out for a walk.

I finally pull myself out of bed to go sign up for unemployment. With odd hours, strange documentation requests, and never-ending lines, Israel even makes being unemployed difficult.

Knowing that the only way I will be able to pull myself out of this hole, I turn to Orli, the only family I have left in Israel for support. I need her to hold my hand. I feel more alone in Israel than ever.

"I don't know what to do," I sob from under my covers.

"Jessica, you need to get up. Start looking for a job. You can't stay under your covers for the rest of your life," she says.

Now weighing under a hundred pounds, I literally do not have the strength to move.

"And you need to eat," she says.

At least I didn't get that Jewish gene of overeating when I'm upset.

"Listen, I've discussed this with the other roommate, and I know it's not a good time to mention this, but we don't want to live with a dog. You're going to have to move out if you want to keep him."

As I pull Jinjy closer, I start sobbing harder. I think back to the night that I had brought her family money for electricity while I was in my volunteer program. That night, I felt like I had family in Israel. Now I feel completely alone.

My real life feels like an over-used chick lit plot, but unlike the strong female protagonist in those books, my strength is gone. I feel limp. I am hopeless. I have nowhere to go and no one to turn to. Most of the *olim hadashim*, new immigrants, I have met along the way, or who had lived with me at Merkaz Hamagshamim, have already been back in the US for years.

Orli gets up and walks out of my room.

*   *   *

Day after day, I sit alone in my apartment with no one to call, no one to lean on, nowhere to go, and no way to get there. Jinjy is the only body that keeps me warm at night, when the darkness, rain, and cold wind penetrate the thick walls of my apartment.

I no longer have the strength for this country. It has worn me down. Even breathing is hard these days. It has destroyed the wide-eyed optimistic girl that got off the plane to make *aliyah*. But this country is still a part of me. Leaving this country would be like cutting off my own arm. I am trapped and I do not know how to get out. I do not know how to move forward.

I look over at the famous poster of the three Israeli paratroopers standing in front of the Western Wall when Jerusalem was first emancipated. Israelis always ask me why I hang that poster up in my room. To me, that picture represents the pride and hope of the Jewish people.

I think back to my teen tour, now nearly fifteen years ago. I remember how many possibilities this country offered. We spent a night at a Bedouin tent, where they made us traditional Bedouin food on the fire, served us strong tea and coffee. They told us about how the Bedouins have preserved their natural way of life as nomads in the desert. And they talked about the coexistence between Jews and Bedouins. I thought it was beautiful. Only a few years ago, I led a Birthright group of twenty-something Americans and we visited the same

Bedouin tent. After listening to the same exact explanation of their custom and their beliefs, I walked in back to discuss logistics with them. And there I saw that their real home had a flat-screen TV, espresso machine, and every other appliance that your heart could desire. They were better equipped in the middle of the desert than I am in Tel Aviv.

I look back at the poster hanging on my wall. I stare into the eyes of those three soldiers, so filled with hope and awe. That is the way that I used to stare at the Western Wall, but now that same site only reminds me of the control the rabbinate has over the country's Jewish identity. The same site that used to represent holiness now represents corruption and discrimination. The picture no longer symbolizes the hope of the Jewish people to be united in one land, it represents everything that is bad about the country. It represents how the secular Jews who fight with their lives for this country only to have it taken over by the ultra-Orthodox.

I get out of my bed. I walk over to the poster. After looking more closely at their faces, I tear it off my wall. With tears blurring my eyes, I look around my room. I see the entire country differently. Even though the national anthem is *HaTikvah*, The Hope, I have lost all hope in this country. I shake with sobs. I can't control myself. It is like the curtain has been lifted to expose the wizard as just an ordinary man.

I'm crying so hard that I can barely breathe. I fall to the floor.

I have nowhere to turn. No one to call. Everyone I ever trusted here has betrayed me. Even though many people turn to religion for hope, religion has caused me to lose it.

I am convulsing. I can't control my tears.

Jinjy looks at me with worried eyes and his head cocked.

Unlike the author of *Eat, Pray, Love*, who heard a little voice telling her to go back to bed and that everything

was going to be okay when she broke down, I hear the
voice of Xanax from my drawer. And that voice is pretty
convincing.

I take one to calm down.

I'm still crying.

I take another one.

I don't want to hurt any more.

I can't stop crying.

I take another one.

I just want to stop hurting.

*   *   *

I open my eyes. Bar is standing in front of me with
light glowing from behind him. He looks like an angel. I
wonder if I'm in heaven.

"Baaaaarrrrrr," I cry. He is sitting right next to me. He
looks at me with tears in his eyes.

Bar moved back to Israel a few weeks ago. He wanted
to give this country another chance.

I look around. I'm no longer in my room. There is a
curtain pulled around the bed. The florescent lights are
flickering above me. I look down. There is an IV in my
arm.

Oops, I think.

"It is okay, Jessica. *Yihyeh b'seder*, everything will be
okay," he says solemnly.

Orli is on my phone talking in English.

She must be talking to my parents. That must mean
that my family is coming for me. For the first time, I
truly believe that *yihyeh b'seder*.

The End of the Tornado

My mom arrived the next day and within the next
week, my entire life in Israel is packed up in boxes. That
is, everything except for my emotional baggage—I'm
stuck carrying that myself.

My mom came to help me pick up the pieces of my life. I'd missed her more than I'd realized. It was her past that I had been running from, but she keeps running to my rescue. Her presence gives me strength. I don't want to run anymore. I want to reclaim my past and stand up for her choice.

Outside everyone is celebrating Israel's Independence Day, but inside we now spend my last few days in the country packing.

As I'm taking the pictures off my wall, I stare at the photo from the day I made *aliyah*, in which I am surrounded by Benjamin Netanyahu, Ariel Sharon, and Sallai Meridor. By now, I've gotten over the fact that the shirt I was wearing that day turned out to be see-through—maybe that was why that religious girl looked at me so strangely on the flight.

Nearly a decade has gone by since I first started my journey in Israel. Things have changed so much. Bibi is prime minister again and will do anything to stay in power, including leading the country into civil unrest and giving the religious more control. Sharon is now at the Tel HaShomar Hospital; he's been in a coma for over three years. And I don't really know what has happened to the other guy, but I don't know if anyone cares.

It makes me wonder, out of all of us in that picture, who is better off now?

I look around my room, the place that has been my home for the past six years. I see all of my memories, both good and bad, all of my accomplishments, packed away in boxes and suitcases. I look in my closet. The only thing hanging there is the pink dress that I bought after my interview in the army. I remember wearing it and thinking about all of the dreams I was going to fulfill. It was the start of many of my path to accomplishing my dreams. The fabric is still soft in my hands. Deciding to leave it here, I put it back in the closet and close the door.

I look back at my empty room. I can't believe that I'm leaving tomorrow. I am terrified to be leaving. To be giving up. But I am going home to the love, comfort, and support of my family, which I have been without for so long.

I look at Jinjy and say, "Don't worry, you are coming with me. And you will have even more room in your kennel than I will in my seat!"

Jinjy comes over and licks my wounds as I hear a knock at the door.

Looking at my watch, I'm surprised that it is already time. I take a deep breath. I'm nervous that I'm making the wrong decision, but it's too late to back out now.

A few months ago, in the deepest depths of despair, I had been sitting alone in my bedroom, looking for answers, when a headline jumped out at me.

Most Israeli Jews Back Religious Freedom, Poll Finds

When I saw the article, my eyes had opened wide. I sat up straight. I devoured the entire article. The statistics made me feel less alone. I read that the poll was conducted by Hiddush, an Israeli organization promoting religious freedom and equality in Israel.

"What is this organization?" I had asked out loud to nobody but Jinjy. He had moaned and then set his head back down on my leg. Suddenly, without thinking, I started writing the organization an email, telling them my story, from growing up in a Zionist family to making *aliyah*, from joining the IDF to being given an ultimatum to convert. My fingers moved across the keyboard without needing to think about what to write. Everything that I had been through poured out of my body through my hands.

Now on my last day in Israel, Hiddush has asked me to share my story with the entire nation. I take a deep breath and open the door. I welcome the journalist, the photographer, and the head of Hiddush into the living room, which is filled with more of my boxes.

I boil some hot water for tea while we make small talk. I find out that the journalist, a reporter from *Yediot Aharonot*, the largest newspaper in Israel, spent a few years in Minneosta where I grew up. I smile to myself, thinking, "Only in Israel."

"Shall we start?" the reporter looks at me.

I look back at her and take another deep breath.

I had agreed to share my story because I wanted to make a difference, to raise awareness, to let others know that they aren't alone, and to help prevent the Knesset from passing a conversion bill that would give the ultra-Orthodox rabbinate more power and make conversion even more difficult. I had decided to try to make some good from everything that I went through.

I took another deep breath and began telling my story. While I sat in front of the reporter, I finally felt the strength coming back into my body. With every word that I said, I felt less like a victim. My story was finally empowering me instead of weighing me down.

*   *   *

My mom and I walk to the gate in silence. This flight leaving Israel feels completely different than the flight coming here. Instead of being filled with hope and endless possibilities, I'm filled with disappointment and uncertainty. I don't feel whole. I feel an emptiness. Leaving Israel is more difficult than moving here.

Our flight begins boarding. I don't want to get up out of my seat in the terminal. I can't believe that my life here is over. As I pick up my bags, they suddenly feel heavier, almost trying to anchor me in the country. I show my ticket at check-in and the agent has to force-fully pull it out of my hands, as if it is stuck between my fingers. As I walk down the boarding bridge, each step gets slower as if I'm walking through deep mud. I can't believe these are going to be my last steps in the country. My mom and I board the plane to a country that I haven't lived in for nearly a decade. Together we find our seats.

Feeling as if I no longer have anyone to call to say goodbye, I quickly turn off my cell phone. It is too hard to call Bar and I know that he hates goodbyes.

Sitting on the plane, I think of all the things that I learned while living in Israel. I learned that it is easier to be a Zionist outside of Israel than inside. Living outside the country, I only had to stand up for it against all the external threats. But living inside Israel, I have to stand up against the internal threats too. I almost wish that I could have held on to my idealistic views of Israel—it was so much simpler.

When I moved to Israel, I thought I could survive on Zionism alone and while this is true in the US if you can get a good job at the Jewish Agency, in Israel you will starve to death on Zionism. You might as well just get in the line for food stamps.

As the plane begins speeding down the runway and the engines get louder than thunder, questions and doubts rush through my mind. I look out the window and see my world disappearing behind me. Is this the right thing to do? Should I really be going?

But as the plane takes off and the wheels lose touch with the land, I realize that I too have lost touch with it.

I look back at the small, twinkling lights of Tel Aviv from the air. Parts of me still want to believe in the Zionist dream of the country being the homeland for all Jews.

But instead I just close my window shade.

13

Badge of Courage

I wake up to three feet of snow on the ground. It is the end of April, but there was a big snow storm last night.

A few days ago, I was lying on the beach in my bikini. Now I have to put on winter boots to walk outside.

This is the first time that Jinjy has ever seen snow. I thought he would hate the snow, but he is prancing and jumping around in it like a puppy. He looks so happy. He scratches at the door for me to let him in. Unlike me, he has already gotten over his jet lag. He curls up on the couch.

I sit down at my parents' kitchen table, the same table we used to have Shabbat dinners at every Friday night. There is a fire burning in the fireplace. The sun shining through the windows warms my skin. Everything feels familiar here.

My mom hands me a cup of tea. My dad gives me a hug.

I look over at the bare wall where there are now two rectangles that are a darker shade than the rest of the paint. The two paintings of Jerusalem's Old City used to hang there—paintings that my parents bought during our first trip to Israel. They were recently moved to some dark and unused closet so they won't be a constant reminder.

I turn my computer on. I go straight to the Israeli news sites. It has been my morning ritual for nearly ten years. But now that I am no longer in Israel it feels even more important. I can't bear the thought that something might happen to the country while I'm not there.

After scanning all the Israeli news sites, I open up Facebook to see what all my friends back in Israel are doing today. To my surprise, I'm greeted with dozens of new messages from people I've never met.

I begin opening them.

"I admire you!"

"You are more Jewish than all of the rabbinate and ultra-Orthodox community."

"In the name of the country, I'm sorry."

"We need more Jews like you here in Israel."

"I want you to know that I am appalled and embarrassed as an Israeli and as a Jew. I firmly believe that the vast majority of the people here would agree with me."

"More than you lose the country, Israel loses you."

"Even if it sounds kitschy, for me and for many others, *you* are the example of a Jewish Zionist."

"I'll marry you!"

I finally got a marriage proposal from an Israeli.

"I guess the article was printed today. Look at all of these messages of support that complete strangers sent me," I say, turning to my parents.

After reading the messages my dad says, "That is wonderful, Jessica" as he gives me another hug.

"It is good to know that there *are* Israelis who are accepting," my mom says quietly.

My phone rings.

"Baaaaarrrrrr," I cry into the phone—happy to hear from him.

"Did you see the article? It is huge! A two page spread!" Bar exclaims.

"I hope that it makes a difference. I hope that some good can come out of everything I went through," I say.

"I bet Meydan regrets ever asking you to do his laundry for him, now that you have aired all of his dirty underwear in front of the entire country," he says and we both laugh.

"I miss you," I say, realizing that what unites us is not what we went through in the army together, but it was our fight to find our Jewish identities in a schizophrenic country.

"I miss you too. I just want to let you know, that I'm so proud of you for speaking out. There are so many people, like me, who don't have the courage to do what you did," he says.

"Thanks," I say, hoping that Bar knows that he should never feel like he has to go through what I did to prove his identity to anyone. "Hey! At least I won't have to hear that Jessica song every day . . . hmmm, I guess I should have paid more attention to those prophetic lyrics . . . because here I am, far away."

"I have to tell you something. Don't be upset, but Tali called me," Bar says hesitantly. "She read the article and told me that she couldn't believe that you would take part in an article that was so critical of Israel."

"I'm not surprised. She doesn't get it. She doesn't understand that participating in this article was more Zionistic than any of my volunteer work, moving to Israel, and serving in the army combined," I say. Speaking up is the first thing I have done to actually try to make Israel a country that lives up to its potential.

"So, what are your plans now? Do you think you'll come back to Israel? " Bar asks, knowing that after he left, he missed the country so much that he returned.

"I'll just take each day at a time," I trail off thinking that if I do move back to Israel, then the next time around, I'll know that no matter how much I will it, the Land of Oz is only a dream.

"We will talk again soon?" he asks.

"Of course," I say, making sure not to say goodbye when I hang up.

I open up the scanned article that Bar just emailed to me. As I read about my experience in the third person, I begin to realize that participating in the article wasn't only about sharing my story. It was about being truthful to myself, accepting my past, and reclaiming my existence so that no one could ever take away my identity again. I had always had that strength inside of me. I never needed a balloon ride or ruby slippers.

Stronger and even more determined, I'm ready to bare my soul to the world. I pick up a pen and pull a notebook in front of me. I embrace all of my struggles while sitting at my childhood kitchen table. Without hesitating, I begin to write. The ink flows out like silk, but I feel like I'm etching something permanent in stone. The black ink is sharp in contrast to the bright white paper.

It's 3:00 A.M. It's August. It's boiling outside.

Afterword

by Rabbi Uri Regev

[Jessica] Doesn't Live Here Anymore

This is the title of the article published in Israel's leading newspaper about Jessica's returning home to the United States, which her book mentions towards the end. I was there that day with Jessica and her mother with the packed suitcases when the journalist recorded her moving story of her failed attempt at *aliyah*. As Jessica stressed in the article, "I love Israel, but Israel betrayed me." Nevertheless, Jessica's genuine Zionist commitment and her love for Israel prevailed, and she is now living in Israel again, havig renewed her *aliyah* and returned in spite of being let down, as she powerfully described.

Jessica's story provides a critical perspective for both Israelis and American Jewry. For all its sharp criticism of different facets of life in Israel, it is a Zionist treatise anchored in a deep love for the State and its people. At the same time, it presents a challenging indictment of the new generation of American Jewry. This is not a story of black and white, but rather of Jewish life's complexity, of core values, and of the realities facing both major Jewish communities.

For Israelis, Jessica's insights are important because just as we don't hear ourselves as others do, so do we not perceive ourselves in the same manner that we are perceived by the rest of the world. The often humorous reminder, and at times biting criticism, which Jessica offers does us a great service by putting a mirror before our eyes and urging us to engage in the necessary soul searching that is so essential for national mending.

Jessica presents the inherent contradictions in the attitude of Israelis to Judaism and the wide gap between the USA's Jewish community-based reality and Israel's consumerist-based reality (without being able to select one's preferred product) in vivid colors. This gap is particularly striking when she describes the reality of Israel only recognizing religious marriages, even though most couples are secular and have no connections with their officiating rabbis, often meeting them for the first time beneath their wedding canopies. Compare this to the longstanding relationships that American Jews develop with the rabbis of their congregations, which build mutual acquaintance, friendship and spiritual meaning. In a lively and compelling way, Jessica conveys the experiences, worries, hopes, and difficulties confronted by the new immigrant: the struggle with the difficult Hebrew language, the atmosphere of the IDF, the military conflict and challenges of security, the divide between religious and secular, and the distinct worlds of Jerusalem and Tel Aviv. The book also serves as a delightful guide for Hebrew terminology.

While the book is multidimensional and covers numerous facets of Israeli life, what brought Jessica and me together on that fateful day when the chapter of her aliyah seemingly ended was the existential dimension of Israel as both a Jewish and a democratic state.

Jessica conveys the pain of the realization that in spite of her family's full Jewish life, their active membership and leadership at their synagogue, her rich Jewish education, her annual Zionist summer camp experiences, her aliyah and the many difficulties she willingly faced out of her deep love for Israel, nevertheless: "my sorority sisters who preferred Prada over Israel would be considered more Jewish than I am in this country." The heart aches when you read her account of feeling that she had to "alter" her parents' Jewish wedding contract, and one cannot fault her. The responsibility for mending Israel's law and reality lies not on her shoulders, but rather with the Israeli public and the Diaspora Jewish leadership.

Jessica quotes her "Otzma" program counselor who explained that soldiers who are not recognized as Jews by Israel's Orthodox Rabbinate are not buried next to other fallen Jewish soldiers in military cemeteries. This is but one example of a scandal that outrages Israelis, as it did when Sgt. Lev Pesachov z"l died in a military confrontation with terrorists and was buried next to the fence of his hometown military cemetery, for his mother was not Jewish according to traditional religious Jewish law. Rabin z"l was the Israeli Defense Minister at the time, and he responded to the public's outrage by ordering that Pesachov's coffin be reburied next to his fallen Jewish comrades. Unfortunately, that did not resolve the problem. Just a few years ago, a female cadet whose family had made aliyah from Russia died in a fire that consumed the Carmel forest, and the military rabbinate pressured her pained family to bury her next to the fence.

This is an example of the battle that we at Hiddush have launched for a more systemic and lasting solution, demanding that the IDF change its rules and provide a dignified solution for soldiers who have made aliyah but do not meet the military rabbinate's Orthodox criteria of Jewish status, and for those whose families wish to bury them in a manner befitting their non-Orthodox beliefs and lifestyles. Much to Jessica's satisfaction, I can report significant progress and remedy unfolding on this front.

A leading Israeli columnist explained some years ago that whereas common democratic discourse deals with the need to protect the minority from the tyranny of the majority, in Israel this is often reversed; the necessary focus is upon how to protect the majority of Israelis from the tyranny of the fundamentalist religious minority. In speaking to audiences in the USA and elsewhere, I am often asked how such a thing is possible. One look at Israel's current government coalition explains this anomaly. With Israel's parliamentary system, no one party has ever been able to win a majority in the national elections. The need to form a coalition to a majority of 61 Knesset seats has been at the core of Israeli politics since its inception.

Looking at Prime Minister Netanyahu's current fragile coalition, which consists of 66 members out of 120, and realizing that if either one of the two ultra-Orthodox parties were to leave his coalition this would topple the government, we can understand how a minority party with only six Knesset members can wield power enough to dictate to the majority such demands as are behind Jessica's vivid account. This is the political reality behind the void between the Israeli public's will, the silent majority, which desires to see Israel live up to its founding promise of religious freedom and equality for all, and the mind boggling reality that Jessica so ably describes, in which Jews enjoy greater levels of religious freedom and choice anywhere in the world outside of Israel. This should signify to both Israelis and Diaspora Jewish leaders that resolving this anomaly will require opening the eyes of all the political powers that be across the political spectrum, urging them to work together to establish a civil coalition and a civil government, which is key to strengthening Israel's civil society. Unsurprisingly, while Israel's politicians are yet to recognize this, the overwhelming majority of the public wants this very end, namely a government that is not dependent upon and does not include the coercive and fundamentalist ultra-Orthodox parties.

Looking at this from a deeper perspective, we must ask the question, "Whose Israel?" The answer given by former Chief Justice Prof. Aharon Barak in a landmark case over "Who is a Jew," which I had the privilege of arguing, was most instructive. In rejecting the State's refusal to register those who converted under non-Orthodox auspices in Israel as Jews in the civil population registry, Barak spoke on behalf of the majority, stating, "Israel is not the state of the 'Jewish community.' Israel is the state of the Jewish people, and is the expression of 'the right of the Jewish people for national revival in its land' (from the Declaration of Independence). Within Judaism there are different streams that operate in Israel and beyond. Each stream operates according to its outlook and views. Each and every Jew in Israel—as well as each and every non-Jewish person—is entitled to freedom of religion, conscience, and association."

Jessica's and Meydan's breakup may not have been avoidable, but it's difficult not to share in her pain and protest regarding his demand that after having lived all her life as a Jewess—born to active leaders in the Jewish community, to a mother who converted to Judaism out of genuine and active existential choice and desire to be Jewish—that Jessica should have to concede to having her Jewish identity revoked and be subjected to Orthodox conversion. Her protest does not emanate from not taking Judaism seriously, but rather the opposite: it rises out of the fact that her attitude towards Judaism is far more serious and consistent than many of the Israelis around her, including Meydan! This gap is, to a great degree, the result of the surrender of the State of Israel, of Israeli politicians who are predominantly secular, and the sale of Judaism to the ultra-Orthodox establishment in return for their votes.

The result of this betrayal of Jessica, of her family, and of the majority of Diaspora Jewry is the foundation of a growing rift between Israel and world Jewry. The current state of Israeli policies carries with it dual significance: 1) Israel officially treats Jessica and the majority of Jews in the USA that she represents as second class Jews, and 2) The fact that Israel refuses to recognize Jessica, her friend Bar from Paris whose mother converted, and the majority of the young generation of American Jews as equals, causes many Israelis, like Meydan, to mistakenly consider such discrimination acceptable. Orli, Jessica's best friend in the book, responds to her pain with a reaction, which Jessica rightly cannot accept: "Don't take it personally; it's not about you." For all their friendship and affinity, many Israelis cannot comprehend how important Jessica's Jewish status and identity—which are recognized by the majority of world Jewry—are to her. A submission to the demand for conversion as a prerequisite for starting a family in Israel is a betrayal of Jessica's own life and family. This is why Jessica cannot understand nor accept Orli's instrumentalist approach to Judaism.

The good news is that Israel's reality is rapidly changing because of the growing awareness of the harm to Israel and Judaism caused by the increasing extremism of the ultra-Orthodox religious establishment to whom Israeli politicians have entrusted the keys to Jewish life in Israel. This changing attitude is also a welcome result of the growing exposure of Israelis to the ideas of pluralism, Jewish renewal, and the open and free Jewish reality of Jewish Diaspora life. These trends lead the majority of Israelis to respond in public opinion surveys, saying that the Orthodox rabbinic monopoly alienates Israeli Jews from Judaism. Also, unlike Orli who explains to Jessica that she is secular but that it's nevertheless important to her to marry via Israel's rabbinate, Hiddush's studies have recently demonstrated that four out of every five secular Israeli Jews wouldn't marry through the rabbinate if given the choice.

Jessica's parting words in her book are "I've lost all hope in this country," but at the same time she describes how she started her days in America with a careful review of the daily Israeli news. Obviously, her loss of hope was temporary, for Jessica has returned and lives in Israel once again. Still, this does not minimize in any way serious challenges that she outlined for us—both for Israelis and for Diaspora Jewish leaders—in her book. On the contrary, she represents a small core of young idealistic Jews who prevail in spite of the obstacles and the rejections. The majority of her peers are moving away from Israel, and if this trend is not reversed, those of us concerned with the future of Israel and committed to the wellbeing of the Jewish people have much to worry about.

Jessica wrote her book and told her story because she hopes to help change this course. As she writes, her friend Tali, having read Jessica's newspaper interview, reacted by saying that she "couldn't believe that [Jessica] would take part in an article that was so critical of Israel." This is a typical reaction of those who want to hide the truth, prefer to maintain the status quo, and don't want to rock the boat. Jessica should be commended because in writing her book and in giving her interview, she demonstrated the necessary opposite view: "Participating in this article was more Zionistic than any of my volunteer work, moving to Israel, and serving in the army combined. Speaking up is the first thing I have done to actually try to make Israel a country that lives up to its potential."

May we all heed to Jessica's call and take part in the pioneering challenge for this phase of Israel's saga: transforming it into a truly Jewish, democratic, compassionate and pluralistic state.

Rabbi Uri Regev, Esq. heads Hiddush, an Israel-Diaspora partnership for religious freedom & equality in Israel.

End reading

Reading Group Guide

1. What do you think drove the author to leave the security of her family and home to move to a foreign country? Do you think the author was running to something or from something?

2. The author struggles with her identity throughout the book. Do you think she needed to have her identity stripped away so she could reclaim it as her own? How does the concept of identity as defined by oneself versus by external forces impact the author? Did the author need to go to a foreign land in order to find herself?

3. This story examines the themes of religion, politics, sex, and identity. Where and how did you see these topics intertwine and come to a head?

4. The theme of fate arose a number of times in the book. Do you think that the author's downfall was destined?

5. The juxtaposition between expectations and reality reoccurs in the book. How do you think this served the story and character development? Is this an effective storytelling tool to emphasize and even foreshadow the disappointments the author experiences? Why or why not?

6. There are a number of allusions to The Wizard of Oz. How do you think the story is similar to this classic? How is it different? Did these references strengthen the story or weaken it? Explain.

7. Meydan was the main antagonist in the book, however his character was never strongly developed nor was he given much depth. Do you think that was an intentional literary tool employed by the author? Why or why not? What could have been the author's goal in turning such a main character into a universal figure?

8. The author uses humor as a tool to release tension during uncomfortable and difficult situations for both herself and the reader. Did this keep you engaged in the story or draw you out of it? Do you think that the inclusion of sarcasm into the text provided greater depth and dimension to the author, possibly giving better insight into her coping mechanisms, or did it conceal her emotions and distance her? Explain.

9. The author built the story using a circular narrative. The ending of the book is also its beginning. Why do you think the author chose this technique? How does this insert the writing process into the story? What role do you think the writing process played for the author herself?

10. Often times it can be difficult for the Jewish community in the Diaspora to be critical of Israel because there is a need to defend the country against condemnations. Does this story cause you to have a more nuanced approach towards the country and its policies? Why or why not? Given the lack of recognition by the Israeli government of the different streams of Judaism, do you think there is a need for the Jewish community in the Diaspora to be more involved in Israel or does this alienate the Jewish Diaspora? Is it the place of the Jewish Diaspora to shape Israeli politics? If so, how?

Appendix

Israeli Driving Rules
Hebrew Slang
Army Slang and Terminology
Israeli Dating Rules

Israeli Driving Rules

1. Never stop for pedestrians, just honk and speed up.
2. Do not use blinkers, as it will only give someone the opportunity to cut you off.
3. The horn is *not* for emergencies.
   - Honking can solve any problem. It can even stop a train that is speeding towards you.
4. The yellow traffic light is a warning for you to go faster.
5. The yellow traffic light with the green light is so that you can get your foot on the gas more quickly after a red light, just like with race car driving.
6. The other driver *never* has the right of way.
7. Roundabouts are there so that drivers never have to stop.
8. Your blind spot is always the other driver's problem.
   - The car mirrors are solely for checking if you have something in your teeth or putting on makeup.
9. The speed bumps are not for you to slow down; they are so you can catch air.
10. If you need to stop, there is no need to pull over. Just put your car in park in the middle of a busy street.
11. If you go the wrong way in reverse down a one-way street, it is okay.
12. There is only one rule in parking: as long as you can get your car in the spot, don't worry about getting out.
13. Big cars and trucks do not watch out for the small cars.
14. Motorbikes do not have to drive within the lanes or follow any of the parking laws.
15. There is no minimum amount of space needed between your car and the car in front of you (this rule applies to both moving and parked cars).
16. The people that put the *shamor merchak*, keep your distance, stickers on their car will be the first ones to tail you.

17. No one slows down when they see a police officer. Police officers are just someone's brother who you know.

    - Popular Israeli joke: A driver makes a U-turn at a red light and is then pulled over by a police officer. The police officer tells the driver that he is being pulled over for making an illegal U-turn. The driver then tells the officer, "Sorry, I didn't notice." The police officer responds, "How did you not notice the sign?" and then the driver says, "No, I saw the sign, I just didn't see you."

18. Finding Osama Bin Laden in the mountains between Pakistan and Afghanistan is easier than finding a parking spot in Tel Aviv.

19. Israelis treat driving like it is a leap of faith. Some even close their eyes while doing it.

Hebrew Slang

Achi or *Ach sheli*: My brother. This can refer to an actual brother, a close friend or a complete stranger. It is a term of endearment and emphasizes that all Israelis are brothers. It is often ironically used by complete strangers in an argument.

Aiya, aiya: Ouch, Ouch!

Al ha'panim: Literally translates as "on the face." Figuratively it means something is really bad.

Ben zonah: Literally translated as "son of a whore," this is the Israeli version of "son of a bitch." Depending on pronunciation, it can figuratively mean something is really good or that someone is really bad.

Chatich: Literally translated as "a piece." Figuratively it means a really hot guy. The female term is *chaticha*, but no one actually uses this term since it is not demeaning or sexist enough. For the actual term used for women, please refer to *koosit*.

Davka: There is no literal translation for this, it is a word to create emphasis, as in:
1. You did that davka to piss me off
2. It does not davka have to be that way

Eichsa, eichs: Eww, gross

Gever: Literally means "man." This word is used twice in a row to describe somebody who is a manly man.

Haval al ha'zman: Literally translated as "a shame of the time." Depending on pronunciation, this phrase can mean that something is really bad or really good.

Koosit: Originates from the Hebrew word *koos*, meaning pussy. The word *koosit* means a really hot girl

Koos'emek: An Arabic term used in Hebrew meaning "your mother's vagina." The word is typically used as a swear word to emphasize frustration. This is Natalie Portman's favorite swear word, as she stated in *Inside the Actor's Studio*.

L'chiot b'seret: Literally translated as "living in a movie." This term is used to tell somebody they are out of touch with reality or completely crazy, example:
Jessica: I am planning on joining the IDF Spokesperson Unit at 23 years old
Typical Israeli: You are living in a movie

La'panim: Literally translated as "to the face." This figuratively means something is really good. This slang term was a reaction to the original *al ha'panim* phrase.

Mami: A term of endearment for a friend, a romantic partner, or a complete stranger.

Ma Pitom?!: Literally translated as "What suddenly?!" and is used to express surprise and outrage. It is the Israeli version of WTF, example:

> Customer: How much is this shirt?
> Store keeper: 50 NIS
> Customer: What suddenly?! That is way too much.

Nu: So, go ahead, well. This can either be used in a friendly way or in a rude way depending on pronunciation and situation.

> 1. Israeli 1: And then after I told him that . . .
>   Israeli 2: *Nu*, and then what happened?
> 2. Israeli 1 is standing at the counter waiting for help from a government employee which is ignoring Israeli 1.
>   Israeli 1: *Nu!*

Pitzuz: Literally meaning "explosion." This term can also be used to say that something that is really good, i.e.:

> Israeli male 1: How was the party last night?
> Israeli male 2: There were so many hot girls, the music was great. It was a *pitzuz!*

Shevah Pigua: Literally meaning "worth a terrorist attack." This is a slang term stating that a girl is really hot, example:

> Israeli male 1: Did you see that hot girl?
> Israeli male 2: Yeah, she is so hot. She is worth being in a terrorist attack.

Tsk!: This is simply a noise that someone makes for saying no. It is a completely acceptable response in any conversation and is not considered rude. An entire interview can be conducted with the prime minister, or any other leader, with this being the only answer.

Yalla: An Arabic term used in everyday Hebrew that means a combination of bye and let's go

Zion: This word is both the name of a letter and an actual word in Hebrew. The word translates to "dick." But strangely enough, in English, people use the word Zion to describe Israel, and the word Zionisim—the settlement of the Jewish people in the country—is rooted in this word/letter. (Sort of puts a Freudian twist on the whole Zionist movement.)

Not surprisingly, in a macho society like Israel, there are many popular phrases that use the word zion, including:

L'zian et ha'sechel: Literally translates as "to fuck the mind," and actually meaning to mess with someone's head, example:
1. Officer: "Do you see a vagina on my forehead?"
   Soldier: "No, Officer!"
   Officer: "So why are you trying to fuck my mind?"
2. Israeli 1: I hope you are wearing a condom.
   Israeli 2: Why?
   Israeli 1: Because you are fucking my mind right now.

Ani lo sam zion: Literally translates as "I don't put dick." The closest equivalent in English is "I don't give a shit."

Le'zrok zion: Literally translates as "to throw dick." This actually means to not put any effort into something.

Al ha'zion shali: Literally translates as "on my dick," which can be used in many circumstances, from expressing disagreement to indifference.

Shavor zion: Abbreviation, *sha'vuz*. Literally means "broken dick." This means that someone is very tired and has been worked too hard or that they are bummed out about something. This expression comes from when soldiers come back from twenty-eight straight days in the army and are so tired they do not even have the energy to fuck.

Army Slang and Terminology

Basa: Bummer

Beitim: IDF terminology for sick leave that is spent on the base. This type of sick leave limits the type of physical activity that a soldier is allowed to do.

Chamshosh: Weekend leave from the army that lasts from Thursday afternoon until Sunday morning.
Choger: A soldier's IDF ID card. This card must be carried by soldiers at all times. The card enables free public transportation, and often eases a soldier's passage through security checks.

Gimmelim: IDF terminology for sick leave spent at home. This can only be granted by an IDF doctor. Many soldiers fake illnesses to try to get *gimmelim*, which is a rare prize.

Jobnikim: Soldiers that are on desk duty and sit in an office all day: known in English as desk jockeys. Warriors look down on *jobnikim*.

Katziz: Abbreviation for *Katzin Tzair*, meaning a new officer who just finished officer training. As used in a sentence: *Ani lo sam zion* on what the *katziz* says. I don't put dick what the young officer says.

Tzair: A new soldier, whose uniform is still green and stiff and gets all of the grunt work.

L'senger: This is to give someone an unpleasant task: usually to a new soldier.

Lilah lavan: A night when you do not go to sleep.

Mashakit: Non-commissioned officer.

Madei Aleph: The formal uniform soldiers wear outside of their base. This is the uniform that *jobnikim* wear on a daily basis and other soldiers wear back and forth to their bases. This uniform feels like cardboard.

Madei Bet: This is the uniform soldiers wear in the field, on base and in combat. Made out of cotton instead of polyester, this uniform is much more comfortable than the madei aleph.

Paz'am: Abbreviation for *Perek Zman*. This means the minimal time in service. The higher a soldier's *paz'am* is, then the less grunt work he has to do in the army.

Profeel: From the English term profile, this is numerical representation of a soldier's physical and mental health. Even though it is measured on a scale of 100, the highest attainable score is 97 due to circumcisions in males and menstruation in females.

P'tor: An exemption from doing duties, most often this is a medical exemption.

Pozah: When somebody tries to act cooler than they actually are. For instance, a desk jockey officer who tries to act tough.

Rimon: In the army, rimon means "grenade." However, in civilian life, it means "pomegranate." This can lead to some unfortunate misunderstandings for new immigrants at the grocery store who learned most of their Hebrew vocabulary during their army service.

Rosh katan: This literally means "small head." This has nothing to do with size. A soldier with a small head is one that tries to avoid responsibility and does not take initiative.

Shvizut yom aleph: Depression experienced when returning to the army on Sunday mornings, much like manic Mondays.

Tash: Abbreviation for *tnaey sherut*, meaning "service conditions."
Mashakit tash: The soldier responsible for ensuring that soldiers receive all of their service conditions. Lone soldiers have a close relationship with their *mashakit tash*.

Totach: This literally means "cannon," but it can refer to a very good soldier or a very intelligent person.

Tzair: In civilian life this means "young," but in military terms, a *tzair* is a soldier whose uniform is still dark green and who has to do all the cleaning and guard duty.

Vatic: In civilian life this means "old," but in military life it is the soldiers whose uniforms are faded and know how to get around all the rules. A *vatic* soldier is nearing the end of his service and gets out of all grunt work.

She'elat kitbeg: An exceptionally stupid question that causes the subordinate/s to receive a harder assignment. The original kitbag question was:
>   Commander: Run around the camp 10 times.
>   Soldier: With my kitbag?
>   Commander: Since you asked, yes with your kitbag

Israeli Dating Rules

1. When an Israeli man says he does not like playing games, then that means he is only looking for a *yazizah*, a fuck friend.

2. Under no circumstance should you date an Israeli man who has served in an elite unit—no matter how intriguing it might be. The reason these men are eligible for elite units is because they are the most fucked up of all.

   - When an Israeli man brags about being a hero or in a dangerous situation in the army, never sound impressed or scared, i.e.:

     Elite soldier: During a patrol in the army this week, a terrorist shot at our Jeep window and cracked it. You know that once the windows are cracked, they are no longer bullet proof?

     Wrong Response:

     Female: Oh my God! I'm so glad you are okay! You could have been killed!

     Right Response:

     Female: Well, there isn't air conditioning in those Jeeps anyhow, so at least you got some ventilation.

3. Be prepared to be invited to a family reunion for a second date.

4. It is completely acceptable to sleep over in your date's childhood bedroom at his parents' house, even after the first date. While in the US, men are embarrassed to admit that they still live at home with their parents, Israeli men are quite proud of it. Just as Israeli moms are completely in love with their sons, so are their sons in love with their mothers. The Oedipus Complex should be renamed the Shlomo Complex.

   Don't be surprised if the next morning the mom will make you breakfast, ask you how good her son was in bed, all while washing the stains off the sheets. This phenomenon was taken to the extreme when one of my boyfriend's moms bought me lingerie.

5. Even on a first date, an Israeli man will invite you to an event that is anywhere from one week to five months in the future. This does not mean that

he intends to marry you. Israelis are simply very inviting people. Do *not* go shopping for a wedding dress.

6. Typically, the cockiness level of an Israeli man is inversely proportional to his skill in bed.

7. While men all over the world hate being wrong, Israeli men treat being wrong as if it physically affects their penis size. Israeli men react to being wrong the same way other men react to cold water.

8. Israeli men have some type of secret radar (I think it is technology developed by the IDF) which helps them detect the moment that you decide that you are no longer going to obsess over them. The very second you stop looking at your phone for a text message or turn the ringer off or decide you are going to meet some other guy, they call—without fail.

9. Sephardic Israeli men are openly primitive and chauvinistic when it comes to women, while Ashkanazi Israeli men will pretend to be progressive, but they will still expect to have their food cooked, dishes done, clothes washed, and houses cleaned for them.

10. Israeli men are very affectionate, even from the first date and will have no problem calling you *motek*, sweetie; *metukah*, darling or *mammi*, honey. (And yes, I do think *mammi* is quite revealing about their mom hang-ups.) Do not confuse these affectionate terms with love. They will call the waitress, cashier, and parking attendant lady by these same pet names.

   In fact, saying you have a boyfriend or a husband may not even be enough. As many guys will respond, "a boyfriend isn't a wall" or "take my number, just in case things don't work out" or even ask, "but are you happily married?"

11. Never expect a serious relationship with any man whose first name ends with the sound y or i or

ie. They are good at charming you and they are always fun, but they never make good boyfriends or husbands. A list of names are, but not limited to: Adi, Assi, Avi, Benny, Danni, Dudi, Ellie, Sagi, Shlomi, Shuki, Tzachi, Udi, Uri, and Yoni

Recipes

Pelov: Afghani Rice Dish
Israeli Salad
Shakshuka

Pelov: Afghani Rice Dish

INGREDIENTS:
1 cup whole wheat rice
2 cups water
5 teaspoons canola oil
1 white onion, chopped
4 carrots, sliced into small pieces
½ cup yellow raisins

SEASONING:
1 teaspoon turmeric
¾ teaspoon of cinnamon
½ teaspoon of salt

1. Steam rice until soft and fluffy.
2. In frying pan, heat canola oil and put in chopped onion. Sauté onions until soft. Add carrots that have been cut into small slices. Cook carrots until soft. Then add raisins.
3. Combine the rice and vegetables into a bowl. Add seasoning based on desired taste. The rice should take on a yellow/orange color.

Serve with an Israeli salad or tomatoes on the side.

Israeli Salad

INGREDIENTS:
1 tomato
2 small cucumbers
½ small white onion
1 teaspoon olive oil (at least)
½ lemon

Dice tomato, cucumbers and onion. Mix in a bowl. Add olive oil and squeeze lemon. Make sure to not let any of the lemon seeds to fall into the bowl.

Optional: Feta or Bulgarian cheese, Zatar seasoning, or grated carrots.

Eat with warm, fresh bread.

Shakshuka

INGREDIENTS:

Olive oil, enough to cover bottom of pan
1 diced onion
2 cloves of garlic
1 jalapeno pepper
2 bell peppers
2 chopped tomatoes
2 8-ounce cans of tomato sauce
2 eggs
Tomato juice
Vegetable broth
Season to desired taste with a dash of hot paprika, sweet paprika, turmeric, salt, pepper, and a pinch of sugar

Heat oil in a large sauté pan over medium heat. Add onion and sauté until lightly browned.

Then add garlic, jalapeno and bell peppers, and sauté 2 minutes more. Add tomatoes and tomato sauce, reduce heat to low and simmer for 5 minutes. Add hot and sweet paprika, turmeric, salt, pepper and sugar. Stir for 1 minute. Add desired amount of tomato juice and vegetable broth and bring to a full boil.

Reduce heat to low and simmer, uncovered, until mixture is very thick and has little liquid left, about 1 hour; stir occasionally to make sure vegetables do not stick to bottom of pan, and add more tomato juice or vegetable broth as needed. Taste and season with salt and pepper.

Gently crack eggs into pan, taking care not to break yolks. Simmer until whites solidify but yolks remain runny, about 8 minutes, or as per personal preference

Carefully serve in the hot pan with bread.

Acknowledgments

This book has been as much of a healing process for me as it has been an opportunity to try to make a positive change in a country that I love. I want to thank everyone who has helped me through this journey that allowed me to change a negative experience into one that ultimately turned me into a stronger person.

My parents, while dealing with their own pain from the events that transpired, nursed me back to mental and physical health so that I could start my journey to recovery. From feeding me to giving me a home in the peaceful mountains for a year, they gave me a place where I felt loved and accepted (see also: I lived like a teenager in my late twenties early thirties) so I could focus on my writing. Thank you specifically to my mom who dedicated herself to raising a progressive, Jewish family.

Thank you to my sister for being my superhero without a cape and flying over twice when I needed you the most. You made me laugh when I couldn't find the strength to smile.

The process of writing this book started with a writing course taught by Madelyn Kent. Her writing course couldn't have come into my life at a better time—when I needed the tools and framework to learn how to express my experiences and emotions. Without Madelyn Kent's writing class, this book would never have made it past blog format. As my first editor, Madelyn stayed on this journey with me for at least a year past her writing class, helping me shape my writing into a story. Thank you Madelyn for having the courage to read the first draft of my manuscript and seeing a book hidden in it.

Lori DeBoer, my second editor, played an important part in continuing to grow the manuscript into a book. As a true confidant and friend, Lori forced me to look into myself and ask the hard questions about what this book is really about. Lori helped me make this book reach a greater depth so that it is a universal story to which anyone on a search for love and acceptance can relate. A special thank you to her husband, Michael, for unclogging the toilet, and to Max, her son, for his patience.

A big thank you to Sheyna Galyan, my publisher, and her publishing company, Yotzeret Publishing, for giving me the platform to share my story. I first met Sheyna and her family at a Passover seder that my parents hosted while I was in high school. She and her family came as new congregants to our synagogue. She was the first person to bring an orange for our seder plate. Then I had no idea that our paths would cross again. Nearly twenty years later, only after she read the scene in my manuscript about the orange did we both realize that we had met before. To me it feels as if we have come full circle that she is the one to bring my words to light.

I would also like to thank a few organizations and people that supported me and my struggle. Hiddush and its president and CEO, Rabbi Uri Regev. The organization is dedicated to fighting for freedom of religion and opinion in Israel and its activities gave me a voice. Rabbi Morris Allen and his congregation, Beth Jacob, for envisioning and practicing an egalitarian and progressive Judaism. With actions and not words alone, Rabbi Allen taught me a loving, kind, and accepting Judaism.

Thank you to those who read and reacted to early drafts of the manuscript – Aviv B., Erica F., and Tom D.

Last but not least, I want to thank Jinjy—even though every single instruction I read for writing acknowledgments warned me not to. But if it weren't for Jinjy waking me up in the morning to take him out for walks, I never would have bothered getting out of bed to start writing.

About the Author

Having grown up in a Midwestern Jewish and Zionist family, Jessica Fishman moved to Israel after graduating from Indiana University with degrees in journalism and business. She spent her first few years in the country serving in the Israel Defense Forces, learning the Hebrew language, and getting acclimated to the country. Jessica has written a number of articles about Israel, and her story has been featured in leading Israeli and Jewish media.

After developing the popular Aliyah Survival Blog, which is an irreverent portrayal of an American immigrant's first years in Israel, she has written a deeply personal, witty memoir about the difficulties, absurdities, and excitement of making a home in a new country.

She was inspired to write *Chutzpah & High Heels: The Search for Love and Identity in the Holy Land* after a life-changing event in Israel. Her goals are to share her experience and inspire social change.

Visit Jessica at http://jessicafishmanauthor.com.